Intolerable Cruelty

Intolerable Cruelty

Marriage, Law, and Society in Early Twentieth-Century China

Margaret Kuo

ROWMAN & LITTLEFIELD PUBLISHERS, INC.
Lanham • Boulder • New York • Toronto • Plymouth, UK

Published by Rowman & Littlefield Publishers, Inc.
A wholly owned subsidiary of The Rowman & Littlefield Publishing Group, Inc.
4501 Forbes Boulevard, Suite 200, Lanham, Maryland 20706
www.rowman.com

10 Thornbury Road, Plymouth PL6 7PP, United Kingdom

British Library Cataloguing in Publication Information Available

Library of Congress Cataloging-in-Publication Data

Library of Congress Cataloging-in-Publication Data

Kuo, Margaret, 1971–
Intolerable cruelty : marriage, law, and society in early twentieth-century China / Margaret Kuo.
p. cm.
Includes bibliographical references and index.
ISBN 978-1-4422-1840-6 (cloth : alk. paper) — ISBN 978-1-4422-1842-0 (electronic)
1. Marriage--China--History--20th century. 2. Marriage law—China—History—20th century. 3. China—Social life and customs—History—20th century. I. Title.
HQ684.K876 2012
306.81095109'04—dc23
2012026587

™ The paper used in this publication meets the minimum requirements of American National Standard for Information Sciences Permanence of Paper for Printed Library Materials, ANSI/NISO Z39.48-1992.

Contents

List of Tables

List of Figures

Acknowledgments

The research and writing of this book have taken place over a number of years spent living in China, Taiwan, Canada, and the United States. Along the way, I have accumulated mountainous debts of gratitude to individuals and institutions that have lent me their support and encouragement. I have benefited first and foremost from the meticulous criticism and advice of Philip Huang and Kathryn Bernhardt. I have aspired to their rigorous standards, though I fear that I inevitably fall short. I thank the anonymous reviewers of the book manuscript for their careful, detailed comments. I only wish that I could have implemented more of their suggestions. At Rowman & Littlefield I thank Susan McEachern, Grace Baumgartner, and Carrie Broadwell-Tkach for expert editorial guidance. Robert Bickers of Bristol University graciously arranged for permission to reproduce several images. A postdoctoral fellowship at the Center for East Asian Studies, Stanford University, provided optimal conditions early on for thinking about this book project. I am most grateful to the Stanford faculty, graduate students, and librarians, especially Matthew Sommer, Jean Oi, Mark Lewis, Dongfang Shao, Brigid Vance, and Mei-yu Hsieh, for making my year there so pleasant and productive. The book also benefited from my participation in workshops, lecture series, and panel presentations organized by Kathryn Bernhardt, Xiaoping Cong, Neil Diamant, Christina Gilmartin, Matthew Sommer, and Lisa Tran, and from comments by Susan Glosser and Bryna Goodman. The book's shortcomings remain mine alone.

The deep archival research upon which this book relies was made possible through the tremendous assistance provided by librarians and archivists at the Second Historical Archives, Jiangsu Provincial Archives, Hebei Provincial Archives, Beijing Municipal Archives, the Guomindang Party Archives, Academia Historica, the National Library in Beijing and Taipei, and the Shanghai Municipal Library. I am especially grateful to director Ma Zhendu and archivist Sun Yongxin at the No. 2 Archives for their kindness during numerous visits. Zhang Yimin helped me secure proper letters of introduction. I enjoyed spending a summer in Nanjing with Jiang Zhaoxin, who was also conducting research on a legal history topic. It was also at the No. 2 where I first met Helen Schneider, whose friendship and support I greatly appreciate. I must also express my great affection for my Chinese language teachers in Taiwan, especially Fann Meeiyuan.

In Montreal, Rong Dao, Grace Fong, Leonard Moore, Yuzo Ota, Nancy Partner, and Robin Yates warmly welcomed me. As department chair, Brian Lewis amiably guided me through the challenges of my first academic job. I gratefully acknowledge the outstanding research assistance of Victor Seow, Joyce Ng, and Zabrina Law. Kimberly Ens-Manning and the rest of the Montreal Area China Scholars provided a stimulating intellectual community. I enjoyed many conversations, walks, and dinners with Michelle Hsieh, who continues to be a close friend and confidante. My Long Beach colleagues, including Emily Berquist, Marie Kelleher, Guotong Li, Michiko Takeuchi, and Giselle and Dean Toji, have provided a genuine sense of community. I must also thank the faculty and staff at the Center for the Pacific Rim, University of San Francisco, for making my stay a fruitful one. Mark Mir graciously helped locate the cover photo. Chiho Sawada and Ellen Huang were supportive officemates. Nancy Park's camaraderie and shared interest in Chinese legal history have elevated my scholarship as well as my spirits.

Financial support for various stages of this project came from the Fulbright Foundation, Blakemore Foundation, *China Times* Foundation, University of California, Los Angeles Department of History and Center for Chinese Studies, Stanford Center for East Asian Studies, Social Sciences and Humanities Research Council of Canada, McGill University Faculty of Arts, California State University, Long Beach College of Liberal Arts, and the University of San Francisco Center for the Pacific Rim.

Byungil Ahn, Joel Andreas, Norman Apter, Leo Chen, Clayton Dube, Karen Sue Fukushima, Richard Gunde, Li Fangchun, Li Huaiyin, Jennifer Neighbors, Bradly Reed, Lisa Tran, Elizabeth VanderVen, and Zhang Jiayan generously read and commented on draft chapters. Long after graduate school, Sue and Liz remain two of my dearest friends. Special mention must be made for the superb encouragement, advice, and editing supplied by Elena Shulman, who deserves to be singled out for her contributions to this book as well as for introducing me to my husband.

I am happy to thank all the members of the Kuo, Tong, Gershenson, Grzegorczyk, and Haley families. My sister Jenny and her husband Tony, and my brother Mel and his wife Betty, have shared many joys and provided much-needed perspectives on life outside of academia. My nieces and nephews have been sources of welcome fun away from writing. My grandparents, parents, parents-in-law, and godparents deserve my deepest gratitude. I dedicate this book to my grandmothers, my heroines, Tong Chen Yuen-chen and the late Kuo Tsai Bao-chen. My mother and father gamely pored over handwritten court documents with me from graduate school through today. It may go without saying, but I will say it anyway: my endless love and gratitude go to Geoff and Jonah, who are my shining lights.

A version of chapter 3 originally appeared in *Twentieth-Century China* in January 2011, and is here reprinted with its kind permission. James Carter, Christopher Reed, and the journal's anonymous reviewers deserve thanks for helping to improve the work.

A version of chapter 5 originally appeared in *Modern China* and is here reprinted with the publishers' kind permission. I am grateful to Kathryn Bernhardt, Richard Gunde, Jennifer Neighbors, and the journal's anonymous reviewers for suggestions that improved the work.

I

Law and the State

Chapter One

Introduction

In the 1920s, marriage and legal reform constituted key components of the Guomindang's (GMD) self-conscious embrace of modernization. The GMD promoted a pedagogical style of rule, in which it envisioned itself as tutor to the Chinese people, who were like "blank sheets" in desperate need of the GMD's guidance to help "awaken" them and bring about their moral and cultural transformation.[1] In the words of the future GMD lawmaker John C.H. Wu [Wu Jingxiong], writing to the American jurist Oliver Wendell Holmes, Jr., in 1921, "As a Chinese I have a country to save, I have a people to enlighten, I have a race to uplift, I have a civilization to modernize."[2] Although Wu's letter was written several years before he undertook the work of drafting legislation and a constitution for the GMD, the sentiment expressed remained true for Wu and many other GMD lawmakers as well. In the excitement of the early Nanjing Decade (1928–1937), Republican Chinese lawmakers, ever preoccupied with China's low status in the modern world, looked to law and marriage reform as a prime means to fulfill their urgent desire to improve the condition of the Chinese race and thereby strengthen the Chinese nation. The GMD state thus assumed the power to shape marriage and other social institutions according to its vision of modernity. Its policies reflected the utilitarian concerns of state-building as well as the modernizing impulses and social innovations of the early Nationalist era. This meant rearranging marriage and family relationships according to principles associated with liberal modernity like equality, monogamy, and individual rights and duties. The GMD acted as a moral and legal arbiter, in effect, appropriating the authority to determine what constituted a proper marriage and how family relations should be ordered, prescribing when to marry, who could marry, how to marry, and when to permit divorce.

One of the central motivations driving the GMD legal reform movement was the effort to rid China of humiliating foreign privileges, like extraterritoriality, and to that end, the GMD produced the Republican Civil Code (1929–1930), an important expression of the GMD's vision that aligned with Western conceptions of modern law. Although Republican civil law largely reflected the modernizing desires of the state and was certainly not without its failures and shortcomings, overall the code was a remarkably flexible document. Its creators undertook a task of enormous proportions, introducing the principles of individual rights and gender equality to a patriarchy-ridden Chinese society. At the time of the code's promulgation, commentators praised it for rectifying the patriarchal conditions that had long governed the lives of Chinese women. The prominent jurist F.T. Cheng [Zheng Tianxi] (1884–1970), for example, noted that "women have gained their full franchise almost by a stroke of the pen . . . whatever the Chinese might have been guilty of in the past in denying political rights to their sisters, the ready amends that they have made should be a sufficient redemption of their sin!" (1930, 118). While it would take a lot more than the stroke of a pen to implement gender equality in Chinese society, it is important to nonetheless acknowledge the profoundly revolutionary nature of the code. Prior to the implementation of the civil code in May 1931, China was home to an emphatically hierarchical legal system that almost invariably privileged men over women. The new civil code, in contrast, conceived of both women and men as individual civil persons, equal in status, rights, and obligations. In an unprecedented set of legal breakthroughs, daughters obtained equal rights to inherit their fathers' property, wives gained mostly equal rights to marry and divorce, and mothers and fathers shared nearly equal rights over their children. While not all members of the GMD supported granting women greater rights in marriage and other civil contexts as well as liberalizing divorce rules, the resulting code explicitly favored conjugal over patrilineal ideas of marriage; a mutual duty of sexual fidelity over the overwhelming emphasis on female chastity; individual equality over family, gender, and age hierarchy; and the regulation of relationships through rights and duties rather than through moral and ritual obligations. The struggle over marriage principles pitting individual rights against ideas that promoted family interests represented one piece of the much larger puzzle of Chinese modernity in which these ideas worked themselves out in the twentieth and twenty-first centuries. In the arena of marriage and the family, this tension persisted for much longer than in other areas and unfolded in sometimes unexpected ways.

LIBERAL MODERNITY AND THE RESHAPING OF CHINESE STATE-SOCIETY RELATIONS

This book approaches its topic from a particular view of state-society relations. Unlike studies that emphasize the GMD's use of family reform as a vehicle to enlarge its power and reach, this book seeks to highlight how individuals, women and men, transformed marriage by turning to the new courts to address their problems and in doing so attempted to shape the law to fit their needs and interests. Susan Glosser points out that greater state intervention in marriage and family matters privileged state power over individual rights.[3] However, when individual rights were a matter of spouse versus spouse in the marital disputes that are the subject of this book, rather than individual versus the state, the expansion of state power did not necessarily lead to state domination of Chinese society.

The GMD, like its predecessors as well as its successors, was never able to remake society according to its ideological vision. When it came to regulating areas like female chastity, as Janet Theiss has shown, the Qing state had to negotiate among competing agendas of its own as well as those of elites and ordinary people (2004, 9). Recently, Xu Xiaoqun has pointed to the "multiple hierarchies" of the Republican state, arguing that its reach varied across counties according to the degree to which judicial institutions had been established and the various instances in which provincial and local interests took precedence over the centralizing state (2008, 6–8).[4] Neil Diamant, writing about the Communist Marriage Law, has provided a portrait of a "disaggregated" state composed of multiple levels to which individual litigants could appeal and even pit against each other (2000). A similar unevenness, multiplicity, and disaggregation mark the effects of the GMD effort to regulate marriage. The central leadership of the GMD was surely occupied with consolidating its own power, but state interests varied by jurisdiction, judge, and court, and local courts were compelled to take into account the concerns of ordinary litigants. The records examined in this book show that greater state intervention in marriage and the family promoted statist interests while also addressing the interests of individual husbands and wives. What came about was a complicated set of dynamics of state-society relations. In many instances, facilitated by socioeconomic conditions and individual legal action, state laws on marriage helped to bring about changes in marriage practices. In other cases, socioeconomic constraints hindered the ability of the state to transform marriage practices.

In the changed legal landscape of the 1930s and 1940s, litigants were able to adapt quickly and selectively appropriate legal and moral tools that best suited their interests, as well as formulate arguments that cast their grievances in the most positive light, even while not necessarily giving up their customary beliefs and expectations. For individual litigants, the meaning of the law resided not in the ability of the state to oppress them, but in its provision of means to protect and defend their own interests. The process of reinterpretation that the new marriage laws underwent reflected changing perceptions of justice and changing social expectations of marriage, as well as individual grievances and disappointments. Legal changes worked in conjunction with other social changes already set in motion to facilitate greater individual agency over marriage. This was a transitional period during which the Republican Civil Code's definition of marriage was one of multiple ideas about marriage that circulated. The state's prescriptions for marriage were important but did not amount to orthodoxy. As this study demonstrates, far from being able to mold a pliant population's marriages according to state goals, the state's expanded role in these areas may actually have facilitated greater individual agency as new legal mechanisms granted individuals more power over their marriages.

With respect to legal practice, Republican family law opened up entirely new areas of litigation that enabled litigants in the 1930s and 1940s to stake out new legal territory. The ways in which individual litigants adopted the lens of rights and duties provided by the code to express their own grievances illustrate a significant change in the nature of state-society relations. The suits for judicial separation and annulment to be discussed in chapters 7 and 8, for instance, lacked any late imperial counterparts. Late imperial law provided for various types of divorce, including divorce by mutual consent, but wife-initiated divorce was a legal anomaly until the Republican era (1912–1949), as was the idea that money and property could follow a wife and leave the patriline through the awarding of spousal support or alimony. In addition to launching new areas of litigation, Republican family law expanded previously existing areas. Marital cohabitation suits (chapter 6) were civil actions against runaway wives rather than criminal prosecutions. The new provisions for a judicial divorce (chapter 5) also enlarged the scope of issues that could give rise to a valid legal claim to divorce. The range of actions a wife could take in response to a marital dispute, moreover, multiplied. The GMD state presented wives with a new set of legal considerations, options, remedies, opportunities, and possible solutions to age-old domestic disputes.

The 1930s and 1940s diverged markedly from the 1920s and 1950s in the scale of attempted social change and in the actors propelling such changes. The effort to recognize the personhood of women and bring about gender equality during this era was waged in the arena of the courts by individual women on a case-by-case basis at the same that the organized women's movement secured their political rights to representation, to stand for election, and to vote (Edwards 2008). The goal of women's emancipation did not die out, at least not when the number of lawsuits filed by women using the new laws in the 1930s and 1940s is considered. The main agents of change in these years were ordinary women, mostly wives whose concerns revolved around their own marriages and families. Few, if any, of the women who pursued marital disputes in the courts in the 1930s and 1940s had backgrounds that indicated any sort of feminist activism, ideological allegiances, or participation in political life. Female litigants used legal forums to air their domestic grievances in new ways, and lawsuits became important tools with which women could attempt to alleviate their plights. Their legal actions represented instances of ordinary women acting to effect social change by effecting changes within their own families. The use of lawsuits was personalizing the conflict over gender oppression. Litigants targeted their lawsuits not against systemic inequalities lodged in social or economic institutions, but directly against their own family members. As a result, the locus of women's emancipation stretched out from the public realm of party politics to the more personal realm of marriage and family politics.

Even though the establishment of legal gender equality failed to live up entirely to its billing as a corrective to Chinese patriarchy, the GMD, through the Republican Civil Code, devised a legal system that armed litigants with a new set of legal mechanisms to pursue individual interests and stake out new legal territory. Chinese litigants in turn selectively appropriated Republican legal provisions to promote their own interests, often in ways unintended by lawmakers. Late imperial Chinese society, especially in the most commercialized pockets, was hardly the inert, reluctant-to-litigate body that it was typecast as. The new legal system helped change social attitudes as well as enabled individual husbands and wives to enjoy an expanded range of choices and options when it came to their marriages and the handling of disputes that arose within marriage. If not utterly freewheeling, wide segments of the Republican population were at least as engaged with the law in ways both prosaic and extraordinary. As this book will make clear, the Republican Civil Code was a point of origin, opening the door to popular engagement with the law on a much wider scale than ever before.

THE 1930 CIVIL CODE AND REPUBLICAN "LEGAL EXCEPTIONALISM"

The history of the Republican Civil Code has long conformed to the story of modernity deferred, representing yet another frustrating chapter in the protracted nineteenth- and twentieth-century pursuit of Chinese modernity.[5] Compared to other dimensions of the GMD pursuit of modernity, law stands out as an arena in which a series of ideological and institutional transformations succeeded to a large degree in effecting wide-ranging social progress. The painstaking effort by a select band of enlightened elites to bring legal modernity to China by borrowing from modern European and Japanese law codes produced a remarkably progressive civil code based upon the principles of individual rights and gender equality. It is commonly presumed that the combined forces of millennia of tradition, a short-lived period of Nationalist rule, and the reign of reactionary elements within the GMD foiled the code's achievements. So despite the progressive features of the code, scholars have dismissed the largely foreign-inspired code for failing to take root in Chinese soil, citing the code's promise of gender equality as an especially notable example of legal change that did not lead to social change. The dominant image of the code remained that of a foreign import unsuccessfully grafted onto unreceptive Chinese soil.

This view of the code begs an array of questions. Was Chinese law during the Republican era really as irrelevant as this image suggests? How does one make sense of a chronological sequence in which the implementation of legal gender equality was followed by a downturn in women's status? Was the hold of patriarchal tradition in China so unshakable? Was the urban-rural divide so impermeable as to prevent legal change in the cities from influencing the countryside? Were legal elites so ineffectual, so attuned to foreign concepts that they were unable to attend to the needs of their own country? Was GMD rule so oppressive that it was able to quash the nascent rights consciousness and gender equality? Was law only an instrument of the state? What influence did society exercise? How, moreover, did legal and social change interact in the highly transitional Republican era?

Improved access to archival materials, historiographic trends, and theoretical models make this a fitting time to reassess questions about the significance and social impact of the code. Views that dismissed the social impact of the code derived from studies that were conducted without access to archival case records. Such access, at least for Western scholars, was not possible until the 1980s. More recent studies that have been able to draw upon case records to analyze the social impact of the code confirm that there was indeed a wide gap between the ideas associated with legal modernity featured in the code and the understandings, values, expectations, and desires of litigants at the local level, especially those outside of urban centers.[6] Social change did not proceed as quickly or as dramatically as legal change. Instead, the social impact of the new laws unfolded gradually and in more complex ways than the drafting of the law itself anticipated. The existence of this gap and this lag, however, does not justify downplaying the significance of the code, but rather cries out for closer investigation. This gap and other disparities associated with the integration of law and social practice generated crosscurrents of cultural reinterpretation demonstrating that the Chinese legal system was a malleable one and could be put to use for any number of state, familial, or personal purposes.

Before the opening of Chinese archives in the 1980s, Western scholarship on the Republican Civil Code tended to cursorily acknowledge the code's achievement of gender equality before brushing it aside as a breakthrough on paper that never materialized in practice.[7] These assessments usually accorded with evaluations of GMD rule overall as a botched attempt at liberalization and modernization. Arguments stressed the GMD's failure to achieve unified rule, thus discounting GMD accomplishments in the legal realm and playing up the lack of political and military stability during the Republican era that overshadowed ongoing efforts at legal reform and institution building. This negative judgment of the code was linked in part to the GMD's own ineptitude and blatant disregard for the rule of law in other areas. From the party's own violent factionalism, to Chiang Kai-shek's reliance on military tactics, to the brutal purge of activists in the White Terror of 1927, and the ruthless suppression of democratic organizers and the student antiwar movement in the war years, the gruesomeness of GMD rule has not been hard to establish (Isaacs 1962, Eastman 1984, Gilmartin 1995, Pepper 1999, ch. 3). Since GMD failure was manifest in the repression, brutality, and corruption associated with Nationalist rule, scholars in the past saw little need to devote scholarship to questions of women's rights or legal gender equality during the Nationalist period. However, in contrast to the grimness of GMD rule as a whole, the building of modern juridical institutions lends important support to the argument for what I call "legal exceptionalism," positing the Republican Civil Code as an important exception to the GMD's otherwise authoritarian nature.[8]

During the postsocialist period historians have reassessed the nature of GMD rule. This reconsideration of Republican state and society has permitted the emergence of a rather different picture of the GMD state and its relation to Republican society. This more recent scholarly approach treats the GMD years, especially the Nanjing Decade, as a critical period of modernization and nation-building.[9] Numerous studies point to the innovations of the Republican era and areas of continuity between the Republic, the post-Mao era, and even the Maoist era. These studies identify Republican precursors to many contemporary developments and make it possible to transcend the problematic but still important 1949 divide in Chinese history. The continuities rather than the ruptures are striking when it comes to marriage reform. The goal of marriage reform was a twentieth-century goal shared by the various political regimes. Much of what seemed novel in the 1950s, ranging from the expansion of state authority in marriage and family affairs to the consolidation of the trend toward conjugal families, and even the combative peasant legal culture, for instance, had definite roots in the 1930s and 1940s. Because of the developments of the 1930s and 1940s, moreover, Chinese society was perhaps better prepared for the more comprehensive wave of marriage and family legislation that ensued after 1950. Contemporary developments suggest thinking of Republican developments not as modernity deferred or as an interregnum but as a type of "gestational modernity," a time when modern legal institutions and values were formed, though their full growth and implementation was delayed until decades later (see Strand 2011 on the idea of an "unfinished republic").

The recent scholarly trend toward studies of Republican culture, society, and economy, moreover, has also complicated the narrative of Republican politics and shifted attention to developments in urban Chinese society.[10] The frame of liberal modernity in this book has much in common with this more recent scholarship. The implementation of the Republican Civil Code in the 1930s and 1940s took place during a time when Chinese society was undergoing dynamic change in its attitudes toward marriage, divorce, and sexuality, especially in urban areas (Goodman 2006). Not only were social attitudes changing, but social institutions were also in the midst of transformation, especially with urbanization and the emergence of smaller families (Glosser 2003). Changes in women's education afforded women increased occupational opportunities (Cong 2007). And an influential class of professional women contributed to nation-building on various fronts (Wang 1999, Schneider 2011). The impact of Nationalist family laws must be examined in the context of these social changes and their inherent tensions.

WOMEN AND THE LAW

Earlier studies of Chinese law drew upon written codes and model case collections to cast Chinese law in instrumental and ideological terms, giving rise to the conventional trope that law was a tool of state domination.[11] However, more recently available archival evidence tells a different story. Republican breakthroughs in legal ideology helped pave the way for a changing relationship between women and the law, one in which law represented a way to reduce the injustices of married life. The primary purpose of late imperial law, according to this older scholarship, was the enforcement of the state's authoritarian control over society through the strict and harsh punishment of crimes. Law was regarded as something to be feared, and litigation was to be avoided by good, circumspect people if at all possible. Prevailing attitudes emphasized popular dread and fear of the law and the belief that people should only turn to law as a last resort. For women, especially, the law was no friend. If anything, women were portrayed as victims of the law, deprived of any formal rights and treated as subordinate and inferior. Imperial marriage regulations mirrored the Confucian preoccupation with the perpetuation of the family line and ancestor worship, with the status of women correspondingly low. Litigious women from the late imperial period were generally cast as "shrewish" and otherwise deviant.

In the early twentieth century, the role of law and attitudes toward the law changed as the idea of the law as a tool of patriarchal oppression was challenged by the Republican notion of law as a tool of women's liberation. Republican lawmakers believed that the surest way to improve the legal status of women was to begin with the traditional patrilineal family system, which had been targeted as the site of the worst inequalities, both for women and for youth. By dismantling the legal basis for the Confucian patrilineal family and replacing it with conjugal and nuclear family ideas, Chinese lawmakers hoped to recast an individual's relationship with the family unit on a more gender-equal basis, especially when compared to Confucian gender hierarchy.

Liberal modernity, moreover, rested upon the foundation of newly bestowed individual rights and the corresponding legal actions to which they gave rise. The prevailing logic seemed to approximate the idea that if only women were granted rights, then those rights would set them free. One might even argue that it was Republican family law that granted Chinese women (and men) formal rights for the first time in history. These formal rights, in turn, provided women with direct access to the state and its judicial system and vice versa. A woman could now represent herself before the law, without the contrivance of a male proxy. A domestic civil dispute, moreover, was no longer a "minor matter" to be determined with finality at the local level. Determined (or disgruntled) litigants in the Republican era began to exercise the right of appeal. The safeguarding of formal rights in some cases also led to the reapportionment of money and property in separation and support cases (this is fully discussed in chapter 7). Courts too became more amenable and available to women who sought redress for marital wrongs. The number of marital disputes handled by the state certainly escalated during the late Republican period. Judges resolved marital disputes and other matters that may previously have been the purview of lineage elders through the use of mediation. Wider access to the state, in addition, meant that a wife's suit for annulment could prompt a judicial investigation and medical examination of her husband's ability to engage in sexual relations (chapter 8). Overall, these changes fostered a shift in popular attitudes toward the law. Compared to the past, there seemed to be more willingness to turn to the law, to resort to litigation, and to engage with the state. This study of Republican marital disputes will trace how and why women in particular turned to the law to pursue their interests and how their willingness to use the legal system to press their personal goals simultaneously enhanced the prestige of civil law more generally.

AGAINST THE "DARK YEARS" THESIS

This book's focus on women and the law suggests a new way of thinking about women's history in China. According to the main narrative of Chinese women's history, the women's movement reached its peak in the mid-1920s, experienced a serious decline in the 1930s and 1940s, and picked up again only after 1949. This interpretation of Chinese women's history during the Republican era takes a grim view of the period after 1927 when the purge of activists during the White Terror signaled a tragic end to the radical Chinese women's movement, which had accomplished heroic feats of mobilizing large numbers of women into military, peasant, and labor organizations in the mid-1920s. The decades that followed supposedly represent years of retrenchment, when both of the major political parties, the GMD and the Chinese Communist Party (CCP), withdrew their sponsorship of the women's movement. The New Life Movement cast a conservative shadow over the women's movement, while the women's movement itself turned its focus to supporting the Chinese war effort.[12] This periodization, with an emphasis on the demise of the Chinese women's movement in the late 1920s and its delayed resurgence in the 1950s, obscures developments taking place during the intervening two decades. As a result, the 1930s and 1940s are relegated to the status of "lost" or "dark" years of Chinese women's history.

Historiographical trends associated with the 1949 divide in Chinese history have contributed to the relative neglect of the history of Republican marriage law and practice. The CCP master narrative of women's liberation as a subset of socialist revolution, for instance, has worked to expunge GMD contributions from the record of Chinese women's history by glorifying the contributions made by the CCP to the exclusion of those made by other actors.[13] This official insistence upon the CCP's role as liberator requires the concomitant denial of progress made toward gender equality especially in urban China during the 1930s and 1940s when the CCP sought refuge in remote rural areas. On the one hand, the CCP narrative indiscriminately lumps the 1930s and 1940s together with the Qing Dynasty (1644–1912) and the early Republican periods into one all-encompassing, blanket "bad old days" category of "feudal society." On the other hand, this narrative disparages the 1930s and 1940s in particular as an era of "bourgeois feminism."[14] The presumed bleakness of the prerevolutionary years for Chinese women, whether "feudal" or "bourgeois," makes their eventual rescue by the CCP seem more meaningful and poignant but does so at the expense of a clear understanding of the developments of the 1930s and 1940s. After 1949, as CCP-sponsored campaigns took center stage, the complexities of marriage and women's lives in the transitional and experimental 1930s and 1940s were largely pushed into the background. Support for the CCP master narrative came perhaps unwittingly from the now-vulnerable but still influential paradigm of revolution and its derivatives.[15] The paradigm of revolution maintains that progress is achieved through wholesale change (usually of a violent nature) and thereby dismisses, unfortunately, the importance of progress made under the rubric of reform, like the Republican-era legal reforms. Historians not associated with the CCP also usually tap 1949 as the major turning point in the emancipation of women in China. With the foregrounding of the 1949 Revolution, GMD marriage law and practice tends to be overshadowed in the historiographic treatment by the much more thoroughly implemented CCP Marriage Law of 1950.

One of the major tasks of this study will be to question this oversight and to recover the significance of this period in Chinese women's history by examining the changes in marriage law and practice that transpired in the 1930s and 1940s. In contrast to the mass mobilization of women in the mid-1920s and the early 1950s, which featured brief spikes of organized, radical change, the transformation of gender relations in the 1930s and 1940s unfolded in a different pattern with a landmark legal act percolating through society over an extended period of time. The social impact of the Republican Civil Code did not sweep over the nation in one comprehensive and intensive upsurge but took hold incrementally and spread selectively. Progress was made, to be sure, but on a case-by-case basis, more appropriately measured by the cumulative effect of thousands of individual legal actions. As individual, incremental, and selective efforts directed at ameliorating personal domestic situations, these legal actions might have been harder to detect, but in the history of Chinese women it is perhaps the more mundane stuff of marital and family life that most directly affected the lives of the majority of women. This work will demonstrate that the late Republican era undeniably marked a formative period for Chinese women's history. During this period both a significant transformation of the legal regulation of marriage and family relations and a more gradual change in actual marriage and family relationships were well under way.

I propose to fill in the historiographic lacuna regarding the 1930s and 1940s by thinking of the late 1920s and early 1930s in terms of an expansion or broadening rather than a detumescence. This period certainly marked the end of an era in Chinese women's history. The marginalization of comprehensive, systematic efforts to combat gender oppression, in my view, however, did not signal the inevitable decline of efforts to propel Chinese women's emancipation. Rather, with the passage of the Republican Civil Code in 1930 and the eradication of legal discrimination against women, a new phase in the history of Chinese women's emancipation was initiated spanning the early 1930s to the late 1940s. This was a period in which definitions of marriage and family were shifting according to fundamental ideological changes, like the partial repudiation of Confucian patrilinealism and the emergence of an essentially modern, liberal framework of individual rights and equality under the law, as well as to continuing socioeconomic changes, such as urbanization and industrialization. When an expansion rather than demise is envisioned, then the sequel to the women's movement of the mid-1920s is no longer the CCP-sponsored feminism of the 1950s but rather the liberal modernity of the late Republican period.

The social dislocations arising from the two wars complicated marriage and family dynamics in unpredictable ways. The war years brought about changes in women's roles and expanded economic opportunities for women, especially in regions in the process of urbanization and industrialization. Throughout these years, many women enthusiastically participated in the war effort in various capacities. Although marriage remained the primary source of economic security for women, other options emerged as socially acceptable alternatives, especially in urban areas where a greater number of women and men sought to defy traditional expectations about marriage.

The law played a crucial role in reinforcing a vision of marriage based upon gender equality, women's rights, conjugal fidelity, and mutual support and companionship. Retrieving the records of marital disputes from the 1930s and 1940s gives a voice to ordinary women who might not otherwise appear in the historical record. Hearing these voices makes it possible then to see questions of periodization and the nature of change in Chinese women's history in new ways. For instance, the 1930s and 1940s appear as a formative period in Chinese women's history when individual women actively engaged with the law to assert their interests, rather than as "dark years" during which women's mobilization declined. In the Republican era, legal and social changes made it possible for women who sought to escape oppressive marriages to approach domestic conflicts with a broad range of legal devices at their disposal. Ultimately, the book demonstrates that the availability of legal recourses and women's willingness to use the law bespeak a new and different form of agency and female empowerment.

THEORIZING THE NATURE OF LEGAL CHANGE IN LATE IMPERIAL AND REPUBLICAN CHINA

To do justice to recent North American, Chinese, Japanese, and European scholarship on Chinese legal history would require an entire review article at least.[16] With the inclinations of social and cultural historians as well as legal historians, for example, the editors and contributors to the path-breaking series on "Law, Society, and Culture in China" mined a trove of previously unavailable archival legal documents that brought to light new understandings of the intersection of law and society.[17] I am extremely grateful for this rich and diverse body of scholarship and seek to expand upon it temporally and thematically. Very little past scholarship, for instance, has confronted the massive transformations presented by the modernization of Chinese law in the early twentieth century. By locating my study in the early twentieth century, I am able to examine how the modernization of Chinese law involved both adopting modern European continental law and drawing upon late imperial legal and social trends. In this section, I draw upon past scholarship mainly to help theorize the relationship between legal change in the late imperial and Republican periods.

During the late imperial period, changes in the legal status of women were mostly designed to accommodate changing social realities. Although these shifts promoted state interests in social order, for the most part they were not ideologically driven or directed toward a grand scheme in the way that characterized legal change during the Republican era.[18] The late imperial assumption was that the basic contours of legal ideology had long been established (back in the early imperial period), and any subsequent changes constituted minor modifications or changes in emphasis directed to respond to particular developments. Changes to the various dynastic codes, for example, most commonly took the form of substatutes or stipulations added on to the original statutes, which were left intact. The substatutes were often narrowly tailored to specific factual situations and sometimes contradicted other provisions. For the most part, during the late imperial period law lagged behind practice, playing catch-up with practice. A number of examples illustrate the trailing function of law. For example, as Kathryn Bernhardt (1996, 56) demonstrates in her study of women and the law during the Ming-Qing transition, a process of "peasantization of the law" had taken place in which peasant practices, which regarded betrothal as nearly equivalent to marriage (to protect the large financial consideration involved in the acquisition of a daughter-in-law), gradually assumed the status of formal law. Matthew Sommer (2000) interprets Yongzheng-era legal reforms that erased status distinctions between "servile" people and "commoners" as measures designed to create a uniform marital order to reduce the social instability generated by a swelling lower class of young, single men. Janet Theiss (2004) also detects mid-Qing legal trends toward conjugal patriarchy, with tensions between conjugal and patrilineal authority increasingly favoring the conjugal relationship. Melissa Macauley (1998) demonstrates that state anxieties about "litigation masters" (*songshi*) corresponded to periods of intense commercialization in the late Song and mid-Qing periods. Each of these legal innovations illustrates plainly that late imperial law functioned both to enforce state ideology and to respond to changing socioeconomic conditions, such as increasing commercialization, rural impoverishment, and social instability. By the early twentieth century, moreover, these socioeconomic factors also made Qing law grossly inadequate in a number of areas, mostly involving civil disputes (Huang 1996).

Republican legal change was of a different nature. Legal reform came as part of a grand, comprehensive plan for modernization, formulated specifically to abide by concerns with liberal modernity. Indeed, in order to eliminate the imperialist contrivance of extraterritoriality, Chinese lawmakers had no choice but to abide by Western legal principles. As noted, the elite group of lawmakers who spearheaded the reforms thought of themselves, above all, as modernizers, and the changes they pushed through were not minor adjustments limited to certain situations but rather accompanied a completely revamped ideological framework. In fact, the nature of the Republican changes required a fundamental reconceptualization of the entire legal system, and no area of the law was to be left untouched. In the area of marriage, legal modernity required a total revamping of existing laws according to the principles of individual rights and gender equality. Republican lawmakers had to dismantle the basic Confucian framework that underlay late imperial marriage provisions, to "de-Confucianize" the law, so to speak, and rewrite the laws according to the principles of liberal modernity.

The totalistic nature of these legal changes and the truism that social change did not simply follow legal change reinforce the impression that Republican law changed on paper but not in practice. This perception is partially true. No one would argue that modern Republican law reached every corner of rural China. Nevertheless, to dismiss Republican law as a superficial change misses the important point that Republican legal reform consisted not just of Chinese adaptations of modern Western law, but to a substantial degree corresponded to legal and social pressures for reform dating from at least the mid-Qing. The legal system, in other words, would probably have needed an overhaul even without the intervention of the West in order to accommodate the changes wrought by urbanization, commercialization, and industrialization. As such, Republican legal changes undertaken in the name of liberal modernity were in fact also rooted in Qing legal trends, though they were not packaged as such. Thus, the de-Confucianization of the law may not have been as draconian a measure as it sounds. It can be interpreted as the consolidation of Qing legal trends under a new ideological label. This point is worth belaboring. The striking ideological changes in Republican law have obscured the fact that Republican legal reform also embodied legal and social trends dating from at least the mid-Qing.

Qing legal and social trends served as important precedents, as deeper roots for Republican legal changes, and also eased the acceptance of Republican changes, as the examples below illustrate. Kathryn Bernhardt and Philip Huang (1994, 10) note that the legacy of Qing civil law provided "hospitable soil" for the Republican Civil Code, pointing to similarities in the content of civil cases. Huang (1996, 8) also posits an "essential continuity" between Qing and Republican civil law. I have found that although Republican lawmakers heralded the major shift in the law from patrilineal to the conjugal models of marriage and family, the changes may not have been as groundbreaking as the lawmakers thought. Lawmakers, for instance, intentionally targeted patrilineal ideology as a blatant marker of "traditional" law that enforced hierarchy and stifled individual productivity and happiness. However, when viewed from the perspective of legal practice, the abandonment of the patriline had definite roots in the Qing. Several scholars have noted how the late imperial cult of chastity shifted the balance between conjugal and patrilineal notions of family in favor of the conjugal bond. Examples include the late Ming shift in inheritance laws from mandatory nephew succession to a widow's preferred nephew (Bernhardt 1999) and the emergence of the conjugally based family as the foil in mid-Qing regulations of sexuality (Sommer 2000 and Theiss 2004).

The divorce provisions of the Republican Civil Code that were so remarkable for their gender-equal applicability also arguably overlapped with several Qing provisions in content. Both codes permitted (and in the Qing sometimes required) divorce in cases of bigamy, adultery, abuse, illness, desertion, murderous intent, and criminal behavior. The changes in Republican law were rooted in shifting definitions of these same basic categories of Qing law. Under the Republican Civil Code, for example, dual branch marriage—in which one man maintaining two families in order to succeed both his father and a sonless uncle had formerly been perfectly legal behavior—now came to constitute bigamy. The definition of adultery, in addition, expanded to encompass a much wider range of behavior by a husband; the focus was not overwhelmingly on a wife's potential to pollute her husband's patriline. And finally, the standard for abuse shifted from requiring "a broken bone or tooth" under late imperial law to abuse that made living together "intolerable" under Republican law.

These examples support the notion of the Republican paradigm of liberal modernity as an important transitional period in modern Chinese law that also served as a way to organize disparate legal and social developments in evidence since the mid-Qing. The link to Qing socioeconomic precedents suggests that the Republican Civil Code was not as "alien" as its packaging appeared.

SOURCES FOR THE STUDY OF REPUBLICAN MARRIAGE, LAW, AND SOCIETY

Historians across a wide range of fields have drawn upon legal documents to provide insight into early-modern and modern societies.[19] The records of actual marital disputes that found their way to Republican courtrooms help us more fully appreciate the significance of the Republican Civil Code and understand how legal-political change from above interacted with developments from below. The concrete examples in archival records of actual marital disputes allow historians to go beyond theoretical and ideological statements of Chinese law and view the operation of law "on the ground."

This study is based on over 400 marital cases mostly dating from the 1930s and 1940s, all of which fall under the category of civil lawsuits. The cases originated from the Beijing District Court (*Beijing difang fayuan*) (roughly 150 cases), Hebei Superior Court (*Hebei sheng gaodeng fayuan*) (over 100 cases), Jiangsu Superior Court (*Jiangsu sheng gaodeng fayuan*) (approximately 80 cases), and Supreme Court (*Zuigao fayuan*) (just under 100 cases). The cases from the Supreme Court originate from nearly every province in China. As described in more detail in the litigation overview in chapter 4, there were three levels in the Republican judicial system. At the lowest level, district courts and county-level judicial organs heard cases in the first instance. Provincial superior courts resided at the intermediate level. For instance, the Jiangsu Superior Court heard appeals from the important cities of Nanjing and Shanghai as well as Suzhou and Wuxi. The Hebei Superior Court heard appeals predominantly from Beijing, but also from neighboring counties. The highest level of the Republican judicial system was the Supreme Court, known as the Daliyuan before 1927. The Supreme Court/Daliyuan was physically located in Beijing from 1906 to 1927, then in Nanjing from 1927 to 1937, then relocated to Chongqing during the War of Resistance from 1938 to 1945, before finally being restored to Nanjing from 1945 to 1949. Litigants did not have to appear in person and had the option to mail their appeals and answers to the Supreme Court. The documents generated by a court case, moreover, usually included a petition, answer, record of oral interrogation, witness testimonials, and court-mediated settlements or judgments. Of these documents, the deposition/interrogation is especially relevant because it allows the historian to read the words of actual litigants. Unlike imperial depositions, Republican-era ones generally constituted verbatim records of questions posed by a judge and answered by litigants, lawyers, and witnesses.

One of the most valuable features of case records from the 1930s and 1940s is that they afford a sample of the pleas and grievances of ordinary Chinese husbands and wives. We "hear" their voices, or at least something close to their voices. Some petitions were drafted by professional lawyers, and their pleas were couched in the more polished legal arguments. In the majority of marital cases, however, litigants had no legal representation, and their petitions and testimonies get us a little bit closer to how they thought about marriage, what aggrieved ordinary people, and what upset their sense of justice. We get a fascinating glimpse into their perceptions of their marriages.

These newly audible voices from the archives disclose how the emergence of liberal modernity contributed to the development of a nascent "rights consciousness," albeit one that was detached from the premises of European liberalism. The grievances of Republican husbands and wives may have been very similar to the grievances of late imperial husbands and wives.

Yet the modern liberal lens of rights and duties recast Republican grievances into legally actionable claims. The spread of this rights consciousness helped reshape individual expectations, values, and disappointments with marriage.

These records also reveal socioeconomic constraints that worked to limit how far legal changes could be implemented. Despite the best of legislative intentions, gender inequality in China persisted in large part because the liberal legal framework ignored the fact that individuals were embedded in existing social relationships of inequality. The preferred liberal solution of creating rights-bearing individuals could not succeed very far within the patrilineally organized Chinese family. Republican subjects were hardly the blank sheets of paper that theorists imagined. They were individuals in marriages shaped by social structures already layered, perhaps even sedimented, with inequalities.

The driving forces behind changing attitudes, expectations, and practices of marriage did not necessarily derive from the state's plans, which often just affirmed trends already under way. Although the state abandoned the patrilineal ideology of yore, the socioeconomic necessity of patrilocal marriage was not addressed. The passage of the Republican Civil Code represented a radical point of departure, but it did not bring about quick solutions in legal or social practice, nor did it launch a revolution in itself. It bestowed rights, but it did not, for instance, secure the immediate, unimpeded exercise of these newly granted rights. Existing social structures like the patrilineal family impeded the exercise of formal rights even under the new Western liberal legal framework.

Wives' relationships with their natal (birth) families also shaped litigation outcomes. The success of a female litigant in a marital dispute often depended on whether or not she could count on the support of her natal family. Wives who could count on natal family help and influence generally fared better than wives without such help. The greatest obstacles to making gender equality a social reality in China was in part the continued potency of the Confucian patrilineal family system, which remained to some extent entrenched in the new laws. The other particularly formidable obstacles to gender equality were the deeply rooted practices of patrilocal marriage (where a wife moved into her husband's family home) and dependent family-based economic relationships.

Perhaps even more importantly than a litigant's gender, explicit class biases shaped the adjudication of Republican marriage law. Class played a determining role in the rate of marital litigation success with urban middle-class women benefiting from the new laws in ways that were denied their more rural and impoverished counterparts. Of course, women from natal families of middle- to upper-class standing had access to more resources (lawyers, witnesses) to aid their litigation efforts. When adjudicating cruelty divorce cases, judges explicitly took class into account. Judicial interpretations endorsed different standards for what constituted intolerable cruelty, with opinions holding that physical violence of any kind amounted to grounds for divorce for urban, educated couples, while occasional violence did not amount to intolerable cruelty in a marriage between uneducated peasants. Class considerations also shaped the types of judicial remedies sought. Bourgeois women were able to sue for separation and support in contrast to women from lower-class families, who often had no choice but to sue for divorce, thereby freeing themselves to remarry and find a new husband to support them.

In addition to archival case records, this study draws upon legislative records, which include meeting agendas and minutes from the codification process, as well as legal codes and draft codes. New laws proliferated in China beginning in the late Qing period. The flurry of legislative activity undertaken after the establishment of the GMD government in Nanjing in 1927, moreover, resulted in the promulgation of a new civil code, two criminal codes, new land and labor laws, and codes for civil and criminal procedures, among others. Before and after the promulgation of these laws, legal questions inspired vibrant debate, as evidenced by the proliferation of journals and publication of treatises devoted to the study of law during the Republican era. Examples of the leading journals include *Falü pinglun* (Law Weekly Review), *Faling zhoukan* (Law Weekly), and *Faxue jikan* (Law Journal). Another group of published sources consists of the writings of the leading figures of the legal reform movement, including Hu Hanmin, Hu Changqing, and Wang Chonghui. Many of these debates took place in the women's press, where we find women's voices and reactions to the legalization of gender equality. The broad presence of women readers, writers, and editors distinguishes the twentieth century, especially after 1930, from any earlier period. These sources are particularly useful in my examination of the debates on surname legislation in chapter 3. They are supplemented with general-interest newspapers and magazines.

The marriage provisions of the code derived from a set of modern liberal assumptions that differed from customary and prevailing social attitudes, but they still had meaning for individual litigants. Litigants reappropriated the ideas in the code, shaping their litigation strategies according to the new ideas, translating the ideas into terms that were intelligible to their worldview, and fitting them into their own schemes. Legislative and judicial records require us to revise the old image of Republican law as an ineffective foreign import and to envision instead Republican lawmakers engaged in a lengthy process of carefully sorting through foreign legal concepts and struggling to find the best way to adapt them to Chinese circumstances. Once enacted, this experiment in legal syncretism underwent further processes of reinterpretation. Through the experience of litigation and adjudication, the new marriage and family laws blended with alternative beliefs, transformed others, and produced an unexpected mix of consequences. These hodgepodge combinations of modern forms and traditional concerns defy the typical tradition-modernity dichotomies.

THE ORGANIZATION OF THE BOOK

The book is organized into two parts, the first emphasizing the state and the second society. Part I focuses on the main components of the Republican state's legal system, the civil code and the court system. Part II examines actual marital disputes from the 1930s and 1940s, with each litigation chapter corresponding to a different type of legal remedy: divorce (*lihun*), cohabitation (*tongju*), separation (*bieju*), and annulment. Combined, the two parts illuminate GMD law as ideology and practice.

Chapter 2 explores the pursuit of modernity by Chinese legal elites who scrambled to reshape the institutions of marriage and family according to Western liberal values. The chapter analyzes the conceptual underpinnings of GMD legal ideology as a variant of liberal modernity that emphasized civil law (over criminal law), individual rights and duties (over moral and ritual obligations), and gender equality (over Confucian hierarchy). The chapter further develops the political setting in which the drafting of the Republican Civil Code took place. For example, in the 1920s, the GMD adopted a radical policy toward women and the family. Overall, the chapter supports my contention that GMD rule displayed a form of what I call "legal exceptionalism" in which the newly established, modern civil law system stood in contrast to the more authoritarian elements of GMD rule.

Chapter 3 centers on the controversy over married women's surnames that arose in conjunction with the codification of GMD family law as well as the postcodification debate in the women's press. The chapter reveals the animated process by which GMD lawmakers, legal experts, women's groups, and others grappled with how best to reform longstanding surname practices. Although the outcome of the legislative process basically affirmed patrilineal surname customs (albeit with progressive overtones), the process itself was uniquely radical, with participants thoroughly reevaluating one of the most fundamental and deeply entrenched patriarchal institutions in Chinese society. My analysis of the legislative debate and postlegislative feminist critique illuminates the Nanjing Decade as a singular transitional period in the history of Chinese law and gender. Law was subject to revision and amendment rather than orthodoxy, and GMD policy toward women was subject to deliberation and interpretation rather than dictated by ideology in this era.

Chapter 4 provides the foundation for understanding the institutional structures, namely the courts of law, that comprised the Republican civil law system. The chapter describes the organization of the GMD court system into three levels: local, provincial, and national. In addition, the chapter covers legal procedures, fees, and other steps needed to file lawsuits, to request mediation or adjudication, to summon witnesses, to marshal other types of evidence, and to appeal disappointing decisions. Aside from the empirical foundation about the juridical system, the chapter supports my larger contention that the civil law framework for marital litigation helped to elevate these disputes, making the legal system more responsive to women's interests and reducing to some extent the stigma of legal involvement.

The four types of marriage cases explored in part II probe the social impact of the Republican Civil Code and appear in order of frequency of litigation, beginning with the most common type of litigation, divorce, in chapter 5.[20] "Spousal Abuse: Divorce Litigation and the Emergence of Rights Consciousness" probes the change in people's consciousness about domestic cruelty. It explores how the introduction of rights through the civil code affected what women and men thought about their marriages. Drawing on the sociology of law literature on grievances, the chapter shows how what might have constituted an ordinary grievance under late imperial law was transformed into a legally actionable claim. The framing of domestic cruelty as an issue of women's rights may have lent poignancy to narratives of marital oppression, but it did not guarantee a favorable legal judgment. Thus, the main argument of the chapter demonstrates that although lawmakers dismantled the patrilineal basis of marriage, individual rights ironically affirmed patriarchy, albeit in a modern, conjugal form.

Chapter 6 focuses on cohabitation lawsuits brought by husbands whose wives refused to live with them. Unlike men in the late imperial period who could press for the criminal prosecution of runaway wives, Republican men's recourse was limited to civil cohabitation suits. And unlike runaway women in the late imperial period who could be beaten under the law for their behavior, in the Republican period women could defy court orders for their return without any criminal legal consequences. This chapter also shows how women continued to negotiate the underlying social tensions between their natal and marital families. These disputes over the physical location of the marriage reveal challenges to both virilocality (when a wife transfers her residence to that of her husband and his family) and the affirmation of patriarchy in its conjugal form.

Chapter 7 examines how bourgeois women navigated the Republican legal terrain. With the help of lawyers, bourgeois women carved out novel suits for judicial separation and support that were transitional measures not explicitly enumerated in the civil code. This alternative to judicial divorce arose largely from legal recognition of the "injury" suffered by innocent wives whose husbands took in concubines or committed other acts of sexual infidelity (an outgrowth of the idea of a mutual duty of conjugal fidelity) as well as the reluctance of injured wives to divorce. Judicial separation and support turned out to be convenient remedies that allowed women to remain formally married and thereby avoid the moral stigma attached to divorce. Under this arrangement, they were at liberty to live apart from their husbands but still entitled to their financial support. These cases also help demonstrate the conjugal and capitalist logic of Republican civil law. Judgments that granted judicial separation and support essentially redirected money and property from husbands and patrilines to separated wives.

Chapter 8 explores how the imported idea of the conjugal debt spawned an infamous genre of lawsuits in Republican China. These cases involved enterprising women who pushed the litigation envelope, often by using impotence allegations as a pretext to address other marital woes that were not otherwise acknowledged by the Republican Civil Code. Impotence cases directly attacked the masculinity of husbands while also capturing the public's imagination. These so-called "natural eunuch" cases provide a fascinating lens by which to analyze changing attitudes toward sexuality. The chapter also analyzes the state's role in conducting these investigations. The state appears as seriously intrusive, armed with modern legal and medical devices, intervening in intimate matters through judicial interrogations and, most notoriously, through invasive medical examinations.

Chapter 9 recaps the key findings and expands on the book's implications for future work. The conclusion reflects upon how mining the intersection of gender and law gives rise to new insights about the problem of Chinese modernity. I suggest ways of thinking about gender, law, and modernity in terms of changes in legal consciousness and popular consciousness. Domestic problems, like cruelty, undoubtedly had a long history in China and elsewhere. Modern legal theory, however, views human relations in terms of rights and duties. Thus the Republican Civil Code approached domestic cruelty as a matter of claims and counterclaims, establishing innovative legal tools, based on the idea of individual liberty, designed to alleviate the problem. The ways in which people in the Republican period came to think about domestic cruelty as a form of oppression that could be remedied through law went beyond late imperial notions of violence as undesirable. Modern Chinese women departed from their forebears in their attitudes toward domestic oppression as well as their sense of personhood. This discussion of changes in law and popular consciousness is emblematic of the larger set of changes that ushered in the period known as modern China. This study makes clear that the political uncertainties of the 1930s and 1940s (and corresponding breakdown of traditional authority) did not preclude the possibility for the advancement of women, built upon the foundation of legal gender equality. Far-reaching social change was possible even in the absence of corresponding political progress and the presence of foreign occupation and civil war. It may even have been facilitated by the wartime pressure wearing down entrenched social patterns.

NOTES

1. The notion of the Chinese people as blank sheets, though popularized by Mao Zedong, originated with the GMD ideologue Dai Jitao. See Fitzgerald 1996, 18.
2. Letter to Oliver Wendell Holmes Jr., dated 23 November 1921 cited by Alford and Shen 1993, 45. Wu served as a law professor and dean in Shanghai and served in the Legislative Yuan beginning in 1933. Wu was widely regarded as one of the most prominent Chinese legal scholars, involved with drafting a constitution, compiling an authoritative dictionary of Chinese law, publishing the law journal *Faxue jikan* (Law Journal), writing numerous essays and books on Chinese law, especially from a comparative perspective, and co-editing and compiling the *Liu fa quan shu* (Complete version of the six laws). See Alford and Shen 1993 and Greiff 1985.
3. Glosser 2003. Glosser's work has been particularly illuminating regarding the family-state nexus. She identifies the connection between family reform and state-strengthening as one of the main reasons for the failure of individual rights to take hold in China. She argues that this pattern of greater state intervention in marriage and family matters only intensified after 1949 during the Maoist era, paving the way for the totalitarian state. See also Schwartz 1964.
4. For additional studies on the nature of the Republican state, see Shue 1988, Strauss 1998, and Huang 2008.
5. Following the pandectist German and Japanese models, the Republican Civil Code was promulgated in five sections or books (General Principles, Obligations, Rights over Things, Family, and Succession) over 1929–1930. The last two books went into effect on May 5, 1931. All references are to the *Civil Code of the Republic of China.*
6. Bernhardt 1994 and 1999 and Huang 2001.
7. An early exception to the general neglect of the Republican Civil Code was the dissertation of Bernice J. Lee (1975). Bergère 1997 and Esherick 2001 provide excellent analyses of the historiographic issues at stake for studies of the Republican era. The failure theme ignores the possibility that failure and disintegration themselves may serve as important catalysts for certain types of change.
8. In his study of Republican legal reform Huang 2001 distinguishes between the GMD "center-stage political story" and a "second-line sphere" that includes law, education, transportation, communication, and industry, where developments took place despite the obstacles that plagued the very top of the GMD leadership. Xu 2008 adopts a mostly positive evaluation of GMD state and institution-building efforts, though he identifies chronic underfunding as one of the biggest obstacles to judicial modernity. The goal of my study is not to celebrate the legal achievements of the GMD period, but first to understand them, then to interrogate them and place them in the proper social and political context.
9. For the larger reevaluation of the Republican period taking place in recent years see Lary 2007, Zarrow 2005, Leutner and Spakowski, eds. 2005, Brødsgaard and Strand, eds. 1998, Wakeman and Edmonds, eds. 2000 (the essays by Loren Brandt, William Kirby, and Julia Strauss emphasize continuity in the areas of economics, foreign relations, and politics; and Strauss and Kirby credit the GMD for some of the state-building success usually accorded to the CCP). Cohen 2002 interrogates the problematic nature of the 1949 divide to the attention of scholars. Esherick 2001 underscored the continuity between the 1930s and 1940s and the period after the 1949 Revolution.
10. Bergère 1989, Fitzgerald 1996, Goodman 1995, Harrison 2000, Hershatter 1986 and 1997, Lean 2007, Lipkin 2006, Lu 1999 and 2005, Nedostup 2010, Stapleton 2000, Strand 1989, Yeh 2007, and Zanasi 2006.
11. For examples of works that underscore the ideological foundations of Chinese law, see Bodde and Morris 1967, Ch'ü 1961, Meijer [1950] 1976, Michael 1962, van der Sprenkel 1962. On the notion of Republican law as a tool of women's liberation, see Buxbaum 1978.
12. Christina Gilmartin analyzes women's participation in the revolutionary movement of the mid-1920s. She also discusses the GMD and CCP's withdrawal of support for the women's movement (1995, 211–215). Wang Zheng examines the sphere of independent feminist activity maintained by a small group of urban career women. She locates the high point of Chinese feminism in the years after 1919 and describes its decline in the 1930s (1999, 13, 24). Louise Edwards challenges this periodization by pointing to the sustained nature of the movement for

women's political participation in the first half of the twentieth century (2008). For recent studies on women in the Republican period, see the contributions to Leutner and Spakowski, eds. 2005. See also Collins 1976, ch. 7; Davin 1976, 15–16; and Witke 1970. On the CCP-controlled areas, see Goodman 2000, Hu 1974, and Stranahan 1983. On Chinese women's history after 1949, see Andors 1975, Croll 1980, Davin 1976, Diamant 2000, Johnson 1983, and Stacey 1983. Hershatter 2007 sketches the contours of the main narrative of Chinese women's history in the twentieth century. These pioneering works have served as inspiration for this study of gender and law.

13. Like the beleaguered but still current paradigm of revolution, the CCP master narrative of Chinese women's liberation has been duly attacked (by Ko 1994, Wang 1999, and others, see Luo 1996) but continues to enjoy a degree of popularity by default, since an obvious successor has yet to be agreed upon. For a critical view of attempts to appropriate both feminist universalism and essentialism as counterdiscourses to the CCP view, see Yeh 2005.

14. Wang 1999 laments this elision of bourgeois feminism from the historical record. On the CCP portrayal of the Republican Civil Code as a "semi-feudal and semi-colonial" instrument, see Hua 1993, 16.

15. The disillusionment with the Maoist era and its historiography has bred diminished reverence for the revolution (and enhanced the status of the modernization paradigm). But on the durability of the paradigm of revolution see Dirlik 1996, 255, where he asserts "that for all the repudiation of the revolution, the historical legacy of the revolution continues to shape much of this work [the contemporary historiography of China], for the simple reason that the revolution as an historical event was, and is, crucial to modern Chinese history," and 276: "in spite of efforts to erase it, revolution remains as the central problem of Chinese history." See also Perry 2008b, who attempts to salvage the more positive aspects of the Chinese revolution (nonviolent, collective action to benefit the poor and disadvantaged).

16. A cluster of recently published volumes has addressed the intersection of law and a wide variety of other areas, like judicial reform (Xu 2008), female chastity (Theiss 2004), women's property (Birge 2002), rural society (Li 2005), economic history (Isett 2007), literature (Hegel and Carlitz, eds. 2007), medicine (Furth, Zeitlin, and Hsiung, eds. 2007), property rights (Zelin, Ocko, and Gardella, eds., 2004), political liberty (Kirby, ed. 2004), political reform (Turner, Feinerman, and Guy, eds. 2000), and contemporary rights (Diamant, Lubman, and O'Brien, eds. 2005). These works suggest approaches to law that go well beyond legal specialists.

Chinese and Japanese scholars, like Tai Yen-hui [Dai Yanhui], Chang Wejen [Zhang Weiren], Jing Junjian, Shiga Shūzō, Kishimoto Mio, Niida Noburu, have also been influential, especially with respect to imperial law. See the *International Journal of Asian Studies* (2004–2008) series on "Law, State and Society in China," which translates important Japanese-language works into English. Though less central to this book, fine studies have also advanced the field of criminal justice originally established in the 1960s by pioneers like Jerome Cohen. See McKnight 1981, Kuhn 1990, Antony 1995, Bouye 2000, Mühlhahn 2009, Neighbors 2009, and Tran 2009.

For reviews of the field of Chinese legal history, see Alford 1997 and Lubman 2003.

17. Armed with evidence from local court cases that included a substantial number of civil matters, Philip Huang (1996) overturned previous claims that civil matters constituted an insignificant part of the Qing justice system. In demonstrating the important transformations that shaped household divisions over the late imperial and Republican periods, Kathryn Bernhardt (1999) pointed out how Chinese property law was far more dynamic than previous assumptions recognized. Matthew Sommer (2000) illustrated the Qing state's attempt to use the regulation of sexuality to enforce social order in an era of an intensifying subsistence crisis. Melissa Macauley (1998) examined the gap in official and popular perceptions of litigation masters, a preprofessional group of lawyers who were reviled but served important functions, especially during periods of increasing litigation. Bradly Reed (2000) studied county clerks and runners to provide a detailed look at local government that revealed the tensions between the central Qing state and local society.

David Buxbaum (1971) was the first to challenge the received wisdom about Qing law in a pioneering journal article. Mark Allee (1994) drew from the same Dan-Xin archives as Buxbaum to provide a complex picture of how Qing law in northern Taiwan adapted alongside socioeconomic changes. Jérôme Bourgon (2002 and 2004) disagrees with Philip Huang's conclusions about the relationship between Chinese law and custom.

18. One exception to this claim might be during the Yuan Dynasty when, according to Bettine Birge (2002), Mongol rulers implemented steppe principles that required a fundamental revision of late imperial law.

19. A few examples outside of the China field include Davis 1983 (sixteenth-century France); Reddy 2001 (nineteenth-century France); Hardwick 2009 (early modern France); Hanawalt 2007 (late medieval London); Stone 1990 and 1993 (early modern and modern England); Hunefeldt 2000 (nineteenth-century Lima); Wagner 1994 (late imperial Russia); and Freeze 2002 (nineteenth-century Russia).

20. There were of course other means of opting out of marriage that are not the focus of this study. Couples could divorce by mutual consent, announcing their decision in the newspaper, for example. Other couples were forced to separate by reason of wartime exigency or economic distress.

Chapter Two

Republican Legal Exceptionalism

Conceptual Underpinnings of the 1930 Civil Code

The authoritarian GMD regime, led by Chiang Kai-shek, has long been reviled for its suppression of human rights and political expression. Indeed, this socially conservative, militaristic regime was preoccupied with amassing state power above all else. Under Nationalist rule, the prospects for liberal ideas like individual rights, gender equality, and freedom of marriage seemed dim. And yet in the areas of law reform and family reform, the GMD did set out to promote a cluster of ideas upholding liberty, equality, and freedom. At the Second GMD National Congress held in Guangzhou in 1926, for instance, the party passed a Resolution on the Women's Movement (*Funü yundong jueyi an*) in which it pledged unequivocally to support the principle of gender equality under the law.[1] Although its authoritarian nature has dominated assessments of the GMD state, in the early Nanjing Decade, the GMD produced a strikingly modern and liberal civil code. The Republican Civil Code of 1929–1930 and the Republican civil law system that developed alongside it represent important exceptions to the GMD's general authoritarianism. The Republican Civil Code in particular showcased systematic de-Confucianization (especially the dismantling of legal backing for the patriline) and served as a beacon of GMD liberalism, providing for individual rights and equality under the law. GMD liberalism, though, did not exalt the individual. The GMD promoted liberal ideas frankly and unabashedly because they served the interests of the nation-state. Social and statist interests meshed to help liberal formulations gain acceptance, but they might also have worked to limit the more emancipatory possibilities of ideas like gender equality.

Through an examination of the conceptual underpinnings of the Republican Civil Code, this chapter aims to show how law was a key arena of GMD modernization efforts and how the establishment of a formal civil law system was indispensable to the creation of women's rights, for example. What might seem at first like a mere technical change, the establishment of a formal civil law system was in fact an absolutely essential underpinning to the more important changes in state-society relations generated by the establishment of a formal system of rights and duties. Under liberal theory, civil law assumed a much greater role and became much more prominent than during the late imperial period, when civil matters were downplayed as "minor matters." Law, civil law in particular, became the guarantor of individual rights. The emergence of an autonomous, formal civil law system (in contrast to a system in which civil and criminal matters were mixed) gave rise to a new conception of state-society relations, one that allowed more room for disputes among private individuals without the infringement of direct state interests.

CIVIL LAW AND LEGAL MODERNIZATION

The enactment of the Republican Civil Code of 1929–1930, China's first civil code to take effect, took place in the context of a vibrant, cosmopolitan, and far-reaching movement for legal modernization in early twentieth-century China. Launched, at least initially, under the external compulsion to rid China of extraterritoriality, and bolstered by the circulation of international ideas of law and modernity, the project of legal modernization grew to encompass a multitude of spheres. These spheres included the movement for constitutionalism, the cultivation of a modern diplomatic core, the emergence of professional bar associations, the establishment of modern legal education, ongoing efforts at judicial reform, and the erection of a modern prison system. In the area of constitutionalism, believed to occupy the first order of importance in creating a stable political system, Chinese proponents of democracy actively sought to ratify a national constitution as well as provincial-level constitutions that would secure basic political rights. Outstanding figures like Wang Chonghui (1881–1958), expertly trained in multiple legal systems and languages, translator of the German Civil Code into English, and justice of the Permanent Court of International Justice, boosted China's international profile in law and diplomacy. Meanwhile, an emerging stratum of modern Chinese lawyers organized locally and nationally to form China's first professional bar associations. These modern-style lawyers obtained an elite, high professional status that distinguished them from the lower status of the litigation masters or "tricksters" of the past. Likewise, a growing coterie of Chinese students traveled abroad to Japan, North America, and Europe to

Figure 2.1. Minister of Justice Wang Chonghui and Chair of the Civil Codification Commission Fu Bingchang posing in front of an automobile (date unknown). Courtesy of Visualising China, http://visualisingchina.net

receive their legal training, increasing their international outlook. And in China itself, foreigners and Chinese alike participated in the founding of the first modern-style law schools, like the Comparative Law School of China, established in Shanghai in 1915, and the numerous law schools (*faxueyuan*) and colleges of law and politics (*zhengfa* or *fazheng xueyuan*). The number of journals devoted to legal studies also proliferated and helped promote the exchange of ideas of law and modernity. Efforts to reform the judicial system constituted another important part of legal modernization in Republican China. Judicial reformers directed their energies toward changes that would promote the rule of law, increase judicial autonomy, improve the quality of judicial training, and formalize the processes of judicial administration. Legal modernization also included the establishment of a modern prison system and system of criminal prosecution, featuring model prisons, drawing upon modern sciences of penology and criminology, and promoting principles like rehabilitation and regeneration in the place of traditional notions of retribution. Highly publicized trials further raised public awareness of legal proceedings throughout the Republican era.[2] The movement for legal modernization in short was a multipronged effort that reshaped the place of law in society.

The Republican Civil Code of 1929–1930 itself marked the crowning achievement of decades of effort and numerous drafts undertaken by Chinese law reformers to establish a formal civil law system. Two previous draft civil codes, from 1910 and 1925, had failed to be enacted into law. Efforts to modernize China's law codes began several decades earlier in the late Qing when officials like Shen Jiaben undertook initial attempts to revise the Qing Code in accordance with international legal models. Japanese legal experts contributed greatly to additional Qing efforts at drafting a new civil code that was completed in 1910 but not formally adopted. Republican efforts at codification went a step further than late Qing reformers by working to institute a conscious, deliberate break with the past. The 1925 "Second Draft Civil Code" (*Di'erci minfa cao'an*) was transmitted to the courts for implementation but also never enacted into formal law. The Republican Civil Code, sometimes referred to as the GMD Civil Code, was structured along German pandectist lines and promulgated in five books (General Principles, Obligations, Rights over Things, Family, and Succession) over 1929–1930, though the last two books were not made effective until May 1931.

As examined in more detail in chapter 3, beginning in January 1929, the Civil Codification Commission (*Minfa qicao weiyuanhui*) of the Legislative Yuan served as the primary drafters of the Republican Civil Code. The commission was chaired by Fu Bingchang and also included Jiao Yitang, Shi Shangkuan, Lin Bin, and Zheng Yuxiu (though she was replaced by Wang Yongbin in the drafting of Books IV and V). The commission was advised by Wang Chonghui, president of the Judicial Yuan; Dai Jitao, president of the Examination Yuan; French lawyer Georges Padoux, councillor of the Legislative and Judicial Yuan; and later on American lawyer Ferno J. Schuhl, honorary adviser to the Civil Codification Commission. The commission shepherded the five books of the code through the Legislative Yuan's three-step process of deliberation, adoption, and promulgation.

The civil code embodied several modern legal principles. One of the first steps toward legal modernization taken by Chinese legal reformers involved the formal division of the legal system into civil and criminal parts. Legal reformers had proclaimed the need for a separate civil code as early as 1907.[3] Republican critics of "traditional" Chinese law cited the absence of a formal distinction between criminal and civil law as conclusive, unambiguous proof of the "primitive" state of Chinese law. Twentieth-century reformers prioritized the establishment of a formal distinction between civil and criminal, separating the two by carving out an autonomous space for civil law. The achievement of legal modernity hinged in large part on this formal separation. As late imperial officials were concerned mostly with the use of the law as a tool to keep the people in line, they did not devote much attention to the potential use of the law as a system of rules that could foster commercial development. Before the twentieth century, late imperial law did not recog-

Figure 2.2. Zheng Yuxiu (Soumay Tcheng) of the Civil Codification Commission in 1930. Photo by Fu Bingchang. Courtesy of Visualising China, http://visualisingchina.net

nize a distinction between civil and criminal law, though there were distinct procedural differences in how different types of cases were handled. Civil matters concerning family and economic disputes had been set apart from criminal matters by the designation "people's" matters (*minshi*) or "minor" matters (*xishi*), but the distinction rested largely on informal grounds and was not made explicit.[4] Because these distinctions already operated in late imperial legal practice, the work of twentieth-century lawmakers largely consisted of formalizing already-recognized procedural distinctions, making the changes they advocated under the name of legal modernity more easily accepted.

The act of formalization, however, proved to be of crucial importance, for it did more than simply create a separate civil law. The establishment of a formal civil law system also enhanced the prestige of civil law. This system implied that civil law was autonomous from state authority. Western legal theorists perceived the primacy of civil law as the distinguishing factor between traditional and modern law. Especially influential here was Henry Maine, who theorized that the relative balance between criminal and civil law corresponded to the degree of legal development, with less-developed countries relying upon criminal more than civil law, and more-developed countries tending to emphasize civil over criminal law.[5] Republican Chinese legal reformers, like Wang Chonghui, took Maine's words to heart. Wang interpreted Maine's thesis as an impetus to pay particular attention to civil matters in law reform, as a clearly formulated civil code was an essential marker of a developed nation.[6] Thus, within the new Chinese legal system composed of multiple elements, civil law would assume the position of honor. Matters once classified as "minor" or "trivial" in late imperial law were elevated to prominence in the Republican period as matters of civil law, because civil law (family law but more so contract and property law) was the crux of modern law.

Significantly, the formal division of civil and criminal law destroyed the unity of traditional Chinese law, which had been rooted in cosmological notions and ideas of Confucian harmony. This formal recognition of a separate system of law authorized the establishment of a civil law system with its own distinct operating logic, set of tools, and unique purposes. The allowance for differentiation was key, as it codified the differences between criminal and civil law, and in the process it legitimized the new characteristics of civil law. What were those new characteristics? In logic, civil law depended far more upon economic rationality than Confucian morality. The purpose or role of civil law, furthermore, had more to do with the capitalist promotion of commercial development than with the preservation of the natural order. The key apparatuses of civil law, moreover, were legal rights rather than moral obligations. In terms of remedies, the new civil law favored monetary compensation over the physical punishment and specific performance of the old Qing Code. The basic unit of reference of the Republican Civil Code shifted as well from the ritual patriline to the biological individual. Civil law deals with disagreements between private individuals (commercial or personal injury disputes, for example), while criminal law deals with acts deemed illegal by the state.

In the twentieth century the logic of civil law shifted from the reinforcement of morality and order to the promotion of economic rationality; the new logic clearly differentiated between law and morality. Wu Jingxiong (John C.H. Wu), an important figure in the modernization of Chinese law, argued that "[E]ver since the legalization of Confucianism during the Han Dynasty . . . the interests of morality were recognized and protected by the law to the exclusion of almost all other interests, such as general progress and the development of commercial and industrial enterprises."[7] Traditionally, law was supposedly subservient to morality. For example, the catch-all provision of the Qing Code stated, "whoever does what ought not to be done shall be punished." Of course, Western law also embodied moral elements. But morality as an independent force was not supposed to sway the judgment of cases on legal principles exclusively. The strong influence of legalism in the modern West made it imperative that Chinese law also be more clearly distinguished from morality and not remain a mere incarnation of Confucian morality. The traditional elite Confucian disdain for the law and legal methods of regulating human behavior (a disdain that was often breached in practice), moreover, had to be overturned, and the Confucian notion that morality represented a superior method of regulating human behavior to law had to be debunked. Confucian officials of course relied heavily upon law (despite their claims of doing otherwise). Republican lawmakers gave law not just an autonomous, independent status but also an elevated one.

The newly elevated standing of modern civil law derived from its rational character. The prescribed changes in form, like this move from morality to autonomous law, did not stir up the same type of debate as the question of what shape the ideological basis of a modern Chinese legal system should take. The reorganization of legal forms was less controversial partly because it took place under the auspices of what lawmakers termed "juridical science." For instance, the legal scholar Boyer P.H. Chu in a commentary on Chinese civil law praised the Republican Civil Code as "the latest as well as the ablest expression of scientific law-making."[8] This scientific veneer endowed the changes in legal form with an incontrovertible and inevitable air. Lawmakers took the changes in legal form for granted. They approached these changes as technical advances that were in a different category than the cultural debates that the reformers raised when tampering with the Confucian values of late imperial law. Legal reformers as well as others not in favor of reform seemed far more amenable to tossing out the organizational structure of the Qing Code in favor of the legal format of the continental European (and other modern) civil law countries.

In addition to the charge that late imperial law reinforced Confucian morality, the disparagement of traditional law also derived from the related contention that late imperial Chinese law was principally penal in nature and operated to preserve natural harmony.[9] For example, Jean Escarra, the French legal expert and counselor to the National Government, wrote that "[I]n regard to juridical institutions, China would recognize only natural order, would exalt only 'moral rule.'" For Escarra, Chinese law was uniquely penal in nature and very severe; the sanctions had chiefly a role of intimidation.[10] Western criticism of the uniformly penal nature of traditional Chinese law found similar expression among Chinese counterparts who also subscribed to modern legal theories of formalism and rationality. In his speech upon assuming the position of president of the Legislative Yuan in December

Figure 2.3. Hu Hanmin and his daughter Hu Mulan in 1928. Photo by Fu Bing-chang. Courtesy of Visualising China, http://visualisingchina.net

1928, Hu Hanmin, widely regarded as the major theoretician of GMD law, lamented that "We cannot deny the fact that China's laws are incomplete: there is virtually no civil law . . . ."[11]

The oft-cited penal emphasis of traditional law relegated civil matters to a relatively minor position,[12] at least in the GMD lawmakers' construction of traditional law. As Hu Hanmin explained, "With respect to the organization

Figure 2.4. Hu Hanmin traveling in Egypt in 1928. Photo by Fu Bingchang. Courtesy of Visualising China, http://visualisingchina.net

of society, the state and the family, the law of China in former days was an amalgam of public and private laws in which the former took precedent over the latter."[13] The private activities of Chinese people were supposed to be governed by custom and morality. Modern legal theories, in contrast, privi-

Figure 2.5. Hu Hanmin just before he was appointed president of the Legislative Yuan in 1928. Photo by Fu Bingchang. Courtesy of Visualising China, http://visualisingchina.net

leged formalism and rationality. According to jurist and diplomat F.T. Cheng (Zheng Tianxi),

> However workable the old code might have been in the days when steam was not yet discovered, it must have appeared to be ever increasingly out of date after the bridge between East and West had been opened, because of its ancient character and also because of its scanty provisions in civil matters, which did not go beyond marriage, succession and debts. In other words, the scarcity of civil provisions in particular rendered the old code incompatible with the needs of a society gradually becoming modern.[14]

Cheng's comment implied that modern economic development required a more sophisticated legal system when it came to commercial matters. This incompatibility between the Qing Code and modernization arose not just as an effect of Western imperialism; urbanization and commercialization during the Qing were already rendering the old code less effective, especially in areas of higher population density. Theoreticians of GMD law agreed that one of the key shortcomings of traditional Chinese law was its overwhelming penal emphasis and lack of detailed laws governing civil matters. By singling out civil law and removing the moral overtones from the regulation of civil matters, Chinese lawmakers cleared the way for the creation of a much more elaborate system of rules to govern economic transactions, marital and family relationships, and inheritance procedures. The spare and stark declarations of the Qing Code on these matters were deemed by the legal reformers as inadequate for the more complex, sophisticated transactions of the modern (capitalist) world.

With the promulgation of the new civil code, the basic conceptions of Chinese law no longer rested upon all-embracing cosmological notions of harmony and the natural world. Criminal matters that affected the public order and deserved to be met by punitive measures were separated out from civil matters that concerned private individuals. The formal division of the law into separate criminal and civil codes also marked an important point of departure for Chinese law because once civil law was freed from the penal emphasis of criminal law it was allowed to acquire an essentially new purpose—to regulate behavior among private individuals without the interposition of the state interest. In the introduction to the civil code, the chair of the Civil Codification Commission, Fu Bingchang, noted, "It is quite characteristic of the old traditional conception of Chinese Civil Law that it is not so much to regulate private intercourse between individuals and to delimit their respective rights as to preserve the general harmony of the universe."[15] With the enactment of the new civil law, therefore, the GMD legislators carved out a new space in the legal system that formally protected private interests from the authority of the state.[16] In this case, the profusion of civil provisions in Republican law contributed to the shift from a traditional society governed by the rules of Confucian morality to a modern capitalist society based upon monetary compensation and the rationality of the market. The provisions of the civil code conveyed an especially strong economic cast, especially since GMD legislators decided not to create a separate commercial law code apart from the civil code.

Indeed, John C.H. Wu blamed China's underdeveloped civil law as a key explanation for her economic weakness. The overwhelming penal nature and purpose of the law in the late imperial period, in Wu's opinion, precluded the development of the law as a means of encouraging commerce. Wu saw civil law not only as a sign of a progressive nation, but as a catalyst for progress. Like today's law and economic development advocates who believe that the rule of law is a prerequisite for economic development, Wu espoused the view that a strong civil law tradition could facilitate economic progress back in the 1930s. In his uncompromising view,

> It is clear that in the legal system of old China, [the] atmosphere of the business meeting was entirely missing. *Indeed, the existence of an ethically neutral margin in the map of social life and the recognition of the 'cash-nexus' as one*

> *of the legitimate and principal relations between man and man, are conditions precedent to the rise and blossoming of the civil law, which . . . is primarily the law of property* [italics added].[17]

Although the conception of civil law embodied by this quote superficially appears little to do with women's rights, it was an absolutely essential condition for formal gender equality. For it was this capitalist conception of civil law that liberated the concept of property from the ideological principles that previously governed property relations along Confucian lines. Property under Confucian law mainly concerned real property (house and land), the most important type of property for an agrarian society, and tied this property closely to the patriline. Property under modern law could take on numerous forms, including but not limited to cash, business interests, goods, stocks, bonds, and so on, all of which should be freely alienable (one should be able to buy and sell freely, etc.). Wu's conception embodied the theoretical adjustment needed to enable property inheritance, for instance, to be separated from the continuation of the patriline, thus granting women (and others outside the patriline) the legal right to inherit property. A wife's right to property after divorce, judicial separation, or her husband's death also could only be possible under such a conception of the primacy of economic relations above patrilineal ones.

Rights and Duties

The formal division of the written law into penal and civil systems also marked the crucial first step in the state's recognition of individual rights. As John C.H. Wu had insisted, "the very fact that the law was now divided into penal and civil was a tremendous gain for the rights of the individual."[18] The emergence of a rights discourse in civil matters alluded to by Wu bespoke a transition from a system of moral obligations to a system of legal rights. Wu's words highlight the differences in the purposes of criminal and civil law. In Wu's liberal-minded construction, criminal justice aimed to punish wrongs. It was only in the realm of civil justice that the law aimed to regulate private behavior and enforce individual rights. The problem with the legal system of old China, according to Wu, was that "it is a system of duties rather than rights . . . the emphasis is markedly on duties, so much so that the notion of rights was not as freely developed as in the Common Law and Roman Law. The emphasis being on duties, the law has never been freed from its dependence on morality."[19] The language of rights translated from the West thus facilitated the resolution of civil disputes according to private interests, independent of the moral consequences. These codified private interests (usually economic in nature) represented a new source of law that in effect superseded moral notions not expressly provided for in the code.

Women's rights derived from this basic sphere of private rights. The formalism embodied by the separation of civil and criminal law was a prerequisite to a rights-based notion of equality. It was the creation of the new civil space that enabled women to obtain legal rights.

Shifts in property law help illustrate the dismantling of the Confucian structure and erection of modern property rules. As Kathryn Bernhardt demonstrates in her work on women and property, women gained their rights as part of the transition to an entirely different property complex and legal system. "The structure of rights that daughters were now to share equally with sons was not the one of old, but a new set based on the Western concept of individual property," she writes.[20] Moreover, under the imperial legal regime neither men nor women had any rights to speak of against the state. In this sense, women gained formal rights at the same time that men did. The modern law concept of individual property did not pay heed to the Confucian patriline. The greatest gain of legal power for individuals came at the expense of the Confucian patrilineal family. Many of the provisions designed to implement gender equality actually afforded greater rights to both men and women. To take freedom of marriage as an example again, the right to choose one's own spouse was newly afforded to both men and women. Even the changes in the divorce laws, which had been notoriously weighted in favor of men, granted greater freedom to both men and women. Thus, gender equality made sense not as the equalization of rights between women and men, but as part of the construction of an entirely new rights complex. In this sense, gender equality can be viewed as a by-product of economic rationality, which is not to discount the tremendous push for gender equality from the organized women's movement.

One need not search very far to find multiple rationalities at work in the Republican-era discussions of rights. By the 1930s, a number of commentators believed that the word "rights" had become so ordinary, that they feared the word had become a mere platitude. In an effort to avoid the empty talk about rights, John C.H. Wu delivered a lecture titled "Rights and Duties in the Constitution," in which he set forth his definition of rights and their origin and function.[21] First, he located the origins of rights in the American and French Revolutions. Over time, two schools of thought about rights developed. The first school he called the theory of "natural rights" (*tianfu renquan).* Under this theory, rights possess a sacred and absolute quality. The second theory he associated with Sun Yat-sen's theory of people's rights. According to Sun's theory, rights do not arise from nature. Rather, they are produced by historical circumstances and the current of public opinion. Wu aligned himself with Sun and insisted that the exercise and meaning of rights are not naturally given but are rather heavily influenced by society and the times. As he put it elsewhere, "with the Chinese all rights are relative . . . 'limited by the neighborhood of principles of policy which are other than those on which the particular right is founded, and which become strong enough to hold their own when a certain point is reached.'"[22] Because rights could be defined as historically relative rather than timeless and universal, they could inadvertently serve as a vehicle by which persistent Confucian hierarchies could infringe upon the new principle of gender equality.

Innovations in legal remedies like the reliance upon monetary damages and compensation rather than physical punishment, moreover, derived from the creation of a formal civil law system. As explained in the civil code, Article 184 (English version), furthermore, the notion of civil liability arose from the belief that "A Person, who, intentionally or by negligence, unlawfully infringes upon the rights of another, is bound to compensate him for any damage arising therefrom . . . ."[23] This notion of civil liability thus reflects the differences in the purpose of the law. Violations of the law with respect to civil matters no longer required state action in the form of punishment like beating, but could be resolved through the payment of money from one private party to another. The breakup of a betrothal agreement, for example, could no longer be legally redressed by specific performance or the enforcement of the agreement, i.e., requiring that the marriage take place against the will of one of the parties. Instead, the party responsible for breaking the agreement under the Republican Civil Code was also responsible for monetary compensation to cover any economic losses or damages suffered by the other party. Modern civil law conceived of monetary compensation rather than criminal penalties as the main means to remedy the injury to an individual's rights.

De-Confucianization of the Law

The dismantling of the Confucian basis for Chinese law led to a new conception of state-society relations in which the conjugal unit rather than the patrilineal family mediated between individual, family, society, and state. Beginning with Ch'ü T'ung-ts'u [Qu Tongzu], Chinese and Western scholars of imperial law have described the effort by Confucian officials to codify moral principles into imperial legal codes as the "Confucianization of law."[24] What has been left out of these accounts of Chinese law is the Republican-era effort to disentangle law from Confucian morality and to create a rational, rule-based system of governance based on codified law without reference to moral principles not explicitly embodied in law. Republican lawmakers intentionally set out to undermine the Confucian basis of traditional Chinese law because the emphasis on Confucian values hindered the elaboration of a general principle of equality. Their efforts were part of the wider discourse that blamed traditional law for China's backwardness. John C.H. Wu, for instance, described Confucian ethics as the spiritual counterpart to footbinding.[25] His comparison served to underscore the manner in which traditional ethics had restrained the free development and creative energies of the Chinese people.

The GMD's official censure of the patrilineal basis of traditional family law in favor of an emerging modern liberal model of law best exemplified the ideological shift from Confucianized family law to a modern liberal family law. Republican lawmakers abandoned one of the main principles of Confucianized law, the emphasis on the patrilineal family. According to Wu, the hierarchical organizing principle of Confucianism bore two legal consequences: "In the first place, this gave rise to inequality of persons before the law. . . . In the second place, it was responsible for the emphasis upon the family institution, in which there was a pigeonhole for everybody."[26] Aside from the general hierarchical principles, the Confucian Three Obediences (*sancong*) further relegated the legal existence of women to a perpetual coverture. As often repeated, a daughter was supposed to follow the command of her father, a wife her husband, and a widow her son.[27] So long as Chinese law reinforced the dictates of Confucianism, legal equality for women (or men for that matter) could never be achieved.

Against the Patriline

GMD legislators believed that by targeting the intermingling of civil and criminal law under traditional law, the convergence of lineage and state interest could be broken down. Republican Chinese observers decried the intermingling of civil and criminal in traditional Chinese law on the ground that it enabled patrilineal principles to be enshrined in the law. Hu Hanmin criticized the imperial system on account that "private law was entirely contained within public law."[28] Hu attributed this lack of distinction between public and private to the entrenchment of the lineage interest, contending that "Given the long history and entrenched position of the idea of the lineage in China, the private laws associated with an individual's relationships had long come under the jurisdiction of public law. Naturally, such a primitive legal system would not be suitable for the present age in which a sharp distinction is made between public and private law."[29] Accordingly, Hu differentiated between imperial law and Republican law on the basis that the new civil code clearly distinguished between public and private law.[30] To Hu, the key to this distinction meant that the interests of the lineage no longer received legal backing.

The GMD goal of gender equality under the law depended upon the prior separation of civil and criminal law and the corresponding disentanglement of state and private (meaning patrilineal) interests. The patriline had received the highest legal sanction under late imperial or "Confucianized" law.[31] Republican law, in contrast, rendered the patriline of no legal significance. Even before the May Fourth period, Hu and other future GMD legislators had already identified this link between lineage and state as the key "feudal" element of imperial law and blamed the unity of state and lineage interest for the perpetuation of the subordination of women in traditional China. The formal division of civil and criminal law, then, worked against the intermingling of state and patrilineal interests. The basic unit of reference for civil law was the individual, not the patriline, though it was not the abstract individual of classical liberalism but the socially embedded individual of early twentieth-century liberalism after "the social turn."

The Republican rejection of the patriline meant that the morally constituted, hierarchically placed Confucian family/patriline member gave way for the most part to the equal-rights-bearing abstract, liberal individual. Take the regulation of sexuality and infertility for example. Republican lawmakers removed related questions of infertility and impotence from the purview of the patriline and melded them instead to the concerns of the individual husband and wife. Under late imperial law, female infertility had constituted one of the Seven Conditions for divorce because a wife's inability to produce sons threatened the extinction of the patriline.[32] The law made no mention of male infertility or impotence. Husband impotence (the topic of chapter 8), however, assumed legal consequences under Republican family law. It became a ground for annulment not because it had anything to do with the patriline but because it prevented the physical consummation of the bond between husband and wife, a new logic that will be discussed further in chapter 8.[33]

Republican lawmakers dismissed the patriline and sanctioned the individual husband and wife elsewhere in the family law as well. Aside from sexuality, the detachment of property from the patriline also corresponds to a major break with the past.[34] The provision for judicial separation and spousal support, examined in chapter 7, exemplifies how property, which conceptually belonged to the patriline under late imperial law, belonged to the conjugal unit under Republican law. This conceptual breakthrough allowed for property to pass from a husband's hands into his wife's according to an apportionment of the mutual duties and responsibilities owed by spouses. The redistribution of property to a wife through alimony or support meant that a wife seeking to break away from the patriline (either through separation or divorce) could permanently sever the link between patriline and property. A wife could siphon property away from the patriline because property no longer belonged to the patrilineal unit but to individual persons.

The transfer of legal sanction from the patriline to the individual husband and wife also affected marriage itself. The conception of marriage as the patriline's acquisition of a daughter-in-law gave way to the conception of marriage as a union of husband and wife. This change in definition required a corresponding reformulation of the grounds upon which a marriage could be terminated. Legal recognition of mutual-consent divorce continued from late imperial to Republican law. But the Republican conditions for a judicial divorce for the most part endorsed the interests of the individual husband and wife equally rather than the patriline. This change is clearly seen in the provision for divorce in cases of "intolerable cruelty" examined in chapter 5. The freedom of marriage and divorce offered by the Republican Civil Code was freedom from the patriline.

The breakthroughs in legal form, especially the creation of a formal and discrete civil law complex, were indispensable steps in the implementation of formal gender equality. These structural changes were more than cosmetic, and their implications reached much deeper. Measures like the division of law into civil and criminal systems, for instance, were not characterized as cultural threats or "de-Confucianization" even though it was these procedures that made steps like the abandonment of the patriline and the emergence of individual rights possible in law.

THE THREE PEOPLE'S PRINCIPLES AND LIBERALISM AFTER THE "SOCIAL TURN"

When the Nationalist government turned its attention to the drafting of a civil code, its lawmakers sought rights and equality for women within an ideology that stressed the Three People's Principles and the primacy of the collective social or national interest. Hu Hanmin, Fu Bingchang, John C.H. Wu, and many others repeated the refrain that Sun Yat-sen's Three People's Principles were the most authoritative guidelines for lawmaking. Republican lawmakers understood the dramatic turn from hierarchy to equality through the substitution of the idea of the patrilineal society (*zongfa shehui*) of traditional Chinese law by the new category of the social or people's interest (*shehui* or *renmin liyi*). This new idea of the social or people's interest (not individualism or individual autonomy) came to serve as the underlying arbiter (and highest value) of the modern legal conception of Chinese women.

Notions of the "whole people" underlying the GMD's official ideology of the Three People's Principles placed limitations upon the individual. The implication of the Three People's Principles for men and women are clear in Fu Bingchang's view that both men and women are located within and subordinate to society.[35] According to Fu,

> The GMD doctrine considers therefore men not as self contained entities but in relation to the society in which they form. It assigns to them rights and duties only in so far as the exercise of such rights and duties tend to the pacific and orderly progress of the community. It restricts their activities when they would be harmful to the group. Rights and morals in the GMD doctrine are purely social notions, which may eventually be subject to evolution, just as society itself evolves.[36]

Individual liberty, in short, was not inviolable. Likewise, Hu Hanmin stressed that "In drafting a marriage law, we are guided by the principle of gender equality, while [also] taking into account human sentiment and social reality."[37]

The making of the GMD Civil Code lays bare the process by which the emergence of liberal modernity loosened the grip of the traditional patrilineal family. However, the move from patrilineal authority to individual liberation never took place given the simultaneous advent of social solidarity, which limited the extent of that liberation by directing it toward the purpose of enhancing the common social and national good. The liberal modernity championed by the GMD was of a decidedly social rather than individual nature. To speak of liberalism after the "social turn" sounds like a contradiction if one thinks of liberalism as inherently individual. Liberalism after the social turn makes sense, however, when we turn to the 1920s, when liberal theory itself was changing partly in response to the assorted challenges posed by the rise of nationalism, industrial capitalism, and social Darwinism. In the post–World War I period, moreover, disillusionment with liberalism ran especially high as extreme individualism was blamed as one of the contributing causes of the war.[38]

Before and after the promulgation of the civil code, moreover, the legal world buzzed about the latest legal theory: "the socialization of law." As Chinese legal philosophers understood it, this theory of law held that historically law was essentially a system of duties through which the rulers could enrich themselves. This stage of legal development was exemplified by the feudal system. With the development of the theory of natural rights and the American and French Revolutions, especially the Declaration of the Rights of Man, however, law was transformed from a duty-based to a rights-based core. This liberal, individualistic, rights-based law continued until the early twentieth century, when the intensification of capitalism and the widening gap between the laboring and capitalist classes gave rise to various forms of socialism (syndicalism, social democracy, communism, guild socialism, solidarism, etc.).[39] Under this model of legal development, it would be fruitless to promote liberal individualism (an already outdated concept) in Chinese law. GMD legislators wished to place the new Chinese Civil Code at the cutting edge of international legal trends by conceiving of Chinese law in terms of the social interest. This brand of post–social turn liberalism embraced by GMD lawmakers, consequently, severely modified if not repudiated the central notion of individual liberty.

Chinese intellectuals were well aware that by the late 1920s the West itself had turned away from individualism and toward various forms of collectivism.[40] Thus GMD lawmakers proposed to selectively temper the "rampant" individualism of the West through a nationalist version of liberalism. For example, Republican Chinese legal scholars considered the Swiss Civil

Code as more inclined toward social solidarity than individuality, and therefore more modern.[41] For as GMD legislators attempted to discard the patrilineal basis of late imperial Chinese law, they also endeavored to distance Republican law from the individual basis of Western law. As one of the key Western advisers to Chinese legal reformers, Jean Escarra, declared, "[T]he new legislation should be, not individualistic like the old western bodies of law, not purely pertaining to the family, like traditional Chinese legislation, but *social*."[42] For John C.H. Wu, it was "a fortunate coincidence, the Chinese civil code was produced at a time when Western juristic thought had for several decades been turning away from the extreme individualism of the nineteenth century and heading steadily toward a humanistic and sociological position strikingly similar, in spirit, to the Chinese philosophy of the human-minded and well-integrated individual, who thinks of his duties more than his rights."[43] Chinese lawmakers viewed the advent of this adopted category of the social or national interest as an advance over purely individualistic legal codes. Social solidarity was now conceived as more fully modern than atomistic forms of individualism.

The creation of the rights-bearing individual was expected to overcome the two major Confucian obstacles to modernity: hierarchy and the emphasis on the patriline. But in both cases as well, the rights-bearing individual needed to be circumscribed, reined in by an even higher authority. In both undertakings, the mediation of the "social," an abstract form of collectivism that had been introduced in the late nineteenth century, was crucial. First, the social enabled equality through the reorganization of human relations according to a horizontal model consisting of the individual, society, and the state. This horizontal model conceived of individuals as equally located in relation to society and the state. It replaced the former, vertical model of individual, family/patriline, and state, under which individuals were hierarchically situated in relation to the patriline and the state.[44] As Fu Bingchang put it in his introduction to Books IV and V (Family and Succession) of the civil code:

> In order to turn China into a real State, in the modern sense of the word, Dr. Sun Yat-sen thought it necessary to substitute for the primitive notion of unity of clan or family, the notion of unity of the population formed by these clans or families. The particular interest of the isolated groups had to yield to the general interest of the nation. To put it into practice this new ideal and to enable the citizens to make use of their personal abilities to the best interest of their country, it was imperative that the excessive grip of the old family ties over the individuals should be loosened.[45]

The reshaping of the individual through "the social" thus portended both liberation from the patrilineal family and a qualification of that newfound liberty. The provisions of the Republican Civil Code affirmed GMD support for individual liberty ("every human being is or ought to be free") but with an important qualification: individual liberty must be circumscribed by social solidarity.[46] In his commentary on the civil code, Boyer P.H. Chu stated bluntly that "With the advent of social solidarity as the main object of legal order, liberty as a subjective right of the individual is delimited."[47] It is through this notion of social solidarity or the social/national interest that GMD legislators intended to transcend the individual interest of Western law, the class interest of Soviet law, and the lineage-family interest of traditional Chinese law. According to Hu Hanmin, "by embodying in it the principles of the [GMD] the Code is given a decidedly social turn. The personal activity of the citizen is directed by the Codes so that it may be most advantageous for the community to which the individual belongs. This particular feature distinguishes the new code from the individualistic legislations of Europe and America as well as from the former Chinese legislation of the old familial type."[48]

The social utility found in the discussion above, moreover, supported the claims for gender equality. The model of gender equality in fact derived from arguments stemming from social utility. Greater freedom in family matters, for instance, was justified not on the basis of any inherent rights of the individual, but on the best interests of society. The new civil code was to "permit freedom of love, freedom of marriage, happiness of man and wife, so they can produce lively, clever, and strong little citizens, enabling the race to gradually turn weakness into strength."[49] In addition to social utility, it was critical for the code's authors that the trend of world legal systems also favored gender equality. From their point of view, the laws of the Soviet Union exhibited the greatest gender equality. The laws of Germany, Switzerland, and Sweden offered degrees of gender equality. Japan and France offered less. The laws of Thailand, Brazil, Turkey, and Argentina also served as models and references. Chinese legal scholars even cited the examples of the post–World War I League of Nations, German, Austrian, Latvian, Lithuanian, and Czech constitutions as evidence of the trend toward gender equality.[50]

Although the adoption of the category of "the social" interest as the basis of the law provided the rationale and framework of understanding for the implementation of gender equality, at the same time it limited the scope of gender equality, since the individual rights of a woman (or man) could be subordinated under the social group. The only female member of the Civil Codification Commission, Wei Zheng Yuxiu [Soumay Tcheng], praised the achievement of women's rights but was also quick to stress the duties that accompanied these newfound rights. In her words, "under the New Civil Code, the women of China not only enjoy absolute equality in civil and property rights but also bear equal responsibilities and obligations—a real equality with men and not preference over them."[51]

CONCLUSION

The argument for legal exceptionalism advanced in this chapter rests largely upon the conceptual underpinnings of the Republican Civil Code and how its creation reflected the discourses of legal and liberal modernity, in contrast to the authoritarian politics adopted by the GMD in other spheres. The civil code was a unique legislative accomplishment, to be sure, and we should not infer too much from it given the other policies of the GMD. And yet it implemented a system of individual legal rights and duties and equality that was both startlingly modern and liberal. These liberal formulations helped "loosen the grip" of the patrilineal family on the individual. At the same time, however, Republican Chinese liberalism reined in the individual through new constructs of the national and the social interest.

NOTES

1. The GMD Resolution on the Women's Movement explicitly spelled out the GMD's commitment to the principle of gender equality under the law. In the resolution the GMD pledged to "enact laws upholding the principle of gender equality," among other state-feminist guidelines. This pledge enshrined legal gender equality in the party platform. It was passed under the leadership of He Xiangning and the influence of Michael Borodin. Two years earlier, in 1924, at the First GMD National Congress, the party had introduced a similar manifesto. See *Zhonghua minguo minfa zhiding shiliao huibian* 1976, vol. 2, pp. 317–320. See also Ono 1989, pp. 87–88, and Wang 1999.

2. On the constitutionalism movement during the Beiyang government period, see Tseng 1930, ch. 6, and Nathan 1976. On Wang Chonghui's many contributions to legal modernization in China, see Yu 1987. On Chinese bar associations, see Xu 1998. On legal education, see Conner 2003. On judicial reform in early twentieth-century China, see Xu 2008 (describing judicial reform especially in Jiangsu Province). On the emergence of the modern penal system in early twentieth-century China, see Dikötter 2002. On trials and the rising public awareness of law, see Goodman 2005 and Lean 2007.

3. See the 1907 memorial by the Ministry of Civil Affairs (*Minzheng bu*) in Xie 1937, 899. For a general overview of Chinese legal reform efforts, see Xie 1937, Escarra 1936, and Cheng 1976.

4. See Buxbaum 1971, Huang 1996, 1–2. For a different view, see Bourgon 2002, who argues that late imperial law lacked a separate notion of civil law.

5. Maine (1864) 1986. This thesis is usually summarized as the transformation from status to contract. Although Maine's thesis has since come under attack for its Eurocentric point of view and empirical inadequacies, it has retained much of its conceptual currency. See Scogin 1994.

6. A native of Guangdong, Wang graduated from Beiyang University and then went abroad for further study in Japan, France, Germany, the United States (Berkeley and Yale), and England. On Wang's contribution to the legal development of China, see Yu 1987.

7. Wu 1936, p. 47.

8. Chu 1935, Foreword.

9. See Jamieson 1921, Preface: " . . . the conception of civil as distinguished from criminal proceedings is entirely absent in Chinese legislation;" Riasanovsky (1938) 1976; Bodde and Morris 1967, 49. See also Bourgon 2002. Most observers, however, also recognized that while legal provisions adopted the form of penal laws, in essence they dealt with civil matters as well. What are now generally considered civil matters of course were dealt with in the Qing Code, and as Kathryn Bernhardt and Philip Huang have demonstrated, civil matters constituted a

major part of legal practice at the local level and among ordinary households. See Bernhardt and Huang, eds., 1994, and Huang 1996. See also Buxbaum 1971 for the argument that Qing courts uniformly disposed of civil and criminal cases in noticeably different ways.

10. Escarra 1936, 11.

11. Hu Hanmin 1928.12.5. 1978, vol. 4, p. 772. "Jinhou lifa de yan yu su."

12. Bodde and Morris 1967, Ch'ü 1961, Escarra 1936. But see Huang 1996, Scogin 1994.

13. Hu 1978, 781.

14. Zheng 1948, 176–177. See also Huang 1996, on the inefficiency of the Qing legal system in more commercialized regions like Danshui-Xinzhu.

15. Fu 1930b.

16. Republican law also differed from imperial law in that it provided greater formality to the distinctive methods for handling "serious" criminal matters and "minor" civil matters. Thus we see in Republican law, for example, the clear separation of criminal and civil codes and additional codes for civil and criminal procedure and the provision of appeal to higher courts for civil cases too.

17. Wu 1936, 49.

18. Wu 1967b, 351.

19. Wu 1967a, 219.

20. Bernhardt 1999, 133.

21. Wu 1935.

22. Wu 1936, 60, quoting American jurist Oliver Wendell Holmes.

23. Civil Code Article 184.

24. Ch'ü 1961, 267–279.

25. Wu 1928, autobiographical sketch. In Wu's later writings he took a more benign attitude toward Confucianism.

26. Wu 1936, 46.

27. Wu 1967b, 357. Wu cautioned, however, against the equation of a woman's legal status with her actual social status. He pointed out that the distinction between the *de facto* (actual) and *de jure* (legal) status of women in traditional Chinese law was especially great: "In actual life, the Chinese woman's role was as important as her legal status was low." Wu made these remarks in relation to his pet theory of "the principle of neutralization," by which he proposed that under any system of inequality, equalities would inevitably creep into the system in actual practice and mitigate the original stark inequality (and vice versa in a system of equality). To illustrate his theory, Wu drew upon the truism that a Chinese woman had no rights of inheritance under traditional law. In fact, Wu writes, daughters of rich families normally received dowries upon marriage, and wives "inherited" together with their husbands from their fathers-in-law.

28. Hu 1978, 781.

29. Hu 1978, 782.

30. Hu 1978, 782.

31. Ch'ü 1961.

32. Tai 1978.

33. See also the legal regulation of sexuality. Since female adultery posed a dire threat to the purity of the patriline, there were harsh penalties for such behavior under late imperial law. A husband engaged in extramarital sex, however, could not pollute the patriline. Therefore the law held that his extramarital sex was not adultery or illicit sex (as long as his partner was not a married woman) (Sommer 2000). Under Republican family law adultery remained a concern. But now that lawmakers had undone the legal foundation of the patriline, the law no longer treated adultery as an offense against the patriline committed by a wife. Adultery was reconceived as extramarital sexual behavior by a wife or husband. The legal harm caused by adultery, moreover, damaged not the patriline but the innocent spouse. Adultery committed by either spouse could thus serve as a cause for divorce.

34. Bernhardt 1999, ch. 4, illustrates the law's departure from the patriline in her extended discussion of how property inheritance was differentiated from patrilineal succession under the Republican Civil Code inheritance provisions.

35. Since the late Qing, legal reform had been spearheaded by a number of different law codification commissions, such as the Bureau of Law Reform (*Falü guan*), commissioned in 1902 and headed by Wu Tingfang and Shen Jiaben; the Committee for the Compilation of Codes (*Fadian bianzuan hui*); the Committee for the Compilation and Investigation of Laws (*Falü biancha hui*); the Law Codification Commission (*Xiuding falü guan*), established in 1918 and chaired by Wang Chonghui and Dong Kang; and the Legal Bureau (*Fazhi ju*). The actual body responsible for the 1929–1931 Civil Code was the Civil Codification Commission, established in 1928 and chaired by Fu Bingchang. A 1928 draft of the family and succession books provided much guidance to the group chaired by Fu. After the establishment of the GMD government in 1928, the work of law codification shifted from the Ministry of Justice (*Sifa bu*) to the newly established Legislative Yuan (*Lifa yuan*). See Escarra 1936.

36. Fu 1930b, xx–xxi.

The subordination of the individual to the group is also reflected in Sun Yat-sen's distinction between *ren* and *min*. The key distinction rested on the fact that *min* signified a person who belonged to a group or society. Apart from society, a person possessed no rights or duties to speak of. See Yu 1932, 169. See also Wu 1936, 130: "rights of man are not given *a priori* but acquired *a posteriori* and therefore subject to modification with changed circumstances. This may be called a theory of relativity of rights. With Dr. Sun as with Holmes, rights are no longer conceived as solid substances existing from eternity to eternity with invariable size and weight, but as little creatures born out of the bowels of history and subject to all the vicissitudes of mortality."

37. Hu 1978, speech delivered on 1930.4.21.

38. See Eastman 1974, 142; Greiff 1985, 453; and Glosser 2003, 20. See also Tsin 1999 on the construction of "the social."

39. Zheng 1931.

40. Zheng 1931.

41. Chu 1935, 112: "As a complete modern code both in theory and in practice, the provision of Art. 27 of the Swiss Civil Code inclines more towards social solidarity than individuality. Likewise the present article should be construed to keep in line with social solidarity—conceiving Liberty as a function rather than a right."

42. Escarra 1936, 249–250.

43. Wu 1967b, 353.

44. See Brødsgaard and Strand 1998, 10.

45. Fu 1930c, vii.

46. Chu 1935, 110.

47. Chu 1935, 111. Chu goes on to explain the difference between the subjective theory of liberty and the doctrine of social solidarity: The subjective theory of liberty ("the State or legislator can in no way infringe the right of the individual to develop his physical, intellectual and moral forces. . . . The State can impose no affirmative obligation upon the individual beyond the payment of taxes established for the needs of the community such as taxes in money, kind or in blood; nor can the State impose upon the individual the obligation to work or to lay aside a provision for the future.") vs. the doctrine of social solidarity ("it is an obligation resting upon each individual to develop his individuality, that is to say, his physical, intellectual and moral activity as fully as possible in order to co-operate with all his forces towards social cohesion . . . .")

48. Civil Code, Books I-III, Preface.

49. Quoted in Greiff 1985, 453.

50. Zheng 1931, 654–655.

51. Wei Zheng 1943, 170. Wei Zheng Yuxiu and her husband the GMD politician Wei Daoming both received doctorates in law at the Sorbonne, and both were regarded as protégés of Wang Chonghui. Wei Daoming had participated in an earlier codification project and served as minister of justice while Wei Zheng sat on the codification commission. Prior to their marriage in August 1927, they had practiced law together in Shanghai's French Concession.

Chapter Three

The Rise of Public Opinion

The Case of GMD Surname Legislation

Over the last century, Chinese women have seemingly catapulted from the ignominy of near namelessness in the patriarchal society of imperial China to the freedom to maintain their own names and surnames. In line with the evolutionary trajectory of the history of Chinese women's liberation in general, this representation of Chinese women's transition from nameless subordination to full name and surname autonomy is, of course, crudely drawn, and therefore in need of careful reconsideration.[1] Past scholarship suggests that this narrative overstates the role of the 1949 Revolution, neglecting to address many questions about the transitional period between the fall of the Qing Dynasty and the establishment of the People's Republic of China.[2] A narrative suggesting a period of ideological darkness before the revolution and an almost magical rupture from the Qing to the PRC obscures the fact that much of the debate, disagreement, and search for surname alternatives and possibilities took place during the Nanjing Decade (1928–1937), a period of growing legal consciousness among the Chinese public.

Scholars have hailed the Republican Civil Code as the first "modern" Chinese civil code, crediting it with introducing the principle of gender equality and helping to convince foreign powers to relinquish the right of extraterritoriality. However, they have also discounted the significance of the code because of the perception that its European-derived ideas did not take root in the Chinese countryside, crediting the 1950 Marriage Law instead with changing popular attitudes.[3] The debate over the value and impact of the Republican Civil Code overlooks something important: When we turn our focus away from the code itself and how modern, foreign, feminist, or patriarchal its provisions were, and begin to interrogate the legislative process that produced the code, we find that it was uniquely radical. In the case of the legislation concerning surnames for married women, distinguishing between the law itself (the brief sentences contained in Article 1000 of the Republican Civil Code) and the protracted legislative debate that shaped the law demonstrates tremendous divergence of opinion over GMD policy toward women and the family among lawmakers, legal experts, and women's organizations. With this approach, we can clearly see the radical nature of the legislative debate and the surprising willingness on the part of the GMD to consider restructuring as sacred and fundamental an institution as patrilineal surnames. In addition, the postlegislative debate carried on primarily by women's periodicals was just as vibrant, if not more so, as the debate leading to the legislation. This postlegislative debate was premised upon the assumption that the law was not fixed, that it was subject to revision and amendment, and that future revision was not just possible but likely. Though it was the 1950 Marriage Law that upheld the right of married women to maintain the use of their own surnames, that law represented the resolution of the surname controversy that reached its hottest point during the Nanjing Decade. The outcome of the 1930 Family Book was certainly eclipsed by the more radical articles of the 1950 Marriage Law, but the legislative process in 1950 was less deliberative than in 1930, projecting an air of *fait accompli* that diverged markedly from the Republican-era debate. In light of the history of Chinese law for much of the rest of the twentieth century, when law and policy were more often than not dictated by ideology, it is hard not to surmise that there was something singular about the extensive exploration of alternatives to traditional surname practices, the space and weight accorded to public opinion, and the possibility for thoughtful disagreement that characterized the GMD legislative process.

The legislative process and the postlegislative debate over married women's surnames (in conjunction with other parts of the Family Law) that took place in 1930 were unheralded in Chinese history in other respects as well. The work of legislation was performed by the Legislative Yuan (*Lifayuan*), a body composed of members who served as representatives of the people. While the members of the Legislative Yuan were still very much legal elites, they also in a sense "popularized" the work of legislation. The public nature of the debate also signaled a departure from late imperial lawmaking. The Legislative Yuan was a deliberative body whose work was to be open to the public. Its proceedings were publicized in official journals like the *Lifayuan gongbao* (Legislative Yuan gazette) as well as in major newspapers. Not only was the work of the Legislative Yuan a matter of public record, its leaders directly solicited public input on controversial issues like married women's surnames. Indeed, correspondence between the Legislative Yuan and the GMD Central Political Council (*Zhongyang zhengzhi huiyi*), the group within the GMD charged with determining the guiding principles for legislation, related to the Family Book was widely and deliberately published in order to spark public debate. Lawmaking, moreover, was open to new groups, including women. Women, for instance, participated in the legislative proceedings for the first time in both formal and informal capacities. Indeed, the committee charged with drafting the law, the Civil Codification Commission, included a woman, Zheng Yuxiu, who was awarded her law degree from the Sorbonne. And women were among the experts whom the Legislative Yuan consulted. Thus a growing legal consciousness during the Republican period both reflected and helped promote these developments.

This chapter investigates the debate over married women's surnames that took place in two key contexts: first, the GMD legislative debate over married women's surnames that reached its climax from April to December 1930, and second, the postlegislative debate in the women's press for changing surname laws and attitudes that continued throughout the 1930s. The sources for this investigation consist of records of the GMD Legislative Yuan, the Central Political Council, legal treatises, legislator memoirs and collected writings, and articles, editorials, and letters published in major newspapers, law journals, and women's periodicals. Newspapers consulted include Nanjing's *Central Daily News* (Zhongyang ribao), the *Shanghai News* (Shenbao), and Tianjin's *L'impartial* (Dagongbao). Major law journals include *Law Weekly Review* (Falü pinglun) published in Beijing then Nanjing and *Law Journal* (Faxue jikan), the Nanjing version. The women's periodical I rely upon most is *Women's Echo* (Funü gongming), published first in Shanghai and later in Nanjing and Chongqing. The legislative and postlegislative debates over married women's surnames help illuminate a number of important issues, including the nature of the GMD state (was it possible for the GMD to be open to exploration and socially progressive, despite its politically repressive aspects?), state-society relations (the role of law in Chinese society and the difficulty of legislating social change), and the paradox of gender presented by a liberal modernity that featured a newly modernized patriarchy centered upon the husband, as opposed to the patriline of Confucian tradition.

COMPARATIVE AND HISTORICAL CONTEXT

While Chinese women were not entirely "nameless" before the twentieth century, they were subject to a naming system that reinforced patrilineal dictates. This naming system was passed down by custom rather than through law, since there were no laws regulating surname usage until the twentieth-century law. An upper-class man might have up to eight different personal names. A woman, by contrast, had fewer personal names, usually getting by with only a "milk name" (*ruming*) that was used by her natal family, though an elite woman might also have a courtesy name. The usual practice upon marriage required a woman to prefix (*cong*) her husband's surname before her natal family surname, symbolizing her incorporation into the husband's patriline, to form a dual surname consisting of her husband's surname first, her natal family name second, and then the designation (*shi*). Women, though, were often referred to by their natal family surname alone, followed by *shi.* A woman's personal name was generally not used. Actual practice of course varied according to class, region, context, and whether it was the written or oral tradition at issue (Watson 1986). Women in the PRC today uniformly do not adopt their husband's surnames upon marriage.

From a comparative perspective, something else emerges as unique about the history of married women's surnames in China. Anthropologist and political scientist James C. Scott famously discusses the role of permanent patronyms in state formation (1998, 64–71). Although Scott primarily discusses the state's need to make its subjects more legible to facilitate taxation, conscription, and other extractive functions in European history, he does cite the Qin (221–206 BCE) and Han (206 BCE–220 CE) Dynasties as early examples of an expanding state's imposition of permanent patronyms to exert greater control over its subjects. Married women's surnames in China complicate Scott's argument about the state's need for legibility in a number of ways. Historically, married women's surnames departed from the need for permanent patronyms, as their surnames were not permanent and changed upon marriage. Although women had surnames, they did not have permanent names combined with surnames to make the women distinct. Perhaps the state did not need to "know" women beyond which family they belonged to, their natal and then their marital families.

Unlike in the United States, where calls to change the practice of married women taking their husbands' surnames arose with the women's rights movement (Stannard 1977 and Million 2003), in China, the controversy over surnames originated in a different context, the context of anarcho-feminist attacks on the family system. Compared to U.S. feminists, Chinese anarcho-feminist critiques of surnames were more radical, attacking the entire family and surname system. The problem was not that women were treated as inferior by the customs related to their family names, but rather that all family names were intrinsically oppressive, even for men. Family names bound individuals to the family system that was the source of oppression. Chinese anarchists aimed to eliminate family names for both men and women in a quest for freedom, not just to change how married women approached their surnames, as U.S. feminists desired. The Guangzhou anarchist Shifu (1884–1915), for example, argued that surnames should be banned in order to promote a more egalitarian family system. Indeed, Shifu singled out family names as "selfish things" that were like the "bricks" used to construct the "prison of great darkness" that was the family.[4] Although such uncompromising condemnations of patrilineal surnames never gained widespread public support, they did prefigure debates that came to a head during the New Culture period and resurfaced in diluted form during the GMD civil codification effort among mainstream figures, such as Cai Yuanpei (1868–1940) (Dirlik 1991, 66–69, 172). Ultimately, perhaps the anarcho-feminist origins of the surname controversy help explain in part historian Gail Hershatter's observation that despite the actual success or failure of Chinese gender policies, China seems to have been uniquely radical in its comprehensive efforts to rethink gender norms in the twentieth century.[5]

NATIONALIST FAMILY LAW REFORM

The actual work of drafting the Republican Civil Code fell onto the shoulders of the Legislative Yuan's five-person Civil Codification Commission (*Minfa qicao weiyuanhui*), chaired by Fu Bingchang (1896–1965).[6] The commission drew upon a number of sources to assist its work: earlier draft civil codes inherited from the late Qing and Beiyang governments, compilations of regional customs, interpretations and opinions of the Daliyuan Supreme Court from 1906 to 1928, the opinions of legal experts like Hu Changqing (1900–1988), a participant in previous codification efforts, foreign advisers,

Figure 3.1. Chair of the Civil Codification Commission Fu Bingchang reading in the library of the Legislative Yuan. Courtesy of Visualising China, http://visualisingchina.net

public opinion, and the ultimate guidance of the Central Political Council. Since it was appointed in 1929, the commission had already accomplished quite a bit, working tirelessly in a few short months to draft the articles that formed the basis of the first three books of the Republican Civil Code (General Principles (*zongze*), Debt/Obligations (*zhaiwu*), and Rights over Things (*wuquan*).[7] The three books were promptly approved by the Yuan and were promulgated shortly thereafter. In contrast to the speedy efficiency by which the commission was able to complete Books One, Two, and Three, work on Books Four and Five (Family [*qinshu*] and Inheritance [*jicheng*]), did not proceed as smoothly. In fact, by April 1930, the commission's work had come to an impasse.

With deliberations stalled at the committee level, Chairman Fu had no choice but to request additional guidance from a higher authority, appealing to Hu Hanmin (1879–1936), GMD veteran and president of the Legislative Yuan. Chairman Fu explained the commission's dilemma when it came to family law in a speech to the members of the Legislative Yuan. First, Chairman Fu stressed the importance of the present undertaking. He made it clear that he considered the work on the Family and Inheritance Books to be the most important pieces of legislation that the Yuan would produce. This was because these laws were most closely related to the "Guiding Principles of the [Nationalist] Party" (*Danggang*) and most relevant to the people and customs of the country, he explained. Why, then, were the Family and Inheritance Books so much more contentious than the other books? Chairman Fu specified the commission's predicament: the Confucian patrilineal system presented the knottiest dilemma. On the one hand, Chairman Fu criticized "patrilineality" (*zongtiaozhuyi*) for reflecting "feudal thinking, violating the GMD principle of gender equality, and encouraging the habit of dependency." On the other hand, he went on in the same speech to celebrate the family as "one of the best features of the Chinese people," the glue holding the people together, and a key building block for national unity.[8] Fu's comments expressed the legislators' ambivalence toward the institution of the family, desiring to eliminate the patrilineal family and its feudal-style oppression while also desiring to maintain and even strengthen the family as a crucial foundation for social stability and political unity.

The need for thorough reform was generally recognized when the GMD set out to formulate its policy on women and the family in conjunction with the family law portion of the Republican Civil Code. In the 1920s, the GMD had adopted New Culture feminism in part as a badge of modernity, and it pledged to struggle against gender inequality in a number of areas, including education, employment, politics, and law.[9] GMD lawmakers were intent on introducing gender equality, yet they were also fearful about the effects of doing so on social order. Liberal elements within the GMD viewed the patriline as a feudal relic that stifled individuality, independence, and equality. At the same time, for elements within the GMD concerned with state-strengthening above all else, the family order, or perhaps an updated version of it, still had its uses.[10] Statist concerns gained prominence in the wake of the party's rightward shift after its 1927 break with the CCP and the ensuing purges that marked a significant setback for the cause of social revolution in general. With the establishment of the Nanjing government in 1927–1928, the GMD further refocused its energies on party consolidation and national unity. In this increasingly statist political context, family reform was reconceived as a vehicle for fostering national unity and loyalty to the nation-state rather than as a vehicle for individual freedom, as Chinese anarchists and liberals had first hoped (Glosser 2003).

Comparing civil code Books One, Two, and Three with Books Four (on family) and Five (on inheritance) highlights the difficulty of legislating social change. With Books One, Two, and Three, the GMD borrowed heavily from the latest codification efforts from Europe and Japan. Perhaps this was because there was little precedent with which to contend. In the absence of a competing, comparable system of formal civil law, the GMD simply supplied the latest, most modern principles in a value-neutral, cultureless way, with science as the model. When surnames emerged as a legislative issue in Book One, one's name and surname were linked to one's identity and personhood. This was not controversial and resulted in an unequivocal affirmation of an individual's right over his or her own surname. In contrast, Books Four and Five invoked cultural attachment rather than scientific rationality. GMD family law was now grappling with topics that had been subject to detailed regulation in the past. Instead of a clean slate, the commission had to contend with a substantial body of family regulations, rituals, prescriptions, customs, and so forth. A series of longstanding precedents could not simply be jettisoned *in toto*, nor could it be allowed to continue in the face of modernization. This dilemma was clear during the deliberations over surnames in the context of Book Four on family. GMD lawmakers distinguished between an individual's rights over his or her name and surname versus a married woman's rights over that same issue. In this case, the GMD had to work out a compromise that would push family and society forward, while keeping an eye on social reality.

Legislative Yuan president Hu and vice president Lin Sen (1864–1943) received Chairman Fu's request and drafted a letter to the GMD's Central Political Council, appealing to that body to clarify the principles that should guide the codification of family (and inheritance) matters.[11] In the letter, President Hu and Vice President Lin pinpointed the nine most controversial issues—spousal and children's surnames constituted point number two, closely related to point number one, kinship classification.[12] President Hu and Vice President Lin's letter was reprinted widely in order to encourage broad public debate and served as the opening salvo in the public portion of

Figure 3.2. Key Guomindang figures: Chiang Kai-shek, Wang Chonghui, Hu Hanmin, and Wu Chaoshu in 1930. Photo by Fu Bingchang. Courtesy of Visualising China, http://visualisingchina.net

the legislative debate over surnames. Over the next three months, while the CPC internally deliberated the future of Chinese surnames, the issue also underwent the intense scrutiny of public opinion.[13]

PUBLIC INPUT IN THE LEGISLATIVE DEBATE (APRIL TO JULY 1930)

Hu and Lin's letter cast a wide net in recognition of Republican society's growing legal consciousness. To further stimulate this consciousness, the public letter called upon the Central Political Council to provide guidance while inviting members of the public to participate in the legislative debate over surnames and other family matters. During the three months between the publication of the letter in April 1930 and the Central Political Council's reply published in July, lawmakers, legal experts, intellectuals, feminists, newspaper editorial writers, and others expressed a wide range of opinion and explored a variety of unconventional alternatives to the surname question. Conservative commentators deferred to the weight of Chinese custom and past practice and stopped there. Others surveyed the laws and customs of other countries in search of better models. Science seemed to hold the answers for another group that looked to apply evolutionary principles to surname usage. Ardent feminists stuck to the principle of absolute gender equality as the only equitable solution. Still others adopted a more flexible approach, suggesting solutions that varied according to marriage type. And not a few commentators dismissed the surname issue altogether as a matter of custom unsuitable for legislative regulation. The atmosphere of the debate over these three months seemed to suggest that almost anything was possible, including the elimination of surnames altogether, but also that any change to such a deeply entrenched practice would be extremely difficult.

Hu Hanmin, who cowrote the letter to the CPC, played an influential role in the legislative debate over family law in general and surname legislation in particular through his positions in the Legislative Yuan and the CPC, the two most important bodies in the GMD legislative process, one authorized to draft legislation and the other authorized to determine the guiding principles for legislation. Hu wasted no time seeking opinions on the surname controversy. On 18 April 1930, two days after sending his letter to the CPC, he brought the issue to the attention of Chinese educators gathered in Nanjing to attend the National Education Conference. At the conference, Hu Hanmin invited the participants, including educators, prominent intellectuals, leading cultural figures, and GMD elder statesmen, to a grand luncheon banquet at the Legislative Yuan, one of the first occasions for a high-profile public discussion of the surname issue, which helped set the parameters for subsequent public debate. After the luncheon, Hu made some general remarks about the close relationship between law and education and then solicited the help of the conference participants in the family law debate. Hu posed his questions starkly as a matter of eliminating or preserving the institutions of surnames, marriage, and the family. If surnames were needed, then should the father's or mother's or a third party's surname be adopted?[14] Hu listened to the views of others and then offered his own perspective.

Cai Yuanpei, the renowned philosopher, former chancellor of Beijing University, president of the Control Yuan, and influential critic of traditional Chinese culture, spoke first at the conference, offering quite radical views that proposed to do away with surnames altogether.[15] Cai argued that "we can do without surnames. To follow either the father's surname or the mother's surname is unfair. An individual in his or her relations with society really only needs a designation. So we can establish a system of assigning signs to people that will work. We don't necessarily have to use surnames." Cai, however, tempered his radical idealism with gradualism, qualifying his views with the proviso that adopting an alternative identification system was a matter for the distant future, not the present.[16] He saw no compelling reason for the use of surnames other than customary practice, but he also recognized

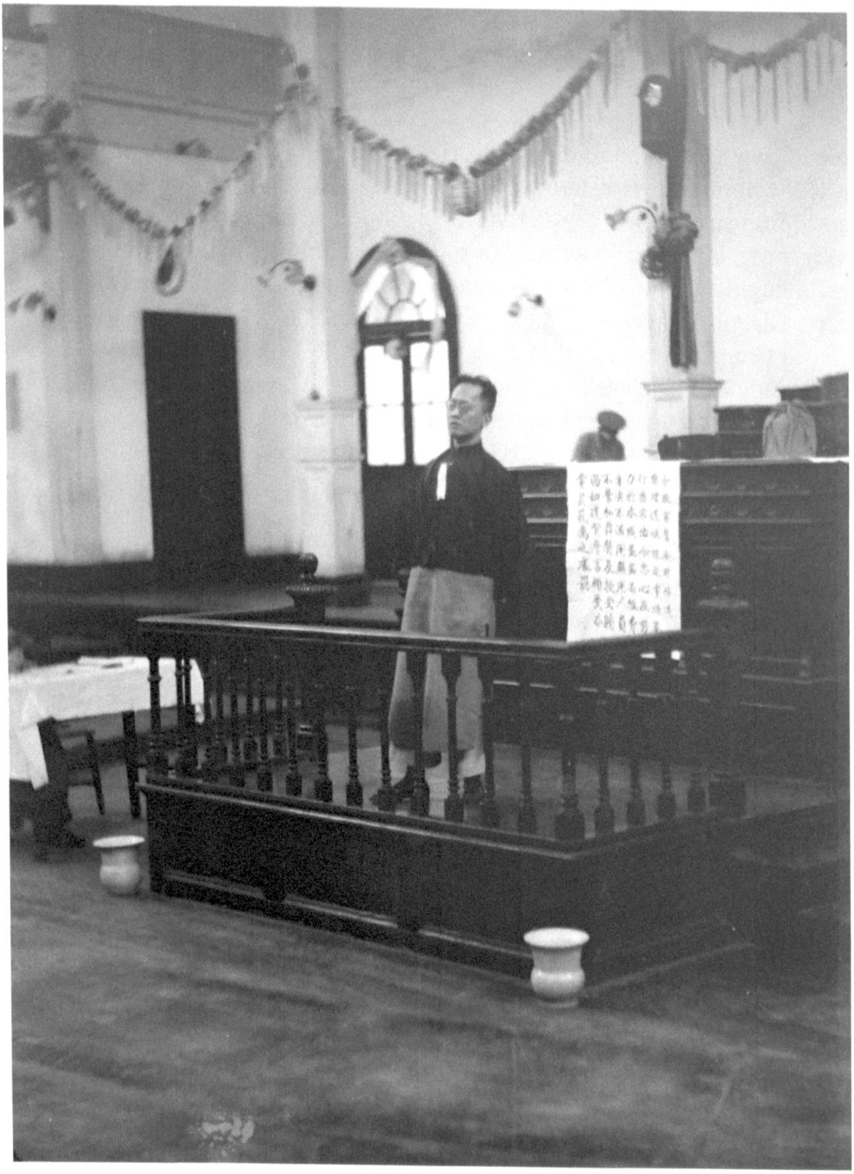

Figure 3.3. President of the Legislative Yuan Hu Hanmin delivering a speech in 1930. Photo by Fu Bingchang. Courtesy of Visualising China, http://visualising-china.net

that the hold of custom was powerful and that patrilineal surnames had become so deeply engrained in Chinese society that it would take much effort over a long period of time before they could be displaced.

Within the GMD, Cai espoused the views of the more radical elements, perhaps reflecting his anarchist background. The radical yet cautionary inclination expressed by Cai was reiterated in the comments by two of his fellow GMD elder statesmen who also had earlier anarchist ties, Li Shizeng (1881–1973) and Wu Zhihui (1865–1953). Li, known for his role in establishing the Paris-based group of Chinese anarchists and for cosponsoring a work-study program with Cai, had spent time in France studying biology and chemistry. Given his training, Li looked to science for answers to the questions raised by the surname debate. In a departure from his anarchist youth,[17] Li argued at the conference that although surnames could be abolished in theory, they should not be eliminated because they played important roles in genetics and evolutionary biology research. A comrade-in-arms from Li's Parisian anarchist days, Wu Zhihui, also preferred deferring the elimination of surnames to some indefinite future date. Wu no longer spoke disparagingly of surnames as Confucian relics as he had in his youth. In 1930, Wu characterized surnames as useful, ideologically neutral customs. He spoke humorously of the practical difficulties that would arise if there were no surnames and gave a hypothetical example dealing with social invitations: when he first arrived in Nanjing, if a stranger wanted to invite him to dine with him, the invitation was possible as long as the stranger knew his name, Wu Zhihui. Without his surname and name, by what means could the potential host reach him?[18] Wu's remarks underscored the present necessity and convenience of surnames, while leaving open the possibility of future change, which he estimated could perhaps take up to 3,000 years.[19] His comments suggested that surnames could be preserved for their functionality, apart from any link to patrilineal ideology. Other delegates to the conference, like the minister of education and Cai's successor as chancellor of Beijing University, the literary scholar Jiang Menglin (1886–1964), also acknowledged the weight of present reality and doubted that any significant changes could be made to customary surname practices for at least another fifty years.[20]

Also at the conference, GMD veteran, feminist educator, accomplished poet and calligrapher, and legislator Zhang Mojun (Sophie M.K. Chang 1884–1964) struggled to find a way to bring the principle of gender equality to bear on the surname system. Like Wu, Li, and Cai, she had joined the Revolutionary Alliance (*Tongmenghui*) before the 1911 Revolution, but unlike her male conference colleagues, she did not bother to contemplate the theoretical abolition of surnames. She instead presented a case for the continued use of surnames, though she wanted children to be able to choose their own surnames.[21] Zhang herself maintained the use of her birth family's surname alone, even after marriage to another prominent GMD figure, Shao Yuanchong (1889–1936). Her views seemed to reflect the belief that surnames in and of themselves were not inherently flawed and should not auto-

Figure 3.4. Nationalist lawmakers and educators (1930), front row: Chiang Kai-shek, Zheng Yuxiu, Hu Hanmin, and Li Shizeng; back row: Wang Chonghui (second from the left). Photo by Fu Bingchang. Courtesy of Visualising China, http://visualisingchina.net

matically be discarded. It was their association with the patriline that made them problematic.

Hu Hanmin concluded the conference discussion of surnames with his own views, which also reflected a thorough consideration of a wide range of attitudes and suggestions as well as the tensions between liberal feminist and family-statist reform. As with Wu and Li, Hu's originally quite radical views on women, marriage, and the family underwent a certain deradicalization by the time of the GMD family law debate in 1930. In his remarks at the education conference, Hu drew a sharp distinction between the nature of legislation and revolutionary theory. Hu expressed a keen appreciation for the practical wisdom exhibited by his old friend Wu Zhihui's comments on social invitations. He believed that Wu's comments hit the mark when it came to the legislative dilemma of how to approach surname practices. Hu's emphasis on a practical approach to the surname question stemmed from the perceived need to maintain social conventions. Those customs, like surnames, which might not be theoretically necessary in the future but which were practically necessary at the moment, should not be abolished.[22] The preservation of surnames, the family, and the patriline, moreover, did not necessarily entail the preservation of their original Confucian rationale. They could be justified instead along nationalist state-strengthening lines. Their Confucian content could perhaps be replaced by family-state connections.

Comments like the ones above reflected the tendency in GMD family law to renounce traditional Confucian patrilineal ideology while maintaining patrilineal customs (like surnames) as a matter of practical necessity. The majority of the conference participants affirmed their desire for a gender-equal naming system (gender equality was modern and liberal), but for practical and logistical reasons, they also conceded their willingness to postpone this scenario to an indefinite future date. Even if the GMD wished to do away with surnames, these comments seemed to suggest that it did not have the power to do so in the face of longstanding social practice. The GMD's ultimate approach to legislating social change was relatively cautious, and the process by which it reached this conclusion reflected an assortment of very thoughtful individual perspectives and contemplation rather than a rigid party-line mentality.

Major newspapers like *Shenbao* and *Dagongbao* covered the National Education Conference and contributed to the growing legal consciousness in Republican society, by for instance publishing summaries of the surname discussion and responses from their readers. Hu Hanmin's consideration of eliminating surnames altogether and Cai Yuanpei's blasphemous suggestion to replace surnames with signs or numbers (at least in theory) generated the most vehement disagreement. Apparently, the legislators' and educators' willingness to even contemplate alternatives to surnames offended the sensibilities of others who opposed any modification to their "sacred and inviolable" (*tianjing diyi*) surname practices. In the following sample of opinions expressed in *Dagongbao,* one commentator rebuked Hu, Cai, and Wu for what he deemed to be their casual remarks on the possibility of eliminating surnames, marriage, and family, as well as their casual disregard of Chinese conditions and customary practices.[23] Another editorial questioned the very need for surname legislation at all, since custom had governed surname usage for so long. For legislators to meddle with surname practices was one thing, but to abolish surnames entirely, as Cai Yuanpei proposed, made people question whether Cai had gone "crazy."[24] Even commentators who supported surname reform recognized that any change to the customary use of patrilineal surnames would lead to popular resistance, given the hold of ancestral sacrifice and clan reverence.[25] Much of the subsequent public commentary underlined the limitations of legal change, especially when the sentiments of the populace ran directly counter to the direction of the proposed legal changes.

Members of the Legislative Yuan also published their opinions on the surname issue in major newspapers. Balancing demands to respect the status quo and to promote gender equality led some lawmakers to flexible and experimental approaches to the surname controversy. Chen Changheng (1888–1987), a member of the Legislative Yuan who was regarded as a finance expert, took into account the diversity of social conditions in China and offered a range of solutions appropriate to different conditions. Chen proposed that the question of which surname to take should be determined according to marriage type. Chen set forth rules for three types of marriage: (1) women who married "out" in traditional patrilocal marriages should prefix their husbands' surnames to their own, (2) men who married matrilocally should prefix their wives' surnames to their own, and (3) men and women who started their own families upon marriage should mutually decide whose surname to take.[26] Chen's proposals corresponded to the conventional view that actual marital residence and financial support were determinative factors. By linking surname regulations to marital residence, Chen's proposals made social conditions the main criterion for surname decisions. Married women would not be required to prefix their husbands' surnames because they were women *per se*, but because they were women who entered their husbands' households and depended upon them for support. In incorporating liberal feminist concerns, respect for custom, and practical adherence to actual marital residence patterns, Chen's proposals attempted to accommodate the many existing types of marriages in the transitional Republican society.

During the three months of open deliberation, legal experts (some affiliated with the GMD and others not) also weighed in on the surname controversy. One group of legal experts adopted a skeptical attitude toward the need for surname legislation. Since Chinese surname usage had always been governed by custom alone in the past, these legal experts questioned whether the legal regulation of surnames was necessary or desirable in the first place. The heated public controversy over surnames led some legal experts to conclude that any legislative intervention would be a mistake because it would only generate more argument. In response to Chen Changheng's essay, Hu Changqing, a leading legal scholar who was a key figure in earlier codification efforts, advocated letting customary practices stand. He dismissed the goal of bringing surname practices in line with the principle of gender equality as not compelling enough to justify legislative intervention. Hu insisted that the practice of "wives taking their husband's surnames is not a great problem because true gender equality does not lie with the trivial issue of surnames."[27] Hu believed that a woman's rights over her surname mattered far less than her education, employment, or property rights.[28]

Newly established social and professional organizations like the Three Five Law Society (*Sanwu faxueshe*), an influential association of Nanjing lawyers and lawmakers that took its name from the Three People's Principles (*Sanmin zhuyi*) and Five Powers Government (*Wuquan xianfa*), also weighed in on the debate. The Three Five Law Society counted key GMD law and policy makers like Hu Hanmin among its board members, and indeed, the society's membership list was a virtual who's who of the Chinese legal world. The society agreed with Hu Changqing that legislating surname equality was not very feasible or even very important. Like Hu, the society concluded that "the expression of the Party's spirit of gender equality applies only to essential matters. It [should] not be used to calculate and then equalize each and every unessential matter." Thus the society agreed with the principle of gender equality in general but concluded that it was not broad enough to cover surnames in this instance, and besides, the society deemed surnames too insignificant an issue on which to apply the principle of gender equality.[29] Instead of questioning the need for surnames, these groups questioned the need for surname legislation. For this group, "minor" vestiges of patrilineality, like surnames, were tolerable in the pursuit of a modern liberal family law.

THE ENACTMENT OF GMD SURNAME LEGISLATION (JULY TO DECEMBER 1930)

In July 1930, after almost three months of public debate, the Central Political Council—the group responsible for the guiding principles for legislation—publicized its findings. Upon receipt of Hu and Lin's request for legislative guidance in April, the CPC initially delegated the task of investigation to its law subcommittee (*falü zu*). In July, the law subcommittee submitted its opinion to the full council, which unanimously approved the opinion. The CPC considered the advantages and disadvantages of six different surname systems: (1) husband and wife both agree to a surname (husband's surname, wife's surname, or a third surname) and children also take it; (2) husband and wife each use their original surname and children combine the father and mother's surnames; (3) husband and wife each use their original surname, sons take the father's surname, and daughters take the mother's surname; (4) wife takes the husband's surname and children take the father's surname; (5) husband takes the wife's surname and children take the mother's surname; and (6) wife places the husband's surname before her own and children take the father's surname.[30]

The CPC applauded the first three possibilities for their fidelity to the principle of gender equality. Method One provided the greatest degree of surname freedom, but the CPC feared that as a result of so much choice, surnames would change every generation, destroying the very usefulness of surnames as durable and reliable identifying markers. The CPC rejected Method Two based on both its lack of uniformity and difficulty of implementation. The CPC disliked Method Three because the prospect of siblings with different surnames was considered too odd. The CPC then disqualified Methods Four and Five as too biased against gender equality. Finally, the CPC approved Method Six because the CPC claimed it seemed easier to implement. Wives would add a surname, but husbands would not have to change anything. The CPC decided children should take the paternal surname mainly because it could not devise a better solution. On the question of spousal and children's surnames, the CPC concluded that while it desired complete gender equality, it found such equality elusive because there was no ideal method for its implementation. In defense of its decision, the CPC, echoing the views of Hu Changqing and the Three Five Law Society, claimed that "gender equality should emphasize reality, like economic, political, and private rights equality rather than empty distinctions. Rather than insisting on surnames having equal weight, which would be impossible, we hope to accord with the main purpose of gender equality within the realm of possibility."[31] In the end, the CPC opinion gave a nod in the direction of liberal, modern gender equality, if only to back away from it for seemingly ideologically neutral reasons of practicality and ease of implementation.

One member of the GMD Civil Codification Commission (and a future minister of justice), Wang Yongbin (1881–1944), provided a thoughtful, extended dissent from the CPC's opinion, upholding a liberal feminist position on surname legislation. He based his critique on a thorough survey of the surname laws of various countries (demonstrating an international legal consciousness) as well as Chinese historical practices. Wang first rejected the codes most influential in the Chinese civil codification effort—German, Swiss, and Japanese—for their blatant gender inequality: all required married women to adopt the surnames of their husbands.[32] The only exception to the use of male surnames came from Soviet law, which allowed spouses to choose whether to adopt the husband or wife's surname or retain one's original surname.[33] Other Chinese legal experts applauded the gender equality embodied in the Soviet code, but declined to follow that model because the Soviet system was deemed unstable. Lawmakers in the Soviet Union had recently been compelled to revise their family law because of the social confusion it had produced. The flux in Soviet regulations indicated to some Chinese lawmakers that fully honoring the principle of gender equality created too much social confusion and disorder. Wang, though, praised the progressive aspects of the Soviet law, especially the code's embodiment of absolute gender equality. In Wang's view, practical considerations related to ease of implementation and the prospect of confusion should be subordinated to the need to fully implement the principle of gender equality.

Wang also investigated the forms of address for married women in works of Chinese literature and philosophy. His literature survey revealed a longstanding tradition by which married women from elite, literary families maintained their own personal names and natal family surnames. Wang believed that this tradition of wives' maintaining their own surnames should now be mandated by law. Wang concluded that the CPC guideline that required a woman to add her husband's surname upon marriage infringed upon the civil personality and very dignity of all women, arguing that "to change surnames upon marriage makes no sense. It's an utterly vile law that insults the human dignity of women . . . . We absolutely must not implement this [type of law]" (Wang 1930). True, the CPC proposal allowed for women to maintain their own surnames, but only in cases where a woman could secure her husband's agreement. Wang maintained a liberal feminist position on the surname issue long after others in the GMD privileged statist concerns with social order. However, although Wang's liberal feminist stance was defeated in the course of GMD surname legislation, feminist concerns dominated the postlegislative debate and efforts to amend the civil code provision.

In accordance with GMD legislative procedures, the Civil Codification Commission set to work drafting a law that conformed to the Central Political Council opinion. The final form of the law on marital surnames reaffirmed the standard of the patriline, albeit without reference to the Confucian patrilineal ideology it had previously supported and with room for other approaches. According to civil code Article 1000, "a wife is to place her husband's surname before her original surname; [an uxorilocal husband] is to place his wife's surname before his original surname. However, parties who have made other arrangements are not hereby limited."[34] In the end, GMD surname legislation did not mandate that all married women maintain their natal family names, nor did it mandate that all married women adopt their husbands' family names. It established that, as a rule, a married woman should prefix her husband's family name to her own family name. For married couples who did not wish to follow this rule, however, the law gave them the freedom to do as they wished. Whether one wishes that the GMD had done more, or less, the process it adopted to determine these rules was thoughtful, careful, and deliberative, incorporating the views of a wider cross-section of Chinese society than any previous lawmaking enterprise.

FEMINIST OPPOSITION AND CALLS FOR REVISION IN THE 1930S

As far as the GMD was concerned, the passage of the civil code at the end of 1930 and its implementation in May 1931 marked the party's achievement of a modern, liberal family law, one that notably weakened patriarchal power with respect to property, inheritance, marriage, and divorce, but not surnames. Chinese feminists were not satisfied with the resulting code and continued to debate the surname issue in the 1930s, adopting a more expansive view of women's rights and the state's duty in legislating women's status, as well as demonstrating a growing legal consciousness. Feminists launched an effort to revise the law with petitions and proposed amendments that highlighted the shortcomings of the surname provision. Feminists also argued that formal gender equality under the law alone was not enough—they demanded that the GMD help end social as well as legal inequality. Recognizing that changes in surname practices had to be accompanied by changes in popular attitudes as well as law, feminists who participated in the postlegislative debate addressed the impact of the surname law on individual women, their status, identity, and personal dignity.

After 1931, most major newspapers and law journals ceased publishing on the surname issue, and women's periodicals became the leading forum for promoting the postlegislative surname debate. Some periodicals, like the journal *Funü gongming*, were loosely affiliated with the GMD, though most occupied what historian Wang Zheng calls the "nonpartisan independent feminist movement."[35] The women who participated in these debates drew upon New Culture themes like independent personhood, women's rights, and gender equality. These women were committed to political and cultural change within and beyond the party.

While the new civil code was widely extolled for its adherence to the principle of gender equality, *Funü gongming* and other women's periodicals offered sharp criticism. To coincide with the effective date of the new Family Book (May 5, 1931), for instance, the *Funü gongming* Society drafted a motion suggesting six different revisions to the Family Book, including a revised marital surname provision that would drop the requirement that a wife prefix her husband's surname upon marriage, allowing both husband and wife to continue to use their own surnames.[36] Several other contributors to *Funü gongming* sounded similar calls to revise the provision on married women's surnames, like the Shanghai lawyer and women's movement activist Jin Shiyin, who criticized GMD family law and its surname provisions in 1931. Jin rejected the notion that surnames were minor matters; she regarded them as integrally related to the question of personhood. The requirement that a person change surnames upon marriage, according to Jin, represented a shameful form of subjugation. Since the law now recognized women's independent personhood, women should not be required to prefix their husbands' surnames as if they were their husbands' "underlings" (*congshuwu*). To place them in such a subordinate position greatly insulted the dignity of women.[37] Her insistence on women's independent personhood situated the debate over surnames within New Culture feminist values, rather than the GMD's framework of social stability and order. Likewise, in *Funü gongming* editor-in-chief and veteran GMD woman revolutionary Tan Sheying's (1891–1978) view, the GMD surname law was out of touch with the revolutionary tide. Tan urged strict adherence to the GMD's revolutionary spirit and the Guiding Principles that promoted gender equality. "How can we set 'sort of equal' (*lüeshi*) as a principle for legislating surnames?" In Tan's analysis, Chinese women had evolved into full members of society and citizens of the nation, enjoying equal rights with men. Women were no longer appendages to the family, and their surnames should reflect this new status as independent persons (Tan 1930).

The other founding editor of *Funü gongming,* Li Zhishan (1896–1939) (who often omitted the use of a surname in her bylines), also opposed the GMD surname law and supported the position that women not be required to change their surnames upon marriage.[38] Li had been interested in the surname question for some time, publishing on the issue in the 1920s and 1930s.[39] In some respects, her views on the surname issue represented a natural outgrowth of her New Culture contempt for Confucian patriarchy.[40] Li interpreted traditional surname practices as degrading women, arguing against patrilineal surnames on the grounds that they violated gender equality. She attributed the practice to "the vile custom of male superiority-patrilineality" (*nanzunnübei de nanxizhidu de louxi),* which she traced back to ancient times when the victors of war took possession of the defeated men and women, turning the captured men into slaves and the captured women into wives and requiring all captives to adopt the surname of the victorious patriline. Li asked, "If the law continues to require women to change their names upon marriage, then isn't it just like continuing to treat them as slaves and captives?" ([Li] Yitao 1930).

She summarized her opposition to the practice of prefixing male surnames again in 1935 in response to renewed interest in the surname question that coincided with the GMD's discussion of amendments to the law (perhaps she and others were also emboldened by the recent success of the women's movement in lobbying for changes that made the adultery laws gender equal).[41] Her objections ranged from the practical harm done to a woman's achievements and undertakings before marriage as well as a woman's career development after marriage, the inconvenience created by changing a woman's name every time she married, to the moral outrage Li felt at the perpetuation of a custom that had arisen when wives were treated more like commodities than human beings. Li forcefully argued that "taking a husband's surname is women's galling shame and humiliation (*qichi dawu*)." Furthermore, Li harshly criticized Chinese women who imitated foreigners and not only prefixed their husbands' surnames but abandoned their own names entirely to become "Mrs. So-and-So (*moumou furen*)." In her view, the English practice of completely obliterating a woman's identity represented an even greater degradation of women than the traditional Chinese system in which married women were at least known by their natal family names. In contrast, Li considered women like Song Meiling (1898–2003), Chen Bijun, (1891–1959), He Xiangning (1879–1972), and Song Qingling (1893–1981) progressive because they were married to prominent men but chose not to prefix their husbands' surnames ([Li] Zhishan 1935).

The lawyer and journalist Deng Jixing (1907–1995) was one of the most vocal and well-qualified critics calling for an amendment to Republican surname law. In 1933 and 1935, Deng published two similarly themed articles attacking the Republican Civil Code's numerous violations of the principle of gender equality (Deng 1933 and 1935). The laws related to marital identity, for instance, reinforced a hierarchal, master-servant relationship between husband and wife, despite the fact that the drafters of the civil code claimed to have abolished the legal force of the patriline. In practical terms, requiring a wife to prefix her husband's surname upon marriage meant that married women might have two-, three-, and even four-character surnames. The CPC Opinion of July 1930, however, had specifically rejected the use of multiple surnames in the context of dual or combined surnames for children (citing the burdensome task of keeping track of dual surnames). Deng pointed out that requiring a wife to adopt an additional surname upon marriage contradicted the CPC's own logic.[42] In that opinion, moreover, the CPC had justified the married women's surname-prefix requirement as an indicator of marital status. Deng questioned the validity of this rationale, especially in the absence of a reciprocal requirement for married men. It did not make sense for the CPC to grant women economic equality (equal property and inheritance rights) but not to recognize status equality. In the face of such faulty legislative reasoning, Deng urged the Ministry of Judicial Administration to amend the law to allow a wife and a husband to each keep her and his own surname (and determine their children's surnames by mutual agreement), respecting a woman's autonomy, both legally and socially. Besides, Deng argued, it was only natural for a wife and husband to have different surnames, since surnames demarcated bloodlines, and wives and husbands were supposed to marry different bloodlines anyway (Deng 1933).

Through personal experience, above all, Deng developed a strong conviction that married women should maintain their own names and surnames even if it meant that members of the same family would have different surnames. Deng married in 1925, then had three children before her husband passed away. In 1933 when she married again, she and her second husband drew up a novel arrangement, printing it on red cards that were passed out to guests at their wedding. Mixing the political and personal, the cards explicitly announced: "Each of us will use our own surname—the husband's surname will not be prefixed; Deng Jixing's three children will remain surnamed Wu as before."[43]

In their effort to reform the law, women discussed the surname issue in terms of popular attitudes, personal practices, and women's status. In 1934 and 1935, Shanghai's *Women's Voice* (Nü sheng) and Nanjing's *New Women's Weekly* (Xin funü zhoubao) published issues devoted to the surname question, prompted by the decision by prominent women's movement leaders, like the writer, editor, organizer, and educator Liu Wang Liming

(1898–1970, known in the English-speaking world as Frances Wong before marriage and Mrs. Herman C.E. Liu after marriage) and one of the few women appointed to the Legislative Yuan, Liang Zhao Maohua (1898–?), to prefix their husbands' surnames. A *Nü sheng* writer using the pseudonym Qian noted that although a few women refused to change their surnames after marriage, the surname situation looked bleak for the vast majority of women. She analyzed the problem from multiple perspectives. First, she grouped women who continued to take on their husbands' surnames into different categories. Uneducated women, Qian claimed, were too ignorant and powerless to oppose traditional surname practices. Most of these women did not even recognize the correlation between their names and their human rights. Even if they did, they would still be powerless to change the situation. In contrast, according to Qian, educated women changed their surnames because of socialization and environmental pressures. Despite their educations, these women succumbed to a mindset that taught them to aspire only to become someone's wife and to seek the vainglory and material comforts of wifehood. Next, Qian analyzed the submission to traditional surname practices by a group of women who were not only educated but had received superior educations and considered themselves to be "civilized" and "noble" persons. Qian accused these women of mistaking the mark of possession and ownership inherent in patrilineal surname practices for an "expression of love" (*aiqing de biaoxian*). Qian described the dilemma these women faced between, on the one hand, wanting to pursue their own independent personhood, and on the other hand, craving their husbands' "love" and therefore adopting their surnames. She especially faulted the high-profile Liu Wang Liming for conforming to the dual surname requirement. In addition, according to Qian, there were too few men who understood and supported women's independence and human rights. Qian lamented that "many, many men are not willing to let go of even one tiny bit of their proprietary interests in their wives." Qian identified this correlation between surname usage and economic subordination and dependency as the main obstacle to surname equality.[44]

Another disagreement over married women's surnames erupted between the prominent woman writer Chen Hengzhe (Sophia H. Chen Zen 1890–1976) and *Funü gongming*'s "Yun'er" (perhaps the journal's manager, Chen Yiyun 1910–1969). Like Qian, Chen distinguished between uneducated and educated women in her views on married women's surnames. But unlike Qian, Chen argued that a housewife who "only knows how to rest on her husbands' shoulders" should be straightforwardly referred to as "*taitai*," (a wife of a man of high status). Only women acting on occasions that showcased their own independent personalities (acting, playing music, painting, teaching, writing, working for the nation or society, or other activities) should maintain the use of their own name. Instead of *taitai*, these occasions called for the designation *nüshi*. Even this second group of women could at times use their husbands' names in order to demonstrate marital solidarity.[45] Chen's compromise provoked Yun'er to protest. Yun'er responded to Chen by resolutely stating: "Dogs have dog names, cats have cat names, only married Chinese women do not have their own names and surnames." Yun'er adamantly believed that there should be no compromise on this issue because women were either "completely independent, autonomous persons" or "male slaves and dependents (*nanzi de nuli fuyong*)" (1936).

In the 1930s, the GMD moved on to more pressing issues like war, which seemingly absolved it from the need to demonstrate how modern and liberal its social policies were, but issues of modernity, law, and gender did not fade away. These issues were taken up, expanded upon, and reshaped by women's rights advocates. As the debate by women's rights advocates illustrates, the meaning of surnames lay not only with their function as a means of organizing and classifying people in society, but also with their significance as markers of independent personhood and as important means of negotiating one's identity as an individual, in marriage, in the family, and in the patriline.

The question of women's status under the law posed a paradox of sorts. Under Books One, Two, and Three of the Republican Civil Code, the status of women was simple: women were "civil persons" the same as men. In Books Four and Five, however, women were treated not just as persons, but as family members, as daughters, wives, and mothers. As daughters, women fared well, attaining equality with sons in matters of inheritance, for instance. As wives, though, women were accorded different legal rights than their husbands. The provisions regarding marital surnames, marital residence, and marital property clearly distinguished between wives and husbands. Marriage changed the legal status of women in a way that allowed for their rights to be subordinated to those of their husbands. In a departure from Confucian ideology, the different treatment of wives and husbands was justified by reason of the location of the marital home (not cosmological differences or different inherent moral capacities). In some respects, Republican Chinese lawmakers encountered a paradox of gender similar to the one that operated in the modern West, a paradox embedded in liberal theory.[46] Whether wittingly or unwittingly, Republican lawmakers helped create a modern patriarchal order of politics and society that eliminated the power of the patriline yet preserved gender inequality on the new basis of conjugality.

CONCLUSION

This episode in GMD legislative history fascinates for several reasons. First, the surname debate invoked fundamental issues of identity and personhood, the stakes of which are almost universal. Second, the public nature of the legislative and postlegislative debate opened lawmaking to voices that had previously had no place in the making of Chinese law, marking this period as one of growing legal consciousness in Chinese society. Third, the vehemence of the arguments pressed by lawmakers, scholars, advocates, and others shows a vibrancy that seems notably absent in the legislative history of China in the rest of the twentieth century. Perhaps some qualification is needed here. The surname debate may be striking in part for its exceptionalism, departing from the usual legislative pattern. Regardless, in the legislative process that culminated in the 1930 Family Book, the GMD demonstrated a great willingness to thoroughly reconsider fundamental elements of family and social organization, even deeply entrenched customs like patrilineal surnames. There was also a wide divergence of opinion among reformers. Some reformers thought the issue of married women's surnames was essential, while others thought surnames were trivial markers that did not merit so much attention and debate. While the resulting Republican law on surnames was not strictly gender equal, the code did provide for an unprecedentedly flexible approach to regulating surnames. These measures accorded with the transitional nature of this period in Chinese history and recognized the durability of customary practices while providing enough flexibility to allow couples to pursue modern alternatives. When compared to the surname practices of other countries, moreover, the surname system that the GMD produced was remarkably progressive for its time. Finally, the longevity and importance of anarchism within twentieth-century Chinese debates on women and the family vividly distinguish the Chinese case from other historical contexts.

NOTES

1. On the trajectory of Chinese women's history in the twentieth century, see Hershatter 2007, 7–8. This trajectory coincides with the main outlines of two other influential paradigms, that of modernization and revolution. See Dirlik 1996, esp. 249–251.
2. See Wang 1999, 1–3, for a critique of the Chinese Communist Party master narrative of women's liberation.
3. Another group of scholars who discuss the 1950 Communist Marriage Law tend to diminish the significance of the Republican Civil Code as a change in law that was never implemented in practice. See Diamant 2000 and Johnson 1983. See also Meijer 1971.
4. Shifu, born Liu Shaobin, first changed his name to Liu Sifu, then Liu Shifu, and finally just Shifu, dropping the use of his family name altogether. While most other elite men also selected personal names that departed from the names chosen for them by their families, Shifu's name and surname choices represented more than just his literary and aesthetic tastes, they symbolized his opposition to family names altogether. See Krebs 1998, 104–105.
5. It is presumptuous to make the case solely on the basis of the history of Chinese surname legislation, but the anarcho-feminist origins of the surname controversy are important to understanding how questions of women and gender have unfolded in a uniquely radical way in twentieth-century China. The scholar who has most powerfully advanced the argument that anarchism has served as the source and influence of a wide cross-section of revolutionary ideas in Chinese history (especially in the period from 1905–1930) is Arif Dirlik. See Dirlik 1991. See also Zarrow 1988.

6. The other members were Jiao Yitang, Shi Shangkuan, Lin Bin, and Wang Yongbin. Zheng Yuxiu, China's first female lawyer, served on the commission during the drafting for the first three books. For a fuller treatment of GMD legislative history as well as pre-GMD codification efforts, see Yang 1936 [1989] and van der Valk 1939.

7. The Republican Civil Code was divided into five books in accordance with the structure of the German Civil Code.

8. Fu 1930a. As with most other important speeches and official documents related to the codification process, Fu's speech was widely disseminated in the mainstream press and legal periodicals. It was reprinted under slightly different titles, for instance, in *Dagongbao* (1930.4.28) and *Falü pinglun* 342 (1930.5.4).

9. The GMD Resolution on the Women's Movement was proposed by the director of the Central Women's Department, He Xiangning, and passed unanimously at the Second National Congress, 16 January 1926. The resolution obliged the GMD to "enact laws upholding the principle of gender equality," among other state-feminist guidelines. See the GMD "Resolution on the Women's Movement," reprinted in *Zhongguo Guomindang dangwu fazhan shiliao—funü gongzuo* 1996.

10. Although GMD founder Sun Yat-sen had decreed that excessive emphasis on loyalty to the family and patriline had retarded the development of nationalist feeling in China, instead of seeking to destroy those ties, he sought to use them as the building blocks of nationalism. See Strand 1997.

11. The Central Political Council, a unit of the Central Executive Committee, supervised legislative policy. In the legislative scheme at the time, the powerful CPC law subcommittee bore the initial task of drafting the opinion on the preliminary questions on family law. The CPC as a whole then debated these proposals and passed the agreed-upon proposals along to the Legislative Yuan as guiding principles of legislation. On the legislative role of the CPC, see Wu 1934, 149–151, and Ch'ien 1950, 139–149.

12. Hu Hanmin and Lin Sen, "Minfa qinshu jicheng bian ying zhuyi gedian (Aspects of the Civil Code family and inheritance books requiring attention)," letter to the CPC, reprinted in *Zhongyang ribao* (1930.4.16–17). Many newspapers and law journals published the letter in an effort to encourage legal experts and the public in general to send their opinion to the CPC during the period of deliberation.

13. On the rise of public opinion during the Republic, see Lean 2007 and Goodman 2005 and 2006.

14. *Shenbao* 1930.4.19.

15. Cai had long envisioned the possibility of a society without names or surnames. Back in 1904, he wrote a short story describing a utopian society in which people were identified by numbers instead of names and surnames. In 1918, Cai also helped establish the Promote Virtue Society (*Jinde hui)* at Beijing University, which adopted Shifu's ban on surnames discussed above. See Cai 1984 [1904] and Dirlik 1991, 66–69, 172.

16. *Shenbao* 1930.4.19.

17. See Li 1907, discussed in Dirlik 1991, 98–99.

18. *Shenbao* 1930.4.19.

19. Dirlik 1991, 233 and Krebs 1998, 29.

20. *Shenbao* 1930.4.19.

21. *Shenbao* 1930.4.19.

22. Hu 1930.4.21. See also Hu 1930.4.25.

23. Mei 1930.5.10.

24. Chen Ganyi, "Wo duiyu suowei 'minfa shang de san ge wenti' de yijian (My opinion on the 'three questions on the Civil Code')," *Dagongbao* (1930.5.9).

25. Chen Liren, "Minfa qinshu bian jige wenti (A few questions on the Civil Code Family Book)," three-part article, *Dagongbao* (1930.5.22–24).

26. Chen Changheng, "Duiyu minfa qinshu jicheng liang bian yuanze shang ying xianjue gedian zhi yijian (Opinion on the Civil Code family and inheritance books' preliminary principles)," *Falü pinglun* 347–348 (1930. 6.8 and 6.15): 30–32, 25–30. Reprinted in slightly different form in *Zhongyang ribao* (1930.7.3–5). Among GMD lawmakers, discussion of the sur-

name issue was not limited to formal sessions of the Legislative Yuan. As Chen's article shows, they also wrote in law journals and newspapers to publicize their views.

27. Hu Changqing, "Du Chen Changheng shi 'duiyu minfa qinshu jicheng liang bian ying xian jue ge dian zhi yijian' (On reading Chen Changheng's 'opinion on the Civil Code family and inheritance books' preliminary principles')," *Falü pinglun* 352 (1930.7.13): 9–13, 12. Hu wrote voluminously on civil and criminal law. As a member of the Legal Systems Bureau (*Fazhi ju*), he helped write earlier civil code drafts. Hu also translated Japanese legal works into Chinese. From 1928–1936, Hu served as editor of China's most influential law journal, *Falü pinglun*. For more on Hu, see Hu Changqing's son's reflections in Hu 1997.

28. Hu's comments on the triviality of the surname question for women were remarkable for their hypocrisy. Just one year earlier, when discussing surnames for men, Hu wrote: "Surnames and names are two of life's most important commodities . . . , " see Hu Changqing, "Mingyu quan zhi benzhi (The essence of rights over one's reputation)," *Falü pinglun* 274 (1929.1.13): 5.

29. Three Five Law Society 1930.

30. CPC, "Qinshufa xianjue gedian shencha yijian shu (Opinion on the Preliminary Problems of Family Law)." van der Valk 1939, appendix III, conveniently reprints the CPC's opinion in both Chinese and English.

31. The dean of China's legal profession, Wang Chonghui, played a key role in drafting the CPC Opinion. The CPC Opinion was published widely in newspapers, law journals, and women's periodicals.

32. German Civil Code, Section 1355, Swiss Civil Code, Section 161, Japanese Civil Code, Sections 746 and 788. The Japanese code provided an exception for a Japanese man who married (uxorilocally) into his wife's family, as he would then have to adopt his wife's family name.

33. On surname choice in the Soviet Family Code, see Goldman 1993, 205.

34. *The Civil Code of the Republic of China: Books IV–V*, translated by Ching-lin Hsia, James L.E. Chow, Liu Chieh, and Yukon Chang, reprint edition (Arlington: University Publications of America, [1930–1931] 1976), Civil Code, Article 1000.

35. Wang 1999, 134–135. For a brief history of *Funü gongming*, see Tan 1936, 235–239. The journal was established in Shanghai in 1928 by a group of women who had been affiliated with several recently suspended GMD women's departments. The journal moved to Nanjing in 1930 and then with the GMD to Wuhan and Chongqing in 1937.

36. *Funü gongming* Society, "Xiuzheng minfa qinshu bian an (Proposal to revise the Civil Code Family Book)," *Funü gongming* 47 (1931.5.1): 58–60.

37. Jin 1931. Jin also contributed to other independent feminist journals, like *Nü sheng*.

38. Li Zhishan (aka Li Yitao) and her husband Chen Xiaocen made important contributions to *Nü xing* (Ladies' star) and *Funü ribao* (Women's daily), some of which are reprinted in *Tianjin Nü xing she* 1985. They also helped found the Awakening Society (along with Zhou Enlai and Deng Yingchao), whose members were known not by names or surnames but by a numerical designation. See Levine 1993.

39. See [Li] Zhishan, "Nannü xingshi wenti de taolun (Discussing the problem of male-female surnames)," *Funü gongming* 58 (1931.10.15): 18–22.

40. See [Li] Zhishan, "Kongzi shi nüren de diren (Confucius is the enemy of women)," *Nü xing* 18 (1923.10.15), reprinted in *Tianjin Nü xing she*, 251–252.

41. Many feminists who were involved in the surname controversy in the early 1930s also participated in the 1934–1935 debate over the criminal code adultery provisions. See Liang 1997 and Tran 2009. On the adultery issue, women's groups formed a united front and succeeded in revising the law. In contrast, on the surname issue, women's groups were divided about the importance of the issue and did not succeed in changing the law, at least not during the Republic.

42. An illustration of just this sort of confusion was featured in a short anecdote, which humorously described the effort of one widow to figure out what she should be called upon remarriage. See Fei'e 1933: "There is a woman surnamed Zhang, who married a man surnamed Li. When people asked her name, she would say, 'Li Zhang *shi*.' Later, the man Li died, and the woman remarried a man surnamed Zhao. When people asked her name, she said, 'Li Zhang

shi.' Her husband heard this and scolded her, 'You foolish woman—how can you still be called Li Zhang *shi*?' After this reprimand, she went to ask her neighbor what she should be called. The neighbor laughed and said, 'You're surnamed Zhao, of course!' The woman suddenly saw the light, 'Oh, then I should be called Zhao-Li-Zhang *shi*.'"

43. Deng graduated from law school in Beijing and worked for the Ministry of Judicial Administration in Nanjing. In the mid-1930s, Deng opened her own legal practice and wrote a legal advice column, often omitting her surname in her byline. See Jiang and Lin 2004, ch. 2. On Deng's unique marriage agreement, see 25. Deng also opted to adopt the separate marital property system and to share all household expenses with her husband. One of the three children referred to in the agreement is a prominent economist in China today, Wu Jinglian.

44. Qian (pseud.) 1934. Liu Wang, who edited the same journal that published Qian's article, declined to respond to Qian's piece, stating, "This is a minor issue—I can't spare time to respond." From a different perspective, perhaps Liu Wang's surname decision could be considered progressive. "Liu Wang Liming," after all, departed from traditional kin-inflected forms of addressing married women. In that respect, her name was one step removed from the patriline, but it still indicated a relationship of subordination, not to the patriline but to the conjugal identity. For more on Liu Wang, see Wang 1999, 138–143.

45. Chen 1936. With her BA from Vassar, MA from the University of Chicago, and status as the first female professor at Beida, Chen enjoyed a high profile. For more on Chen, see Ye 1994. Women's publications in Beijing also criticized Chen's article. See "Tan yihun nüzi de xingming (Discussing married women's surnames)," *Shijie ribao* (World news) (1936.3.30).

46. See Pateman 1988 for the argument that a sexual contract is embedded in the social contract.

Chapter Four

The Process of Civil Adjudication

Marital Justice and the Republican Civil Court System

Republican China's civil law framework for handling marital disputes embodied several important changes in the relationship between law and society that lessened the stigma associated with law and made seeking a legal solution to marital disputes more appealing, especially to wives. In addition, the Republican court system made significant strides toward developing along modern lines, lending further support for the notion of Republican legal exceptionalism. This chapter serves as an overview of the GMD legal system that is essential background information for understanding the next four litigation-based chapters. The first section provides a basic description of the organization of the judicial system, covering the processes of civil litigation, mediation, adjudication, and appeal available to litigants in marital disputes. Whenever possible, statistical information is included on the number of marital disputes, the number of civil suits overall, and the geographical distribution of marital disputes. The second section outlines the typology of marital disputes in the Republican period. In its third and final section, the chapter follows the progression of an actual marital dispute through several rounds of litigation. As we shall see in the sample case discussed at length in the last part of this chapter, these legal provisions and procedures constituted part of a relatively flexible civil law system, embodying the GMD state's malleable approach to marital disputes, an approach that made it possible for litigants to air their grievances and often resolve their disputes.

The cases described here and in the next four chapters contribute to our understanding of Chinese law and society in the 1930s and 1940s by examining the social impact of the new civil code. Drawing upon the case records of marital disputes over divorce, cohabitation, separation, and annulment, these chapters seek to examine how the GMD state interacted with society through the legal system and what the implications of that interaction were for changing gender, marriage, and family norms and practices. The familiar account of an expanding state intruding more and more into family life forms part of the story in these chapters, to be sure, but it features less prominently than the more neglected story of the values, priorities, and understandings of marriage held by the individual husbands and wives who brought their conflicts to the courts.

ORGANIZATION OF THE CIVIL COURT SYSTEM

Studies of judicial reform in the early twentieth century by historians Philip Huang (2001, ch. 3) and Xu Xiaoqun (2008, ch. 3) have demonstrated that Republican governments successfully established a modern judicial system that managed in large part to supplant the Qing system of local magistrates with institutions and procedures akin to those of modern continental European courts. As part of the late Qing law reforms, the Qing government decreed that government officials should work toward establishing a modern judicial system. The 1907 Judiciary Act (*Fayuan bianzhi fa*) originally conceived of a four-tier (three-trial) system modeled after the German and Japanese systems, consisting of local courts, district courts, superior courts, and a supreme court (Zheng 1948, 180, and Kiang Yung 1926, 117–118). Because the government lacked the funds and personnel to support such a system, a few years later the local courts were folded into the district courts to create a three-tier system of district courts, superior courts, and a supreme court. The three-tier system was confirmed in the 1932 Judiciary Act. In the 1930s and 1940s, litigants in marital disputes brought suit under this three-tier judicial system. Chronic underfunding of judicial institutions during the Republic left plans for judicial modernization in some areas only partially implemented. A lack of adequate judicial resources translated into the establishment of only 23 superior courts, 83 superior court branches (*fenting*), and 298 district courts by 1937.[1] Nevertheless, by 1948, there was an extensive system of 2,161 courts, county judicial offices, and county government offices (see table 4.1). The buildup of a modern court system in Sichuan Province, Yunnan Province, and other areas occupied by the GMD during the War of Resistance was especially pronounced. Studies have shown, moreover, that for the most part Republican courts handled marital disputes in a relatively efficient and expedient manner despite the shortfall of judicial resources.[2]

District Courts and County Judicial Sections

The first tier of the Republican judicial system consisted of local district courts (*difang fayuan*), county judicial offices (*xian sifachu*), and county

Table 4.1. Courts Established, 1948

Province (35) Municipality (1) Other (1)	*Total*	*Supreme Court*	*Superior Courts*	*Superior Court Branches*	*District Courts*	*County Judicial Offices*	*County Government Offices*
Andong	19	-	1	-	18	-	-
Anhui	68	-	1	6	21	40	-
Chahaer	20	-	1	-	2	17	-
Fujian	74	-	1	5	14	54	-
Gansu	78	-	1	6	30	41	-
Guangdong	105	-	1	9	95	-	-
Guangxi	108	-	1	8	22	77	-
Guizhou	86	-	1	5	26	54	-
Hebei	144	-	1	8	16	119	-
Heilongjiang	28	-	1	-	26	1	-
Hejiang	19	-	1	-	18	-	-
Henan	119	-	1	6	15	96	-
Hubei	78	-	1	6	34	37	-
Hunan	82	-	1	5	17	59	-
Jiangsu	64	-	1	4	31	28	-
Jiangxi	85	-	1	6	22	56	-
Jilin	21	-	1	1	18	1	-
Liaobei	25	-	1	-	18	6	-
Liaoning	28	-	1	1	26	-	-
Nanjiang	21	-	1	-	18	2	-
Ningxia	8	-	1	-	4	3	-
Qinghai	9	-	1	-	7	1	-
Rehe	21	-	1	-	10	10	-
Shaanxi	98	-	1	4	20	73	-
Shandong	117	-	1	7	29	80	-
Shanghai	2	-	1	-	1	-	-
Shanxi	68	-	1	5	8	54	-
Shoudu	3	1	1	-	1	-	-
Sichuan	155	-	1	11	68	75	-
Songjiang	17	-	1	-	16	-	-
Suiyuan	22	-	1	1	4	16	-

Taiwan	10	-	1	1	8	-	-
Yunnan	138	-	1	7	16	114	-
Xikang	40	-	1	2	10	27	-
Xinjiang	80	-	1	-	13	-	66
Xing'an	10	-	1	-	8	1	-
Zhejiang	82	-	1	5	43	33	-
Total	2,151	1	37	119	753	1,175	66

Source: No. 2A 7-7085

government offices (*xian zhengfu*). By 1948, there were 753 district courts, 1,185 county judicial offices, and 66 county government offices. The district courts best exemplified the attributes of modern judicial institutions, while the county government offices most resembled the local yamens of the late imperial period. Most of the interaction between litigants and the judicial system took place at this level. A single judge (*tuishi*) from the district court or adjudicating official (*shenpanguan*) from the county judicial office, assisted by a clerk (*shuji*), was responsible for conducting mediation sessions (*tiaojie* or *hejie*), interrogations (*diaocha xunwen*), oral arguments (*yanci bianlun*), and trials. The district court cases I draw upon in this study come from marital disputes brought before the Beijing District Court (*Beiping difang fayuan*) in the early 1940s.

Provincial Superior Courts

Litigants who disagreed with the outcome of the trial court had the right to appeal the decision within twenty days of the judgment. Just under 20 percent of litigants filed appeals with the superior courts (see the figures in table 4.3). Litigants submitted their appeals to the courts of the second tier of the judicial system, which consisted of provincial high courts, or superior courts (*gaodeng fayuan*). By 1948, there were thirty-seven superior courts, one for each of the thirty-five provinces claimed by the Republic of China, plus an additional one for the capital city of Nanjing, and a separate one for the municipality of Shanghai. In addition to the thirty-seven superior courts located at the provincial capitals, there were 119 superior court branches or divisions to serve areas where travel to the capital was difficult. The superior courts and superior court branches considered appeals and could also serve as a second trial court. A panel of three judges from the superior court usually conducted its own investigation of the facts and issued decisions that either affirmed or reversed those of the court of first instance. Typically, the appeals court ordered the losing party to pay the litigation fees (*susong feiyong*). In case of a split decision, the court usually apportioned the litigation fees between the parties. In this study, I draw upon superior court decisions from the 1930s from the Hebei Superior Court (*Hebei sheng gaodeng fayuan*) located at the Hebei Provincial Archives in Shijiazhuang and cases from the Jiangsu Superior Court (*Jiangsu sheng gaodeng fayuan*) located at the Jiangsu Provincial Archives in Nanjing.

Supreme Court

Litigants who disagreed with the outcome of the appeals process had one more venue in which to make their case. Just under twenty percent of superior court litigants appealed to the Supreme Court (see table 4.3). Litigants had twenty days after receipt of a superior court decision to submit an appeal to the Supreme Court (*Zuigao fayuan*), the third tier of the Republican court system. Appeals that were not filed within twenty days or were not accompanied by payment of the proper court fees were rejected through a summary ruling (*caiding*). Assuming that an appeal satisfied procedural requirements, a panel of five judges from the Supreme Court usually evaluated the case. The panel considered the litigants' arguments through written pleas that litigants generally submitted by mail. The Supreme Court did not conduct oral arguments, and it generally limited itself to deciding questions of law rather than fact. Like the superior courts, the Supreme Court had the authority to affirm or reverse the decision of the lower court. In the alternative, the Supreme Court could vacate the superior court's decision and remand the case to the superior court with instructions to conduct a new trial. The rulings and decisions of the Supreme Court were final, meaning that they were not subject to further appeal.

The decisions and interpretations (*jieshi li*) of the Supreme Court carried additional significance. The same 1907 Judiciary Act that decreed the establishment of the modern judicial system also gave the Supreme Court (the Daliyuan at the time) the right of interpretation, which gave the Daliyuan's rulings the weight of law (after 1929 the authority over judicial interpretations was transferred to the Judicial Yuan).[3] This function was especially important during the interim between the 1910 Qing Code currently in force and the promulgation of the 1930 civil code. During this time, the Daliyuan's rulings helped to generate a body of civil law that largely accorded with modern Western legal principles. These rulings created what might be thought of as "judge-made law" or "indirect legislation" that introduced modern legal principles to Republican China, helping to pave the way and prepare the public for the 1930 civil code. Even after 1930, Supreme Court decisions were published regularly and read by other judges. These decisions provided important guidelines on questions like what constituted "intolerable cruelty," for instance, as discussed in chapter 5. In this study, I rely upon decisions from the 1930s and 1940s from both the Nanjing and Chongqing Supreme Courts collected from the Second Historical Archives in Nanjing.

Fees

The costs associated with bringing a marital dispute before the Republican courts were not exorbitant. The fee system in the 1930s and early 1940s required litigants to submit 4.50 yuan with a petition for court adjudication or 0.75 yuan with a petition for court mediation. Additional fees were set for the plaint form (0.60 yuan), a fee for the use of a scribe (0.10 yuan for 100 characters), a fee for the form notifying the court of representation by a lawyer or other legal representative (0.75 yuan), a graduated fee for summoning witnesses to court, and a fee for obtaining a copy of the settlement agreement or judgment (0.15 yuan per 100 characters). The fee to appeal a case to the superior courts was slightly higher, 6.30 yuan. The fee to appeal a case to the Supreme Court was slight higher again, 7.20 yuan. The fees for forms and scribes remained the same as for the district court. These costs were not insurmountably steep when we consider that earnings for a Beijing rickshaw puller could be as much as two to three yuan a day, for a Shanghai cotton mill worker 0.50 to 0.65 yuan a day, and for an agricultural day laborer in north China 0.50 yuan a day.[4]

The Appeals Process

The appeals process for marital disputes underwent a significant change from the Qing to the Republic. During the late imperial period, the judicial treatment of marital disputes remained consigned to the county magistrates. Under late imperial law, marriage was considered a "minor matter" that was not subject to review by higher-level bodies.[5] Litigants had no formal avenue to appeal a county magistrate's decision to higher courts. It was not until the late Qing and Republican-era legal reforms created a formal system of civil law that avenues of appeal opened up for marital disputes. By making the appeals process available to litigants in marital disputes, the state accorded more formality, attention to procedure, and importance to marriage matters.

The appeals process operated to shape the outcome of marital disputes in various ways. An appeals court had the power to affirm, reverse, and vacate decisions, to remand with instructions for a new trial, and to issue memos ordering further mediation. In 1944, for instance, the Supreme Court agreed with the lower courts' decision to grant a women's petition for divorce. The Supreme Court simply issued a brief decision stating its action to affirm the decision.[6] When an appeals court disagreed with either the factual determinations or the interpretations of law made by a lower court, it could reverse the decision. For instance, in 1939, the Hunan Superior Court disagreed with the trial court on whether the abuse a wife suffered amounted to intolerable cruelty and reversed its judgment.[7] In other situations, a higher court could hold off on issuing a formal decision and send a memo to the lower court to try mediation. In 1939, for instance, the Supreme Court received a divorce case in which the district court and the superior court had reached contradictory decisions. Rather than choose a side, the Supreme Court sent a memo to the Hebei Superior Court with instructions to mediate a settlement between the parties.[8]

The view of state law that emerges from the case records of marital disputes is a rather uneven one, reflecting conflicting agendas and producing often contradictory or unexpected effects. Ensuring that litigants received a fair judicial process was important in reshaping the view of law in Chinese society, especially the relationship between women and the law. In case of procedural violations or other improprieties by the trial court, moreover, an appeals court could vacate the lower court decision and remand the case to the lower court for a retrial. The importance of the remand function of the appeals process in ensuring procedural fairness for marital litigants is clear in the 1945 case of Mrs. Tan-Xue, who sued for divorce on the basis of intolerable cruelty, accusing her husband of beating her on two separate occasions in 1945. In the case the Supreme Court vacated the superior court's decision to deny a woman a divorce because it found that the superior court did not properly investigate the wife's allegations of intolerable cruelty. It remanded the case to the superior court with instructions to retry the case more carefully. At the first trial, Mrs. Tan-Xue was denied her petition for divorce when her witnesses failed to appear in court. She faced another loss at the appeals level to the Guangxi Superior Court even though she explained that her witnesses failed to appear because they were afraid to testify in court.[9] She appealed once again to the Supreme Court, and this time the Supreme Court granted her another hearing.[10] The Supreme Court vacated the superior court's decision, sending the case back to the Guangxi Superior Court and telling that court to do a better job of investigating the wife's allegations of abuse, including summoning the witnesses to court. This and other remanded cases demonstrate that Republican courts took the investigation of women's grievances seriously, especially the Supreme Court. In fact, the failure of lower courts to properly investigate a wife's allegations was one of the most common reasons for the Supreme Court to vacate lower court judgments. As demonstrated in table 4.3, in numerous cases like the one above, the Supreme Court responded to appeals by women whose divorce petitions had been denied by trial courts and superior courts by vacating the superior courts' decisions and instructing them to conduct a more thorough investigation of the abuse allegations. The Supreme Court admonished the superior courts for not following up with witnesses and not conducting careful investigations.

Table 4.2 provides information comparing the number of civil cases in the decade from 1938 to 1947. It points to a burgeoning of civil litigation over this decade, with more and more litigants turning to the court system to resolve their disputes.

Table 4.3 provides statistical information on the percentage of cases that were appealed to the superior court and to the Supreme Court. Table 4.3 shows a pronounced spike in marital disputes after the conclusion of the War of Resistance in 1945, 1946, and 1947.

Table 4.2. Percent Distribution of Civil Cases Received and Resolved, 1938 to 1947

Year	*Courts of 1st Instance*			*Courts of 2nd Instance (Appeals)*		
	Civil Cases Received	*Civil Cases Resolved*	*Percentage Resolved*	*Civil Cases Received*	*Civil Cases Resolved*	*Percentage Resolved*
1938*	74,992	64,534	86	22,339	18,787	84
1939	145,594	133,461	92	44,595	40,570	91
1940	177,765	153,877	86	60,744	51,632	85
1941	216,232	196,863	91	80,087	68,666	86
1942	228,539	210,998	92	92,348	79,034	86
1943	186,096	167,593	90	86,323	72,919	85
1944	247,097	222,050	90	69,795	59,352	85
1945	308,642	267,046	87	69,501	57,666	82
1946	508,091	446,625	88	107,428	86,983	80
1947	524,962	459,719	88	132,190	106,144	80

Source: No. 2A 7-7084. The figures for 1938 cover only the second half of the year.
*The operations of the Supreme Court were disrupted during the first half of 1938 when the court was relocated to Chongqing.

Instance), 1944 to 1947

Litigation Type	*1944*	*1945*	*1946*	*1947*	*1944*	*1945*	*1946*	*1947*	*1944*	*1945*	*1946*	*1947*
Total	15,819	43,671	74,280	86,601	8,482	9,649	13,716	18,846	3,741	2,848	2,737	3,408
Pledge	308	966	1,844	2,005	109	104	309	165	16	8	5	5
Dian	5,274	12,143	17,390	19,123	3,256	3,576	4,667	6,028	1,939	1,151	1,223	1,943
Lien	79	359	743	985	112	43	60	74	21	10	6	8
Occupy	331	1,638	2,873	3,196	196	258	459	559	131	188	112	253
Marriage	**4,916**	**15,429**	**25,945**	**32,162**	**1,778**	**1,950**	**2,941**	**4,942**	**729**	**419**	**389**	**586**
					36%	**12%**	**11%**	**15%**	**24%**	**13%**	**8%**	
Parent-child	276	698	1,284	1,699	157	159	174	254	61	46	58	16
Guardian	92	244	525	474	48	38	55	75	25	59	42	29
Support	982	1,995	2,950	3,342	357	392	505	586	104	86	69	48
Family	493	1,034	1,738	2,235	97	132	216	246	126	55	18	40
Family council	40	124	196	202	14	20	17	36	15	46	81	54
Inheritance	1,629	4,526	6,677	8,327	1,575	1,594	1,885	2,660	381	433	324	269
Will	115	399	620	703	137	91	100	125	45	24	13	18
Other	1,284	4,116	11,495	12,148	646	1,292	2,328	3,096	148	323	397	136

Source: No. 2A 7-7085. The total number of civil cases differs, sometimes quite substantially from table 4.2 above, in part because table 4.3 only includes cases reported to the Ministry of Judicial Administration Statistics Bureau "Sifaxingzhengbu" through annual reports and is therefore not comprehensive. Also, table 4.3 does not include special categories of cases like retrials.

Note: Columns 2–5 (the first set of dates 1944–1947) are numbers for the Court of 1st Instance; columns 6–9 are for the Second Level; columns 10–13 are for the Third Level.

TYPES OF MARITAL DISPUTES

In the 1930s and 1940s the Republican Civil Code made a range of different legal mechanisms available to husbands and wives who experienced marital conflict. As the typology of marital litigation in table 4.4 illustrates, individuals sought a variety of resolutions to their marital problems before the courts. Lawsuits for divorce (discussed in chapter 5) were the most common form of marital litigation. Under the Republican Civil Code divorce became more widely available, but it was by no means the universal remedy for unhappy couples. Aside from divorce, couples brought suit for cohabitation (chapter 6), separation (chapter 7), and annulment (chapter 8) among other legal remedies. Litigants who preferred not to divorce looked for their own solutions, like the wives in cohabitation suits who had simply left or run away from their marital homes without necessarily seeking a formal end to their marriages. It was their husbands who initiated engagement with the judicial system to seek their return. Other litigants who preferred not to divorce fashioned their own legal solutions, as in the case of separation suits in which wives sued for a judicial separation and support that left their marital status intact. In annulment suits, wives sued to dissolve their marriages on grounds that differed from those available to divorcing couples. The variety of marital disputes in Republican China (in contrast to the eventual singular focus upon divorce after 1950) reflected the complexity of marriage litigation in this highly transitional period.

Table 4.4 provides a typology of marital litigation that shows some of the new civil law mechanisms that were made available to Republican husbands and wives.

Table 4.5 shows the outcomes of 6,216 marital disputes from 1936 (one of the only years in which detailed statistics for marital disputes are available). The figures in table 4.5 may be further broken down by province.

Table 4.6 provides detailed information about 230 courts from nineteen provinces that reported their marital disputes from 1936. This table illustrates the geographical spread of these cases. The most complete figures come from Guangdong Province, perhaps a reflection of the longer history of GMD state-building in that province. The compilers of the statistics noted that a significant percentage of cases were resolved through mediation or through withdrawal. The compilers interpreted the high percentage of mediated and withdrawn cases as an indication that many marital disputes were brought in temporary anger and could be resolved without formal adjudication.

Table 4.4. Percent Distribution of Marital Litigation by Case Type, 1936

Type	*Number*	*Percentage*
Divorce	3,103	50%
Annulment	262	4%
Marriage without effect	246	4%
Confirm marriage exists	195	3%
Confirm marriage not established	125	2%
Cohabitation and separation	762	12%
Dissolve engagement	1,032	17%
Unresolved cases of unknown type	491	8%
Total number of cases	6,216	100%

Source: *Sifa tongji: 1936.* This table was compiled using the annual reports (*nianbao*) submitted by individual courts. It is not comprehensive, as not all courts submitted annual reports. In addition, it only includes cases that were resolved in 1936.

THE ANATOMY OF A REPUBLICAN MARITAL DISPUTE

The development of the formal civil law system to handle divorce and other disputes helped to reshape how people thought about the law and to change the relationship between law and society. As we will see in the sample case below and the litigation chapters that follow, the history of Republican marital disputes shows the willingness of women to turn to the law for help. For women, bringing suit no longer required obtaining the agreement of natal family members to serve as proxies. Wives could and indeed were required to bring suit in their own right. The establishment of a formal civil law system to govern marital disputes, moreover, meant that husbands and wives who turned to the law to address their marital grievances engaged with civil law, not criminal law. This shift to civil law meant that a marital dispute was to be conceived of as a dispute among private parties rather than a disturbance of the natural order that required the state to intervene. The civil law framework for resolving marital disputes was also more flexible—allowing for a variety of outcomes—adjudication, yes, but also mediation, withdrawal of the suit, and so forth. This civil law framework arguably helped to lessen the stigma of the law. Civil law was the recourse of ordinary citizens looking to resolve private disputes. Civil law did not carry the connotations of crime and punishment that criminal law did. The reach of the law changed: civil law as opposed to criminal law relied on a different set of enforcement mechanisms. The parties to litigation could not be physically coerced, tortured, or otherwise intimidated into submission. This change in enforcement mechanisms was made abundantly clear in the cohabitation cases in which

Table 4.5. Percent Distribution of Marital Litigation by Outcome, 1936

Outcome	*Number*	*Percentage*
Adjudication	2,697	43%
Mediation	697	11%
Petition denied	1,168	19%
Petition withdrawn	622	10%
Other	541	9%
Not yet resolved	491	8%
Total number of cases	6,216	100%

Source: *Sifa tongji: 1936*

husbands returned to court multiple times to try to get their wives to comply with the judgments.[11] The highly developed nature of the Republican court system may perhaps come as somewhat of a surprise, as may the development of a high degree of legal consciousness evident in the motivations, feelings, and subjectivities of the litigants, as in the case of Fu Baoguang, who sued Yu Xiurong for cohabitation while Yu Xiurong countersued for divorce.

Fu Baoguang vs. Yu Xiurong was a mixed cohabitation and divorce case originating from Beijing and litigated between 1945 and 1947. The case deserves a rather lengthy analysis for a number of reasons. First, the procedural history of the case demonstrates the significant difference that the formal civil law framework for Republican marital disputes made, providing the wife with far greater flexibility and more options than compared to a criminal case against a runaway wife in the late imperial period. The husband's cohabitation suit was countered by the wife's suit for divorce. Even when the first and second courts ruled in favor of the husband and cohabitation, the wife did not obey those decisions and appealed. Second, the records from the case afford a detailed glimpse into the husband and the wife's perceptions of their marriage, their grievances, disappointments, and differing ideas of justice. The husband's pleas and testimony emphasized his family's poverty and the tension that their poverty generated over the question of marital residence. The wife's pleas and testimony catalogued the various forms of physical and emotional abuse she suffered daily as a wife and daughter-in-law. Finally, the parties' extensive use of the legal system illustrates the changing relationship between law and society in the late Republican era. Their actions suggest a greater willingness to engage the law. For the wife, in particular, the law represented a means for her to escape the authority of her estranged husband and have her grievances as an abused wife validated by the state.

Table 4.6. Resolution Status of Marital Disputes by Province, 1936

Court	*Total*	*Deci-sion*	*Medi-ation*	*Rejection/ Denial*	*With-draw*	*Other*	*Not Yet Resolved*
Anhui	97	35	20	19	18	2	3
Chahar	11	8	-	3	-	-	-
Fujian	127	42	9	33	8	26	9
Gansu	183	34	62	14	39	20	14
Guang-dong	1,203	690	55	167	56	89	146
Guangxi	1,027	417	82	304	50	48	126
Guizhou	115	67	6	9	6	22	5
Hebei	284	146	35	9	30	45	19
Henan	195	70	17	37	24	29	18
Hubei	465	180	45	115	60	53	12
Hunan	210	62	15	61	32	17	23
Jiangsu	543	175	54	116	96	67	35
Jiangxi	150	66	16	43	17	4	4
Ningxia	93	21	37	7	25	3	-
Shaanxi	104	47	9	5	15	26	2
Shanxi	93	37	12	30	2	11	1
Shandong	504	273	58	55	59	23	36
Sichuan	281	105	63	50	15	38	10
Suiyuan	41	23	7	1	8	2	-
Zhejiang	490	199	95	90	62	16	28
Total	6,216	2697	697	1,168	622	541	491

Source: *Sifa tongji: 1936*. These statistics are not comprehensive—they only include the figures from the 230 courts that submitted annual reports to the Judicial Yuan. Nevertheless, they provide an empirical richness that is not available for other years in the Republican period. The original table includes information by district court, which has been omitted here in the interest of space.

Fu Baoguang and Yu Xiurong married on October 20, 1943. The couple lived together until August 16, 1944, when Yu Xiurong returned to her natal family home. The domestic dispute between Fu Baoguang and Yu Xiurong ended up working its way through four rounds of litigation in the judicial system.

Fu Baoguang's Petition for Cohabitation, August 1945

Fu Baoguang, twenty-five, a fried-food vendor, represented by a lawyer, initiated the legal proceedings between the couple when he petitioned the Beijing District Court for a cohabitation order in 1945. He hailed from a family that was basically poor with many brothers and sisters vying for the family's limited resources. From his point of view, although his family was not wealthy, "all was happy and harmonious" until his mother-in-law conspired against him and thus "the cause of this case and its past numerous difficulties were all single-handedly constructed by [Yu Xiurong's] mother." In his retelling of the facts, he had no objections when his wife Yu Xiurong returned to her natal family for a visit in 1944; however, he did not anticipate that she would come under the influence of her mother, who convinced her not to return to her marital home. The husband explained that his overly materialistic mother-in-law, who in his words, "hated poverty and loved wealth" had always looked down on his family for its poverty. When he refused her order for the couple to live with the wife's family, she turned against him. "When Yu Xiurong entered our home, the household was harmonious—everybody knew this. It was only Yu Xiurong's mother's constant nagging that my family was poor and had too many members [that caused discord]. She demanded that I separate from my parents and ordered me and Yu Xiurong to move in with her." Although Fu Baoguang repeatedly asked one of the matchmakers to intercede on his behalf, Yu Xiurong completely disregarded his efforts. He told the court that Yu Xiurong clearly ignored her duty to live with him and was thus requesting that the court order her return.[12]

Yu Xiurong's Countersuit for Divorce, August 1945

Yu Xiurong, with the help of a lawyer and her mother, countersued for divorce. Yu Xiurong was seventeen *sui* when she married in 1943 in Beijing, with the expectation that she and her husband "would grow old together" (*baishou xielao*). The marriage was arranged by her parents and two matchmakers and followed a patrilocal pattern in which she went to live with her husband and his family, which in this case included his parents and several brothers and sisters. According to Yu Xiurong, her marital family provided their new bride with a most inhospitable welcome. During the months she lived with her marital family, each of them subjected the young and vulnerable Yu Xiurong to a peculiar form of intimidation and initiation familiar to Chinese daughters-in-law. Her husband did not wait long before he took to regularly beating and scolding his wife, often for trivial reasons like not washing her feet before going to bed. Her mother-in-law was also quick to criticize her daughter-in-law, finding fault with the way in which she prepared steamed buns, for example, and almost every other domestic task she performed. Her sisters-in-law too ganged up on their brother's bride, taunting her verbally and beating her as they pleased.[13]

Yu Xiurong described her marital life in her oral testimony and written petitions as a life of misery and abuse, full of unpleasant encounters, ill treatment, mental torment, and heartbreak. Her in-laws treated her in general as an enemy, like "a nail in the eye," finding all kinds of ways to intimidate her. "As soon as I entered their home, I was bullied . . . . Mother, son, and the others abused me. In the family old and young all badmouthed me. Frequently for no reason whatsoever they tried to find some inadequacy on my part. They beat and scolded me on the slightest provocation."[14] Over the first several months of marriage, she suffered repeated physical abuse. She was beaten so often that she lost count of all the incidents and could not keep track of all of her bodily injuries. Her body sustained one wound after another: as soon as one wound faded, she claimed, another one would appear. Even months afterward as she stood before the various courts, scars of her physical injuries were still visible. To Yu Xiurong, these physical injuries were evidence that her husband behaved in a habitually sinister and cruel way, placing her in a death trap.

Initially, Yu Xiurong tolerated the abusive treatment she received in the hopes that her husband would change and repent. She was, after all, subject to the restrictions of Confucian norms (*shou lijiao zhi su*). However, her injuries multiplied and the need for medical attention became more urgent. Unable to bear the abuse and barred by her marital family from seeking medical treatment, the young woman ran away. She returned to live with her natal family, where she finally received medical treatment for her injuries. In addition to medical attention, she brought her injuries to the attention of the Beijing District Court's procurator, who investigated the case and filed an injury report documenting the extent of her wounds. Yu Xiurong understood the physical abuse she had suffered as a clear indication that the marital bond had been severed (*yijue*) and requested a divorce.

Beijing District Court Decision, September 1945

The Beijing District Court disposed of the case efficiently, taking a little over a month from Fu Baoguang's original petition to issue its judgment. Initially, the Beijing District Court responded to Fu Baoguang's cohabitation suit and Yu Xiurong's divorce countersuit by summoning the parties to a mediation session. When the mediation effort failed, the court took testimony from the couple, their parents, and their lawyers. After another court session for oral arguments, the district court granted the husband's cohabitation petition and rejected the wife's divorce suit. The various beatings recounted by Yu Xiurong did not convince the court that a divorce was in order. Typical of the divorce cases in which a wife's cruelty allegations were denied, the court justified its decision on the ground that Yu Xiurong did not present enough evidence of cruelty. The court dismissed her allegations as merely "empty contentions" (*kongyan*). According to the procurator's investigation report that she submitted, moreover, the court labeled her injuries as "slight" (*qingwei*). Moreover, since she did not press criminal charges and the time to do so had passed, the judge concluded that her abuse was merely occasional, as opposed to habitual, and matters were now basically harmonious. Thus the court's standard for intolerable cruelty had not been satisfied. As for Fu Baoguang's petition, the existence of a valid marriage between Fu Baoguang and Yu Xiurong provided justification enough to grant a cohabitation order.[15]

Yu Xiurong's Appeal to the Hebei Superior Court, November 1945

Yu Xiurong refused to comply with the cohabitation order and appealed the decision to the Hebei Superior Court. Yu Xiurong mainly addressed the lower court's ruling that she lacked proof of her abuse allegations. According to her appeal, during the ten months in which she lived with her husband's family, her husband's beatings were well known in the neighborhood. It would not be difficult to look into the matter. Besides, her scars were still visible. The Beijing District Court procurator's investigation, furthermore, included an injury report that verified her injuries. Even though criminal charges were not brought forward before the statute of limitations had passed, the fact remained that Fu Baoguang's beating had broken the law. Since the district court had held her failure to bring a criminal suit against her, she explained the circumstances surrounding her failure to bring suit. Her injuries limited her ability, on the one hand, and her adherence to Confucian norms hindered her from acting, on the other hand.

> My body is wounded all over. This is definite proof that I suffered [Fu Baoguang's] cruelty. But because I was subjected to cruelty and wounded, I could not immediately bring suit. And because I accepted the restrictions of Confucian teachings, I still hoped that the marital bond between [Fu Baoguang] and me perhaps had not been severed. I still just hoped [Fu Baoguang] would turn [his behavior] around. I had no idea that [Fu Baoguang] would not repent for his evil behavior.

As she explained further, Fu Baoguang's suit for cohabitation represented no more than his desire to further his sinister habits, resume his cruelty, and place her in a death trap. Why else would he and his family not have visited her even once during the year she stayed at her natal family home? And given the fact that her natal family home was located very near the Fu family home, why did they not go to bring her back to their home? In addition, Yu

Xiuruong emphasized that because of Fu Baoguang's evil intentions the marital bond between them ceased to exist: "It is obvious that the marital bond has been severed. Since the bond has been destroyed, we cannot cohabit."[16]

A few months later, in March 1946, the Hebei Superior Court convened the parties for oral interrogations and oral arguments. At the appeals level, the case revolved around the same issues as before and followed a similar outline. Yu Xiurong attempted to prove she had been abused by Fu Baoguang and his family. And Fu Baoguang continued to maintain that spousal relations were fine, and that it was only the interference of Yu Xiurong's mother over where the couple should reside that created marital discord. The Hebei Superior Court was not convinced by the evidence presented by Yu Xiurong. The court asserted that "The testimony is all hearsay. The force of [Yu Xiurong's] evidence is weak. In addition, she cannot prove that the cruelty has reached the degree to which it could not be tolerated." The court concluded, contrary to Yu Xiurong's testimony, that conjugal feelings were "quite good." Thus, the court denied Yu Xiurong's appeal and affirmed Fu Baoguang's cohabitation order.[17]

Fu Baoguang's Enforcement Suits, 1946

Even after the rejection of her appeal, Yu Xiurong continued to resist the courts' orders. In response, Fu Baoguang then filed two more lawsuits in the Beijing District Court seeking enforcement of the judgments for cohabitation that he had obtained. As Fu Baoguang explained, "It's not easy to marry. I want her to return home and live together."[18] However, winning an order for cohabitation and actually having it be enforced were two separate matters for Fu Baoguang. Although the court supported Fu Baoguang's position, its power was limited to issuing judgments. As a civil body, the court could not coerce Yu Xiurong to move back in with Fu Baoguang.

Yu Xiurong's Appeal to the Supreme Court, 1946

Meanwhile, Yu Xiurong appealed again, this time to the Supreme Court. The gist of Yu Xiurong's appeal to the Supreme Court focused on the Hebei Superior Court's finding that she had failed to present sufficient evidence of intolerable cruelty. She argued that the two matchmakers had testified with utmost certainty and without hesitation confirming the cruelty she had suffered. They had seen her bodily injuries with their own eyes. These were matters they had witnessed firsthand—how could the court call it hearsay? She further attacked the court's handling of the evidence. She alleged that the court had not investigated the matter carefully. Instead, it had relied upon generalized statements to hastily form the basis of its opinion, which was biased. The two matchmakers, too, took the unusual step of sending a joint petition to the Supreme Court, arguing that the Hebei Superior Court had misconstrued their testimony.[19]

The Supreme Court took the substantive and procedural concerns raised by Yu Xiurong and the matchmakers quite seriously. In its December 1946 decision, the Supreme Court noted the numerous places in which proof of cruelty existed in the case file but was ignored by the Hebei Superior Court. It, moreover, chastised the Hebei Superior Court for violating investigative objectivity in its selection of evidence. It insisted that the court should not have dismissed the matchmakers' testimony as simple "hearsay" that was not trustworthy. Thus, the Supreme Court upheld Yu Xiurong's complaints that her evidence had been ignored, but it did not grant her a divorce. Instead, it vacated the previous cohabitation order and directed the Hebei Superior Court to retry the case.[20]

"Marital feelings were not good": Remand to the Hebei Superior Court, February and March 1947

With the original Hebei Superior Court decision vacated by the Supreme Court, the Hebei Superior Court reconvened the parties under the stewardship of a new head judge. The judge summoned Fu Baoguang, Yu Xiurong, and the two matchmakers to an interrogation session in February 1947 and summoned Fu Baoguang and Yu Xiurong to yet another oral argument in March 1947. The primary purpose of both hearings was to investigate the emotional state of the couple's marriage, which assumed greater importance in this round of litigation. The judge posed the same question to each of the four individuals: What are conjugal affections like? Yu Xiurong responded adamantly, "They are not good at all—as soon as I entered their home, I was bullied." Fu Baoguang begged to differ. He characterized conjugal feelings as "good," even "very good." The matchmakers' testimony backed Yu Xiurong. Both of them reported that relations were "not good."[21]

The judge then pressed each witness to explain why she or he believed that conjugal affections were good or bad. Again the parties offered conflicting accounts. Yu Xiurong's explanation stressed the physical cruelty she suffered in the Fu family: "My mother-in-law and my husband beat me."[22] At the subsequent hearing she elaborated: "I want a divorce . . . because he beats me . . . . A young chicken died and he used pincers to grab me . . . . My husband has a sister who frequently gave me trouble . . . . She would say bad things about me to my husband . . . . She said everything I did was wrong and everything she did was right."[23] As before, Fu Baoguang rejected the notion that he or his mother ever hit her. He pinned the problem on Yu Xiurong's well-off and avaricious natal family, who he claimed "hate poverty and love wealth" (*xianpin aifu*).[24] He developed his previous accusations further during the oral argument. "We married in October of 1943, and feelings were very good. It was because my family is poor and I have many brothers and sisters that her mother pushed me to move in with them [the Yu family]. I would not agree. She lived at my house for nine months then went to her natal home and never returned."[25]

The judge also elicited explanations from each party's matchmaker. Jia Ming on the wife's side testified that the couple had not had any contact for the last two years: "Yu Xiurong has lived at her natal family home for over two years, and Fu Baoguang never once went there . . . . He never went to bring her back; he must have treated her badly . . . . He hit her . . . . When [the Fus] beat her and sent her back to her natal family, she was injured." The matchmaker for the husband's family, Mrs. Wu-Liu, also confirmed the physical cruelty and the subsequent lack of contact between the two. But when asked who was responsible for the problems, she blamed Yu Xiurong's ineptitude for the troubles. "Yu Xiurong is a little bit stupid, she really was bullied . . . . [Fu Baoguang] hit her . . . . Because she was stupid, he hit her. After nine months of marriage, she returned to her natal family . . . [and Fu Baoguang] never went to pick her up."[26]

Conjugal feelings aside, the judge also took advantage of the oral argument to investigate the details of Yu Xiurong's cruelty, as instructed by the Supreme Court. Based on the questions and answers below, this time around, the court took her claims quite seriously and investigated them accordingly.

Judge: Does your husband treat you well?

Yu: Not well.

Judge: Not well, how?

Yu: He hit me.

Judge: Why did he hit you?

Yu: Because a young chicken was trampled to death by who knows whom? He forced me to kneel before the chicken and took a wooden stick and hit me.

Judge: Did you kneel?

Yu: I kneeled.

Judge: How long did you kneel?

Yu: One hour.

Judge: Where did he hit you?

Yu: He hit my body.

Judge: What did he use to hit you?

Yu: A feather duster handle. When that snapped, he took pincers and pinched me.

Judge: Were you injured?

Yu: My body suffered injuries.

Judge: Was there nobody to make peace?

Yu: It's not good for neighbors to mediate.

Judge: When was this incident?

Yu: About seven months after I entered their home.

Judge: Has Mrs. Wu-Liu [the matchmaker] mediated?

Yu: Yes.

Judge: Did he hit you after this?

Yu: He hit me ten or so times.

Judge: For what reasons?

Yu: One time it was raining and I left a box of soap outside, and my husband hit me.

Judge: What did he hit you with?

Yu: A feather duster handle.

Judge: Where did he hit you?

Yu: He hit my head.

Judge: What sort of feather duster handle?

Yu: A wooden one.

Judge: How long was it?

Yu: A couple of inches.

Judge: Other than that did he hit you?

Yu: There were many incidents over trifling reasons.[27]

On remand the Hebei Superior Court reversed its previous decision. In its March 1947 decision the court first clarified its criteria for a marriage: "The union of husband and wife involves harmonious feelings on both sides which enable living together and growing old together." Such feelings, the court went on to explain, did not exist in the conjugal relationship between Fu Baoguang and Yu Xiurong. Unlike the earlier opinions that emphasized evidentiary inadequacies, this time around, the court placed primary importance upon the emotional shortcomings of the marriage.

Unusual circumstances may have explained Yu Xiurong's ultimate success. Neither Fu Baoguang nor Yu Xiurong's testimony wholly swayed the judges. Yu Xiurong was fortunate that both of the two matchmakers confirmed her story. The three judges on this retrial panel heeded the Supreme Court's recommendation and based their decision primarily upon the testimony of the matchmakers, especially Mrs. Wu-Liu. The judges reasoned that since Mrs. Wu-Liu represented the groom's family in the marriage and was an old friend of the groom's family, her testimony was not biased, and therefore could be trusted. The court's written opinion quoted from her testimony in five different places: "Their marital feelings were not good"; "Yu Xiurong is a little bit stupid, she really was bullied"; "Fu Baoguang hit her"; "Because she was stupid, he hit her. After nine months of marriage, she returned to her natal family"; and "Fu Baoguang never went to pick her up." In addition, the court quoted the testimony of the other matchmaker in three places to confirm that "Their marital feelings are not good"; "Yu Xiurong lived at her natal family home for over two years, and Fu Baoguang never visited. Now all of Yu Xiurong's food and clothing are provided by her natal family"; and "When [the Fus] hit her and sent her back to her natal family, she was injured." Taken together, this testimony convinced the court that Fu Baoguang's cruelty toward Yu Xiurong had reached the point where cohabitation was impossible, and finally granted her request for a divorce.[28]

Yu Xiurong also benefited from a close relationship to her natal family members. They lived nearby, took her back, and looked after her for a long period of time when she experienced marital strife, supported her lawsuit and appeals as co-plaintiffs and witnesses, and hired a lawyer for her in at least one round of litigation. Apart from the degree of actual cruelty suffered by Yu Xiurong, the fact that her family was of some means factored prominently into the outcome of the lawsuit. Perhaps the key to her eventual success lay with her natal family's ability and willingness to support her throughout the four rounds of litigation. Her natal family, moreover, wanted the couple to live with them rather than the husband's family. Unlike wives who could not depend on their natal families for financial support, Yu Xiurong could demonstrate that upon divorce, her family would support her.

"All was happy and harmonious": Fu Baoguang's Ideas of Marriage and Justice

According to Fu Baoguang, the main conflict between his wife and him concerned where he was to live, and the question of where he was to live, in turn, generated a deep conflict between his filial and conjugal obligations. As a filial son, he lived with his parents and used his income to help support them. His family was working class and relied on his income for support. The family did not own property and relied "entirely on our labor to make a living." Fu Baoguang's father and younger brothers worked at a printer's shop. At the oral argument during the first trial before the Hebei Superior Court, Fu Baoguang explained that his wife "disliked my family because we don't have property and because there are a lot of people in my family. She frequently asked me to take leave of my parents. I would not agree."[29] In other words, his wife and in-laws pressured him to take leave of his parents and siblings in order to move in with his in-laws.

Fu Baoguang interpreted the competing demands for patrilocality and neolocality in terms of a tension between his filiality and his conjugality. In his case, he would not violate his filial duty to his parents in order to satisfy the wishes of his wife and in-laws. Fu Baoguang explained to the judge that he could not leave his parents; he just didn't have the heart for it. "Her idea is that I leave the large family and form a small family with her. Because my father is old and my siblings are very young, if I separate from them, not only will it affect their livelihood, it is also contrary to the Chinese notion of 'raising children to take care of you when you're old' and my heart would not be able to endure it."[30]

"I was bullied": Yu Xiurong's Ideas of Marriage and Justice

Yu Xiurong derived her ideas of marriage and justice from various sometimes contradictory sources. In several places, she described herself in traditional terms, as an obedient daughter-in-law who was subject to the constrictions of Confucian teachings. In her marital life, she set about performing domestic tasks like cooking, cleaning, and tending to chickens. In her various legal petitions, she made several references to "the severing of the marital bond," a notion derived from imperial marriage law. As a resident of Beijing, perhaps, she was exposed to changing marital norms and expectations in urban China in the 1940s. Above all, she seems to have been affected by "feelings." These "feelings" were not necessarily tied to a particular ideology but rather related more closely to an innate "sense of personhood" or "personal dignity."[31] She had a definite, though not clearly articulated, sense of how people should treat each other as a married couple and as in-laws; in other words, how she wanted to be treated.

Her grievances laid open ideas of justice and corresponding rights and duties that relied more upon daily experiences and family relationships than upon the abstract principles ruminated upon by lawmakers and legal scholars. Like other female litigants in intolerable cruelty cases, Yu Xiurong's sense of justice did not take shape as a precise, highly articulated exposition on legal rights and duties or other formally recognized principles. In place of theoretical ideas of justice, daily beating, scolding, and "so many different types of cruelty—I cannot list them all . . . "[32] that she experienced firsthand served as the referents for her ideas of justice and the lack thereof. This more visceral sense of justice may be reconstructed from the episodes Yu Xiurong narrated in the course of litigation portraying the various types of mistreatment she endured at her marital home: her husband physically beat her with a wooden duster handle and iron pincers and verbally chastised her over slight mistakes like leaving a soapbox out in the rain or not washing her feet before going to bed. This visceral sense of justice conveyed her belief that she had merely been going about her daily tasks like a good wife and daughter-in-law when she suffered injuries on the pretext of very minor matters. She had particular trouble with the many other more powerful women in the family. "Their family's many sisters-in-law are formidable; there is one that is especially powerful. My mother-in-law listened solely to her. If she was slightly dissatisfied, she just beat me as she pleased."[33]

The cruelty of her husband and her mother-in-law caused her endless grief. "Just after I entered their home, [Fu Baoguang's] mother beat and scolded me daily, and did not give me enough to eat. At first I tolerated it, hoping [Fu Baoguang] would take pity on me. Later it was not to be; on the contrary, he encouraged [the cruelty] even more. Mother and son together intensified the cruelty—beatings in the morning, scoldings in the evening."[34] Among the many matters concerning Yu Xiurong that did not meet her mother-in-law's approval was her cooking. "[My mother-in-law] invariably disparaged me. Take cooking for example. She always said the food I cooked did not taste good."[35] For instance, Yu Xiurong gave an account of an incident in which she was assaulted for her ineptness as a cook:

> Once when I was steaming buns, my mother-in-law complained that the water was too dark and hit me again. My husband took my legs and arms and injured

> them all over. They wanted me to live at my natal family home, but they would not give me any clothes, so I just went there in my rags.[36]

These tirades of her husband and mother-in-law culminated in the incident of cruelty that drove her away from her marital home, the beating that resulted from the death of the chicken.

> Once because a little chicken died, my mother-in-law beat me, and then made me kneel on top of coins. If I kneeled improperly, she hit me again. What's more, she took chicken dung and rubbed it in my mouth. My husband also used pincers and pinched me until I was wounded.[37]

Scars from this incident were still evident during her testimony.[38] When she recounted this chicken incident during oral arguments before the Hebei Superior Court, she added that it was this incident that hurt her feelings the most.[39]

In addition to her husband and mother-in-law's abuse, her sisters-in-law worked against her, told her she was stupid, and complained about the way she cooked and cleaned. According to her description of the treatment she received from her sisters-in-law, they played tricks on her and did her wrong. "Everything I did was wrong, everything they did was right," she explained at one point.[40] Her grievances spoke not only to her quarrels with her in-laws, but also to her deep disappointment with her husband's behavior. She had harbored the hope that her husband would help her in her disputes with her mother-in-law and sisters-in-law. But not only did he not come to her aid, he joined them in the cruelty.

None of these incidents were particularly outrageous. In fact, they might even have been construed as quite common to the experience of any new daughter-in-law. Had not one of the Hebei Superior Court judges even advised her that "minor injuries should not be of much concern"?[41]From these various actual experiences with abuse, Yu Xiurong's sense of justice developed into a highly visceral phenomenon, rather than a cerebral abstraction. Her ordeal as a daughter-in-law in the Fu family drove her to grief. The constant beating and scolding caused her much mental and physical anguish. The cruelty Yu Xiurong suffered violated her bodily integrity as well as her sense of personal dignity. And she went to great lengths to defend these principles, battling through four rounds of litigation before she finally obtained a divorce. The challenge for female litigants like Yu Xiurong was to convince judges that these principles, however personal, emotional, or intrinsic, deserved to be validated, legally recognized, and given the force of the state's authority.

The language of Yu Xiurong's written pleadings and oral testimony provides a further understanding of her sense of justice. She never directly appealed to "justice" (*zhenqyi*) per se. Instead, she poured forth the numerous ways in which she had actually experienced suffering in her marriage. She firmly believed that upon her entrance to the Fu family she had "suffered wrongs" and "been bullied" (*shou qi*). Based on the repetition of this phrase in every round of litigation, it is clear that she had a highly developed sense that she had been wronged. Perhaps she was a little slow or careless in the performance of her domestic chores, but she did not deserve to be treated in such a malicious way. Her complaints amounted to a litany of words for cruelty: "beating and scolding" (*dama*); "beat up" (*ouda*); "twist" (*ning*); "kneel on coins" (*gui qianban*); "nail in the eye" (*yanzhongding*); "either blows or reprimands" (*feida jima*); "beating and scolding day and night" (*zhaoda muma*); and "entire body covered with scars like scales" (*bianti lingshang*). But Yu Xiurong did not experience physical pain alone. The physical and verbal cruelty left her truly "heartbroken" (*shangxin*) as well.

Not only did the Fu family members beat and scold her, but the injustice they dished out also extended to their unwillingness to let her back into their home after a dispute. She described how they left her at one of the matchmakers' homes after one beating. The matchmaker tried to patch things up by bringing her back to her marital home, but they refused to let her in and left her squatting on their doorstep overnight. How could they now, years later, demand her return? Thus her highly developed sense of being victimized was accompanied by an uncompromising attitude toward reconciliation, rebuffing mediation attempts at several levels of the litigation. She insisted that conjugal relations had deteriorated to the point where mediation was useless. Even when a judge reassured her that Fu Baoguang would no longer be able to abuse her if she returned to her marital home, she refused to accept his assurances.[42]

Although this case did not involve large sums of money or prominent public figures, the ultimate stakes in the case did involve matters of great importance. For Yu Xiurong, the stakes concerned life or death. She appealed to the court's humanity "to preserve my very life."[43] To send her back to her marital home would be "to look for trouble and misery."[44] If the courts upheld her husband's demand for cohabitation, she would be subjected to renewed cruelty, in which case, she articulated the stakes to mean that "she would die" and adamantly refused to return because "there would be no good in it for me."[45] From her point of view, the only reason her husband demanded cohabitation was to "further his sinister habits, resume his cruelty, and throw [her] into a death trap."[46] Even the matchmakers likened her plight to "death," "the inside of a fiery pit" and "a death trap."[47] All of this amounted to cruelty to the degree that a wife should no longer have to tolerate.

The parties' extensive involvement with the law also shows a willingness to engage the law, a change in the relationship between law and society, especially for women who could now turn to the law to help assert certain rights and defend their individual interests. Yu Xiurong, for instance, invoked the authority of the law in order to "save my life." She pleaded with the courts to grant her a divorce to rescue her from a life-threatening situation. She looked to the court to back her up, to bolster her claims, to preserve her right to bodily integrity, to defend her personal dignity, to give her the freedom to end a marriage that was far from happy and harmonious. When the courts disagreed with her, dismissing her petition for divorce, she persisted, bringing her case to the next highest court. In these appeals, she freely criticized the lower courts' handling of her case. She attacked the Beijing District Court and the Hebei Superior Court for their evaluation of the evidence of physical abuse. She pointed out the ways she thought the Beijing District Court's judgment was "rash and biased." She alleged that the Hebei Superior Court did not conduct a careful investigation of her case, that it misconstrued the testimony of the couple's matchmakers, that it reached its decision hastily, and that its judgment was overly subjective. Yu Xiurong's persistence before the law may have clinched her divorce.

Fu Baoguang and Yu Xiurong made ample use of the law in attempting to resolve their marital disputes, engaging the law at every level of the judicial system over several years. They resorted to formal lawsuits to press at least two of their claims, his suit for cohabitation and her suit for divorce. They also contemplated criminal suits at various points, although Yu Xiurong declined to press charges. Their suits were initially brought before the local Beijing District Court, heard on appeal by the Hebei Superior Court, appealed again to the Supreme Court, and finally remanded and tried again by the Hebei Superior Court. Each round of litigation involved a relatively elaborate set of procedures and requirements, usually including the submission of written documents (a complaint or appeal and an answer at a minimum), attempts at mediation, the service of warrants and summons, attendance at one or more oral interrogations (*xunwen*), an oral argument (*yanci bianlun*), and a written opinion (*panjue*). The extensive record of litigation in this case suggests in part how seriously the courts took domestic disputes. The expenditure of judicial resources for mediation, interrogations, oral arguments, petitions, responses, appeals, as well as the Supreme Court's admonishment to the Hebei Superior Court for not carefully weighing the evidence illustrate a judicial complex for marital disputes that differed significantly from the late imperial treatment of marriage as a "minor matter" that was settled at the local yamen and not beyond. The contrast between the options available to Yu Xiurong and women in similar circumstances in the imperial period is rather stark. In the late imperial period Yu Xiurong would have been forced to return to her husband as soon as her husband turned to the court to report her missing. She would have no right to countersue him for divorce. And she would not have been able to appeal her case to multiple levels of the late imperial judicial system.

CONCLUSION

During the 1930s and 1940s, the development of a civil legal and judicial system helped to make the law more amenable to litigants in several ways. In civil disputes, for instance, parties were treated equally before the law. Civil law offered an opportunity to resolve a dispute among private parties without the fear of incurring criminal punishment or torture. The state had an interest in resolving the dispute rather than in punishing wrongdoing or restoring the natural order. As illustrated in the case of Fu Baoguang vs. Yu Xiurong, within the civil law framework, moreover, litigants could select a course of action from a range of legal options and procedures that might suit their purposes and fit their circumstances. As a matter of civil law rather than a "minor matter," litigants in marital disputes could also count on layers of oversight through the appeals system. Meanwhile, by the 1930s and 1940s a modern court system had emerged that enabled litigants to pursue their grievances with the expectation of a modicum of fairness.

NOTES

I have taken the liberty of adopting "Mr." and "Mrs." where appropriate to rendering the names of litigants. Even though the English Mr. and Mrs. are not precise equivalents to the Chinese rendering of names, I hope that readers do not object too strongly to this usage. I have chosen to do so after much deliberation in order to help signal to readers the gender of the litigants, which is conveyed by the original Chinese characters but lost in the Romanized pinyin spelling of the names.

1. Xu 2008, 101. Reports differ as to the number of courts during any given year of the Republic. Chih-Fang Wu (T.F. Wu) 1934, for instance, gives the number of modern courts in China in April 1932 as 452: one Supreme Court, 27 superior courts, 38 superior court branches, and 386 county and district courts. He includes county courts as part of the modern judicial system (229).
2. Bernhardt 1994, 195–196. Xu 2008, however, warns that Republican courts often had large backlogs of cases that remained unresolved for years. Such backlogs were also found during the Qing. The evidence of court backlogs does not include marital cases. As table 4.6 shows, the percentage of unresolved marital cases hovered between 8 and 15 percent of all cases.
3. Huang Yuansheng has conducted the most extensive research on the Daliyuan. See Huang 2009 and 2011. Guo Wei, ed. 1946. *Zuigao fayuan jieshi li quanwen.* Introduction explains the influence of the interpretations. Zheng 1948, 182–183. Zheng says: "by the time the Civil Code was promulgated in 1930, the body of legal principles declared in the decisions of the Supreme Court was so comprehensive that it differed little from a modern code," 184. Escarra too praises the work of the Daliyuan as well for easing the transition to modern legal principles (1936, Part III, chapter 2). On the role of the Daliyuan, see Young 2004.
4. Bernhardt 1994, 195–198, citing Niida, ed. 1952 on fees and Honig 1986: 176 and Huang 1985: 197 on comparative earnings; Bernhardt and Huang 1994, 5.
5. Bernhardt and Huang 1994, 2. Liang 2007, ch. 2 provides a good description of the Qing adjudication and appellate system. See also Ocko 1988.
6. No. 2A 16(7)2987-9 Supreme Court decision dated 1944.2.29.
7. No. 2A 16(7)2913-2 Hunan Superior Court decision dated 1939.9.23, and Supreme Court decision dated 1940.3.22.

8. HPA 634-1-368 Supreme Court memo dated 1939.8.26.
9. No. 2A 16(7) 2912-5 Guangxi Superior Court decision dated 1946.1.16.
10. No. 2A 16(7)2912-5 Supreme Court decision dated 1946.10.1.
11. Most marital disputes were litigated under the provisions of the Republican Civil Code. Marital cases, though, sometimes involved related criminal litigation as well. For instance, suits for divorce on the basis of adultery, bigamy, or intolerable cruelty might include a spouse's criminal conviction for adultery, bigamy, or injuring another. The criminal code also contained a separate set of offenses against marriage and family (*fanghai hunyin jiating zui*) that involved crimes like luring a daughter away from her parents. See Glosser 2003, 99–110.
12. Beijing J65-21-3597 petition dated 1945.8 and response dated 1945.11.
13. Beijing J65-21-3597 countersuit dated 1945.8.
14. Beijing J65-21-3597 oral argument dated 1946.3.26.
15. Beijing J65-21-3597 Beijing District Court decision dated 1945.9.18.
16. Beijing J65-21-3597 appeal 1945.11.
17. Beijing J65-21-3597 Hebei Superior Court decision dated 1946.3.27.
18. Beijing J65-22-1148, petition for enforcement dated 1946.5.17, oral interrogation dated 1946.5.25, petitions dated 1946.6.17 and 1946.6.20, and oral interrogation dated 1946.7.8.
19. Beijing J65-21-3597 appeal to Supreme Court by Yu Xiurong dated 1946.4.29, petition to Supreme Court by matchmakers dated 1946.7.29.
20. Beijing J65-21-3597 Supreme Court decision dated 1946.12.14.
21. Beijing J65-21-3597 interrogation dated 1947.2.24.
22. Beijing J65-21-3597 interrogation dated 1947.2.24.
23. Beijing J65-21-3597 oral argument dated 1947.3.26.
24. Beijing J65-21-3597 interrogation dated 1947.2.24.
25. Beijing J65-21-3597 oral argument dated 1947.3.26.
26. Beijing J65-21-3597 interrogation dated 1947.2.24.
27. Beijing J65-21-3597 oral argument dated 1947.3.26.
28. Beijing J65-21-3597 Hebei Superior Court decision dated 1947.3.31.
29. Beijing J65-21-3597 oral argument dated 1946.3.26.
30. Beijing J65-21-3597 oral argument dated 1946.3.26.
31. For mid-Qing precedents for female outrage caused by verbal and social slights, see Theiss 2004. Theiss sees chastity as central to women's identities. But she also speaks of dignity and self-respect. "Whether they were infuriated, ashamed, disgusted, or all three, most women who cared at all about chastity (and there were plenty who did not) felt deeply that it was integral to their sense of being human. To insult a woman's chastity was to deny her humanity" (202–203). Even in cases in which there was no actual sexual violation, the verbal and social slights engendered by the attempt or hint of a sexual violation constituted a violation of a woman's virtue. Perceived insults seem to have been treated very seriously under Qing law.
32. Beijing J65-21-3597 oral argument dated 1946.3.26.
33. Beijing J65-21-3597 interrogation dated 1946.3.14.
34. Beijing J65-21-3597 appeal dated 1945.11.
35. Beijing J65-21-3597 oral argument dated 1946.3.26.
36. Beijing J65-21-3597 interrogation dated 1946.3.14.
37. Beijing J65-21-3597 interrogation dated 1946.3.14.
38. Beijing J65-21-3597 appeal dated 1945.11. This was a painful form of punishment because the surface of the coins was uneven. It caused pain similar to punishments like kneeling on top of a washboard.
39. Beijing J65-21-3597 oral argument dated 1946.3.26.
40. Beijing J65-21-3597 oral argument dated 1947.3.26.
41. Beijing J65-21-3597 interrogation dated 1947.2.24.
42. Beijing J65-21-3597 interrogation dated 1946.3.14.
43. Beijing J65-21-3597 oral argument dated 1945.9.12; and appeal to the Hebei Superior Court dated 1945.11.
44. Beijing J65-21-3597 interrogation dated 1946.3.14.
45. Beijing J65-21-3597 oral argument dated 1946.3.26.

46. Beijing J65-21-3597 appeal to Hebei Superior Court dated 1945.11.
47. Beijing J65-21-3597 appeal to the Supreme Court dated 1946.4.29.

II

Law and Society

Chapter Five

Spousal Abuse

Divorce Litigation and the Emergence of Rights Consciousness

Building upon archives-based research, this chapter and those that follow explore interactions between the civil code and legal practice in order to evaluate the law's role in spurring changes in individual consciousness and the law's social impact more broadly in the Republican era. By examining "intolerable cruelty" divorce lawsuits filed in the two decades after the code went into effect, this chapter aims to outline ways in which legal change contributed to changes in people's consciousness about physical abuse in marriage. To analyze popular attitudes and perceptions is an extremely difficult task, but it is possible to at least begin to delineate the major changes through close readings of the court records. Archival case records from local-level courts, provincial-level superior courts, and the national Supreme Court point to an emerging "legal consciousness" or "rights consciousness" by which the framework of individual rights and duties enshrined in the civil code helped to effect changes in popular expectations of marriage. Rights consciousness refers to the ways in which people came to view themselves as "rights-bearing" beings and to view conflicts in terms of a clash of rights. Case records show that despite the tenuous place of rights-thinking in Republican China, in the 1930s and 1940s litigants began to interpret their marriages through the lens of rights and liabilities and drew upon Republican legal mechanisms to forge various meanings of rights. This chapter will illuminate the ways in which litigants grounded their understandings of rights in light of socioeconomic realities, everyday experiences of injustice, and grievances against family tyranny, wittingly or not, within the frame supplied by liberal modernity. These changing perceptions marked an important break in consciousness associated with liberal modernity.

The rights consciousness revealed in the legal actions taken in the 1930s and 1940s suggests an approach to understanding rights in China that focuses on the way in which ordinary individuals deployed rights to promote their interests, rather than the debates among intellectuals and politicians over the meaning of rights. Past studies have debated the origins of Chinese conceptions of rights and compared Chinese conceptions to European and American ones (Angle 2002; Angle and Svensson 2001; Bourgon 2004; Diamant, Lubman, and O'Brien 2005; Gallagher 2005 and 2006; Nathan 1986; O'Brien and Li 2006; Perry 2008a; Svensson 2002; Weatherly 1999; and Zarrow 2008). Unlike these studies of Chinese rights, my research pertains to legal rights rather than natural, political, constitutional, or human rights.[1] Legal rights refer to those rights that are specifically enumerated in codes of law, like the Republican Civil Code, with no claims to universality. The emergence of liberal ideas of rights and gender equality endorsed by the Republican Civil Code provided a framework and vocabulary with which to label the oppressions experienced by husbands and wives in the course of marriage. The naming of these oppressions gave rise to a certain type of agency by which wives and husbands could turn individual feelings of injury and injustice into lawsuits for divorce, separation, cohabitation, or annulment. Thinking of marriage in terms of rights served as a way for litigants to make sense of their lives, giving substance and poignancy to and in some cases validating their stories of suffering. Mistreated wives readily received these ideas and eagerly took them up in the pursuit of their own interests (the thousands of marital disputes from the 1930s and 1940s attest to this enthusiasm). By pursuing a legal remedy when they felt disgruntled, displaced, or otherwise aggrieved, litigants constructed narratives about their lives that described their suffering, victimization, abuse, fatigue, labor, struggles, deprivations, and other experiences, and in turn reshaped the content of the idea of rights. Rights took on new visceral and practical meanings rooted in family and socioeconomic justice.

As critics of rights have underscored, though, rights are imperfect vehicles that can serve to reinforce existing hierarchies as readily as they serve the interests of justice and equality.[2] Chinese case records of intolerable cruelty marital disputes not only illustrate the emergence of rights consciousness among individual litigants, but also the limitations of individual rights as a means to achieve gender equality. Wife-litigants, husband-litigants, and judges presented divergent interpretations of the new laws. While wives mobilized a new rights discourse to support their petitions for divorce, husbands relied upon older concerns with the hardships created by marriage finance and a fluctuating economy to keep their marriages intact. Although Republican courts adopted the new marriage framework of individual rights and duties and gender equality, GMD judges did not necessarily validate the individual rights of wife-litigants, tending instead to preserve the conjugal unit and thereby reinforce husbands' rights. The process in which litigants and judges contested the nature of intolerable cruelty and the conservative judicial outcomes that mostly denied divorce on the basis of intolerable cruelty helped produce a new, modern, male-dominated conjugal family ideology.[3]

Perhaps, though, the important transformations in women's legal consciousness that were inspired in part by the individual rights framework of the Republican Civil Code have been easy to overlook because most wife-litigants fared poorly in the courts. After all, judges rejected the majority of divorce claims in intolerable cruelty cases. And yet, the mere act of bringing a formal lawsuit against one's husband marked a significant departure in mindset from past practice. Regardless of the ultimate judicial outcome, the individual women who initiated formal legal petitions for divorce during the Republic took perhaps bolder steps than their late imperial counterparts who traditionally complained informally to their relatives, women's communities, or local yamens about abuse. Justified by emerging notions of individual rights and personhood, Republican women litigants lodged stronger forms of protest against abuse by their husbands and marital families.

THE PREVALENCE OF INTOLERABLE CRUELTY DIVORCE LITIGATION

The modernization of Chinese marriage and divorce laws has most commonly been explained in terms of the liberalization of divorce and the expansion of women's rights (Meijer 1971, Tai 1978, Johnson 1983, Bernhardt 1994, Diamant 2000). Before the twentieth century Chinese women had little if any power to divorce and were subject to expulsion for seemingly arbitrary reasons. Beginning in the 1910s, supported by Daliyuan Supreme Court rulings, Chinese women gained the right to initiate divorce and thereby liberate themselves from the fetters of oppressive marriages. Studies caution that women's agency was limited by conservative thinking and socioeconomic constraints, but the general trend toward greater rights for women was unmistakable. Republican lawmakers formalized the configuration of marriage and divorce in terms of individual rights and duties in place of late imperial norms that regulated marriage in terms of Confucian patrilineal ritual, moral obligations, and criminal violations. Republican family law provided a new set of legal tools that bolstered the interests of individual husbands and wives over and against the family unit. Most importantly, Republican family law made divorce available on a gender-equal basis. The increased availability of divorce and the language of rights and equality affirmed changing ideas and practices of marriage. These legal mechanisms helped to consolidate the idea that although marriage should be a lifelong union, the union was conditional, subject to dissolution for a wider range of reasons than in the past. Divorce law offered a viable alternative to "accepting fate" when it came to unhappy marriages. It promoted the idea that certain types of behavior, like egregious or habitual physical abuse, were no longer acceptable in a marriage. The emergence of a formal civil law approach to divorce during the Republic led to a legalization of divorce that reformulated divorce as a problem of Confucian morality to divorce as a problem of civil law. While divorce remained a moral offense with shameful associations under Confucian ideology, it also took on the aspect of a formal legal proceeding adjudicated by the state. Divorce still entailed a stigma, but the new divorce laws streamlined and formalized the process to make it less complicated and less onerous during a period in which law was on its way to becoming a central normative structure in the lives of husbands and wives.

In 1930, the Family Book of the Republican Civil Code expanded the grounds for a judicial divorce and made ten grounds available to the husband or wife on an equal basis: bigamy, adultery, spousal intolerable cruelty, in-law intolerable cruelty, abandonment, intent or attempt to murder a spouse, incurable physical disease, incurable mental disease, lengthy disappearance, and imprisonment or the commission of an infamous crime. As table 5.1 indicates, spousal and in-law cruelty together represented the most common grounds cited by wives who sought a judicial divorce (*susong lihun*).[4]

The frequency of intolerable cruelty litigation as compared to the other categories of divorce suggests that intolerable cruelty divorce was one of the most important components of the new set of Republican legal mechanisms that allowed an individual wife to defend her interests within the conjugal and family unit. The higher rate of cruelty litigation also suggests that something else was afoot. Cruelty was the provision that resonated with wives. It was the number of cruelty cases that generated a litigation "explosion," in part, I would venture to suggest, because of the change in consciousness at work, the shift from viewing abuse as an unfortunate circumstance to be tolerated to viewing abuse as an injustice that should be remedied.[5] Under the Qing Code, a wife's natal family could bring suit to dissolve a marriage only if the wife suffered extreme physical abuse resulting in a "broken bone or tooth." The "broken bone or tooth" served as definite, incontrovertible physical proof of abuse. Like the Qing Code, the Republican Civil Code recognized that extreme physical abuse was unjust and constituted valid grounds to dissolve a marriage. But the Republican standard of "intolerable cruelty" expanded the range of behavior that could justify divorce. The legislature stated in Article 1052-3 and -4 that either spouse could sue for divorce in case of "such ill-treatment from the other spouse as to render it intolerable to live together (*bukan tongju zhi nüedai*)."[6] Both emotional and physical

Table 5.1. Percent Distribution of Reason for Divorce in 774 Cases, 1936

Civil Code Provision	*Reason for Divorce*	*Number of Cases*	*Percent*
1052-1	Bigamy	71	9
1052-2	Adultery	88	11
1052-3	Abuse (spouse)	247	32
1052-4	Abuse (in-laws)	72	9
1052-5	Abandonment	132	17
1052-6	Intent to murder/harm	10	1
1052-7	Disease	23	3
1052-8	Mental illness	12	2
1052-9	Not clear dead or alive	78	10
1052-10	Imprisonment	41	5

Source: *Sifa tongji 1936.* Abuse was the leading cause for judicial divorce until the late 1940s when divorce suits on the basis of intolerable cruelty declined in proportion to divorce suits citing abandonment. Bernhardt estimates that spousal cruelty made up 31 percent of divorce cases nationwide from 1934 to 1939, 41 percent of Shanghai divorce cases from 1940 to 1941, and a whopping 70 percent of Beijing divorce cases from 1942.

cruelty could constitute intolerable cruelty. The underlying idea was that a marriage could be dissolved when one party to the marriage (or in-laws who resided with the married couple) subjected the other party to cruelty that was so severe that it made living together intolerable. Judicial outcomes that adopted a highly circumscribed interpretation of intolerable cruelty, however, show that Republican courts did not depart too far from Qing legal practices.

FROM GRIEVANCE TO INJUSTICE: "NAMING, BLAMING, AND CLAIMING"

The meaning of cruelty and standards for determining what constituted "intolerable cruelty" were debated, contested, and negotiated through the processes of litigation, mediation, and adjudication in Republican courts. Wives objected to everyday instances of cruelty and sued for divorce. Meanwhile husbands proffered denials, defenses, and excuses designed to hold the marriage together. Judges, for the most part, discounted most cruelty allegations, preferring to preserve marriages (as husbands did) rather than break them apart. The inexact meaning of "intolerable" cruelty in the civil code left it to individual plaintiffs, mostly wives, to define the contours of intolerable cruelty each time they recounted in legal petitions the marital injustices they suffered. Wives recounted numerous incidents of cruelty that drove them to file for divorce. Litigant wives understood intolerable cruelty in expansive terms, bringing up myriad grievances under its auspices: complaints about physical abuse, verbal abuse, mental abuse, material deprivation, and emotional deprivation. They accused husbands of feeding them coarse food, slapping them on the face, and gravely injuring them. In intolerable cruelty cases the wives' sense of justice is best captured by the visceral personal experiences of decidedly gender-unequal physical beatings rather than theoretical abstractions about gender equality. These complaints provide a better understanding of women's perceptions of their lives and their marriages, bringing attention to their injuries, disappointments, and grievances, and the ways in which the concept of legal rights reshaped these ordinary complaints into legal actions.

To illuminate the emergence of rights consciousness among women who petitioned for a judicial divorce on the basis of intolerable cruelty after the implementation of the Republican Civil Code, it may be helpful to borrow a theoretical model from American scholarship on the sociology of law.[7] The framework of naming, blaming, and claiming first proposed by Felstiner, Abel, and Sarat (1980–1981) outlines a three-part process by which grievances are transformed into disputes. Naming involves perceiving a particular condition as injurious and labeling the injury (their example is asbestosis). Blaming necessitates moving from the perception of an injury to a grievance directed at a particular cause (an employee comes to hold an employer accountable for the injury, for example). Finally, claiming entails voicing the grievance to those deemed responsible and requesting an appropriate remedy (usually by filing a complaint). With respect to domestic abuse in Republican China, naming was made possible by the intolerable cruelty provision of the Republican Civil Code, which supplied a label for the injuries women had long endured. Blaming was directed at husbands and in-laws as the main parties held accountable for such behavior. And women's petitions for divorce became the main mechanism for claiming.

Chinese women went to the local yamen, government headquarters, to complain about their marriages for centuries, long before the implementation of the Republican Civil Code in 1931. The lawsuits of the 1930s and 1940s partly continued this tradition but also diverged from that pattern of informal grumbling because these modern lawsuits formally invoked the provisions of the civil code and represented instances of formal litigation rather than informal protests. The modern lawsuits, moreover, appealed to principles of conjugality and gender equality rather than Confucian patriarchy. The differences between women's informal protests during the Qing and women's formal legal actions during the Republic highlight the shift in legal and popular perceptions of domestic abuse, from abuse as a misfortune to abuse as an injustice, and illustrate how a sense of injustice developed over domestic abuse.[8] Both Qing and Republican law censured domestic violence, as evidenced in the Qing provision allowing a wife's natal family to sue in case of injury resulting in a "broken bone or tooth" and in the Republican Civil Code's "intolerable cruelty" provision. Unlike the Qing Code, the Republican Civil Code supplied a more expansive legal heading under which women could shape, i.e., "name," a much wider range of erstwhile grievances "intolerable cruelty." The terminology of abuse or "*nüedai*" came to serve as shorthand for oppression in general and became a catch-all for various oppressions, many of which lacked a more specific term, experienced as part of marital life. The idea of *nüedai* alone was not enough to make a difference. But *nüedai* paired with the idea of legal rights made action and alternatives thinkable and possible.

During the Qing, men who were too poor to marry constituted a class of "bare sticks" or "rootless rascals" (*guanggun*) who emerged as potential sources of social unrest (Sommer 2000). Republican judges understood the realities of the "marriage crunch" for poor men and proved sympathetic to them. During the Republic, marriage, despite the transformation from patrilineal to conjugal principles, remained a way to ensure social stability. Judges were reluctant to dissolve marriages so painstakingly arranged over incidents of cruelty. The ideology of modern conjugal patriarchy emerging from judicial rulings affirmed the socioeconomic defenses offered by husbands. Based upon the decisions rendered by judges in the cases presented in this chapter, occasional wife-beating appears to have fallen well within the boundaries of ordinary, acceptable norms for marital behavior. Judicial rulings in intolerable cruelty cases occasionally granted divorce, but most of them denied divorce in favor of preserving the existing marriage.

Nevertheless, thinking about marriage in terms of individual rights (a manifestation of "rights consciousness") helped facilitate changes in legal and popular attitudes toward abuse. Abuse not only constituted a physical injury to a wife's body but also represented an injury to a wife's legal rights. Wives came to believe that they had a legal right not to be abused. When paired with notions of individual rights and duties, the experience of abuse could traverse the course from naming to blaming and claiming. The modern, liberal rubric of conjugality made it possible to "blame" or hold husbands legally accountable for abusive behavior. A wife's right not to be abused corresponded to a husband's duty not to abuse her. Lastly, the Republican civil law framework in general formalized procedures for "claiming," increasing access for women and making it more likely for wives to expect specific relief, divorce, from abusive husbands. Women could come to expect a legal remedy for everyday grievances that in the past simply constituted a part, albeit an unpleasant part, of married life. Together these circumstances added up to more than just a change in terminology; they made it possible for people to think differently about the place of abuse in marriage, which in turn reflected the birth of a form of modern legal consciousness.

"PLEASE PROTECT WOMEN'S RIGHTS": CAO XIUZHEN'S PLEAS

Examining the unfolding of an actual intolerable cruelty divorce case may help illustrate the process of naming, blaming, and claiming at work as well as the changes in individual consciousness and the limitations of this rights consciousness in the context of gendered social expectations. Like other case records from the genre of intolerable cruelty divorce suits, this one suggests how cruelty or "abuse" acquired the status of a legal category that enabled the wife-litigant to transform her previously tacit and inchoate grievances into articulated legal claims. The wife's lawsuit alleging intolerable cruelty helped to give form to the individual injuries she experienced in the course of marriage and family life. The case also demonstrates the interactions between the category of intolerable cruelty in Republican divorce law, the development of rights consciousness, and popular beliefs and expectations of marriage. Thinking of marriage and oppression in terms of rights proved to be a potent combination that prompted women like Cao Xiuzhen, below, to attempt to break out of the patterns that had previously governed the lives of women who endured domestic abuse.

Cao Xiuzhen, twenty-five *sui*, sued her husband for divorce in 1948 in the Xi'an District Court, Shaanxi Province, citing intolerable cruelty, abandonment, and bigamy. Her life story, as narrated and perhaps embellished by her and her lawyer in legal pleadings and courtroom testimony, was a sad one, full of hardship.[9] She was given up for adoption when she was just four *sui.* At fifteen *sui,* her adopted father arranged to hand her over into marriage to a man who was thirty-nine *sui,* twenty-four years her senior. Initially, she thought her marriage was a good one. Unexpectedly, she discovered that her husband had another wife in Hebei Province and that he was addicted to prostitution, gambling, and opium. He treated her poorly, beating her odiously and depriving her of food, drink, and clothing. As she described it, the beatings and deprivations had destroyed any feelings between her and her husband (*ganqing polie*); they treated each other like strangers (*xingtong luren*). Her sadness was compounded by the fact that she had given birth to three children, none of whom survived past infancy. The year before she sued for divorce, her husband went to jail after being convicted of an opium-related offense, and she had no choice but to look for work in a textile factory. Her meager salary from the textile factory work had to be handed over to her husband and father-in-law. Now at twenty-five *sui,* Cao Xiuzhen pleaded with the court to grant her a divorce and free her from a marriage that she had never had any say over.[10]

Her husband, Yang Donglin, forty-nine *sui*, painted a rather different picture of the couple's marriage in his legal pleadings and courtroom testimony. According to Yang Donglin, the couple was engaged in October 1940, through the auspices of a matchmaker. Yang Donglin offered 250 *yuan* in cash as an engagement gift to his wife's adoptive father. At the time of the engagement, Yang Donglin and Cao Xiuzhen met face to face and conversed with each other at the matchmaker's house. She was seventeen *sui*, not fifteen, and expressed her willingness to marry him (*xinqing yiyuan*). They married two months later in December 1940. He admitted he was previously married to a woman in Hebei Province, but declared that she was already deceased when he arranged to marry Cao Xiuzhen. According to Yang Donglin, at the time of his marriage to Cao Xiuzhen, he operated two successful businesses. In 1943, however, he was forced to close down both businesses, and the couple relocated to Li Family Village. Now in 1948 they had been married almost nine years and had three children born to them. During all those years, Yang Donglin was the sole breadwinner of the family. Only in the last year and entirely on her own volition Cao Xiuzhen went to work at the Dahua Textile Factory. After she worked in the factory for twenty days, she had a change of heart (*lingxin*). Yang Donglin accused his wife of "detesting poverty and loving wealth" (*xianpin aifu*). He attributed his wife's divorce suit to the change in his family's economic situation. Yang Donglin testified: "I did not abuse her. I have been married ten years already. In the past my family was well-off and we enjoyed a good life. In recent years, living has become increasingly expensive. Because of this [inflation] our family is not as well-off as before. Last month she quarreled with me and left."[11]

The Xi'an District Court first attempted to mediate the case, asking Cao Xiuzhen if she would be willing to return to Yang Donglin and asking Yang Donglin whether he would be willing to divorce. Both parties refused to give in. The court then interrogated the three witnesses provided by Yang Donglin, all women in their forties who lived in the same village as the couple. The three witnesses testified that the couple seemed to get along just fine and that the marriage appeared to be a good one. They denied that Yang Donglin had ever abused Cao Xiuzhen. A month or so after the hearing, the court clerk read the court's decision to the parties: the court rejected Cao Xiuzhen's divorce petition and ordered her to pay the litigation fees. The court cited the testimony of the three villagers and the fact that the couple had already been married nearly ten years and had three daughters.[12] This emphasis on the long duration of the marriage as cause to deny the divorce illustrates a significant pattern and underscores the role of social expectations for marriage in limiting the scope of rights consciousness. As table 5.2 shows, the majority of divorce suits involved couples who had been married less than five years. The highest rates of divorce litigation came within two or three years of getting married. Cao Xiuzhen's petition after almost ten years of marriage came relatively late.

Table 5.3 suggests that divorce suits were brought mostly by women, like Cao Xiuzhen, who were in their twenties. The youth of the female litigants suggests the vulnerability of new wives, the difficulties of making the transition to a marital home, and the instability of the initial period of marriage. It also suggests that younger women were the greatest beneficiaries of this new rights consciousness. Divorce was also less complicated when children were not involved. Younger women benefited moreover from the availability of additional employment opportunities like factory work.

Within a month, Cao Xiuzhen appealed, begging the superior court to protect her "human rights" (*renquan*). Her appeal again centered upon generating sympathy for the oppression she had suffered since childhood. The circumstances by which her marriage had been arranged proved that she had no say over it. She claimed she was even younger, only fourteen *sui* (twelve or thirteen years old), at the time of her engagement. Her appeal also stressed her current vulnerabilities, portraying herself as an "uneducated woman trying to make ends meet, with no roads open, who can only find factory work." She portrayed herself as dutiful, using her meager salary to buy food and cook for her husband and father-in-law. Given the rising cost of living, she worried that she, a woman alone, could not provide for herself, much less for herself, her husband, and father-in-law. She wanted a divorce to be free from a life that she had not chosen for herself.[13] Despite these pleas, the superior court rejected Cao Xiuzhen's appeal for divorce, ruling that she had presented no new evidence of abuse. The superior court determined that occasional spats between Yang Donglin and his wife did not amount to intolerable cruelty. The superior court too relied on the testimony of the three fellow villagers and found that the marriage was satisfactory, illustrating a great deal about social expectations (shared both by the witnesses and by the court)

Table 5.2. Years Married among Couples in 774 Divorce Cases, 1936

Years married	
Less than one year	86
Less than two years	142
Less than three years	139
Less than four years	111
Less than five years	82
Less than ten years	137
Over ten years	77

Source: *Sifa tongji 1936*

Table 5.3. Age of Litigants in 774 Divorce Cases, 1936

Age (in sui*)*	*Male*	*Female*
11–15	4	6
16–20	96	181
21–25	226	257
26-30	209	206
31–35	123	82
36–40	67	31
41 and up	49	11
Unknown	-	-
Total	774	774

Source: *Sifa tongji 1936*

of relationships between husbands and wives, which included the possibility of conflict and outright occasional violence between married couples that did not in itself make the marriage untenable or the wife a victim of intolerable cruelty.[14]

After two rounds of judicial rejection, Cao Xiuzhen refused to give up and appealed once again, this time to the Supreme Court. This appeal explicitly cited the protection of "women's rights" (*nüquan*) as a reason to grant her a divorce.[15] In response, Yang Donglin repeated his account of the marriage and explanation of his wife's motive. The archival file does not contain the decision of the Supreme Court (the file is located in a category of cases that were on the docket but not yet decided at the time of the 1949 Revolution).

Even with the final outcome in doubt, the case reflects the changed outlook of a woman who claimed she was given up for adoption at four *sui*, handed over into marriage at fifteen *sui* by an adoptive father to a man who was much older than her, suffered through the birth of three children who all died in infancy, tolerated her husband's frequenting of prostitutes, gambling, and opium smoking, forced to rush about searching for work in a textile factory when her husband was arrested, then obliged to hand over her meager cotton mill salary to support her husband and father-in-law. Perhaps her husband guessed correctly when he asserted that it was only after she went to work at the factory that she had a change of heart, a change in her consciousness. Following her employment at the textile factory, she turned to a lawyer to free her from her domestic predicament. Cao Xiuzhen lost her case, but rights-thinking helped her to conceive of the case in the first place, to think that she deserved a different outcome in life, to believe that a better life was possible through divorce.

Although the weight of the evidence in this chapter leans more toward the limitations of rights consciousness, that does not mean that rights did not have some transformative effects. As legal scholars have noted, rights can make an important difference to the powerless as a protection against oppression. Rights can transform an individual's sense of self. And rights may also serve as a means to challenge repressive practices.[16] The lens of individual rights provided a new way of framing Cao Xiuzhen's life story, lending it a certain poignancy and moral weight. The idea that women were entitled to certain basic rights, including the right to determine their own marriages, gave substance to her personal history of suffering. However difficult her plight, it probably did not differ that much from the predicaments of many other women in the late imperial and Republican eras. Cao Xiuzhen's options, however, were different. Unlike women in the past who had no choice but to resign themselves to fate and find methods of coping with their dissatisfactions, by the time Cao Xiuzhen filed her divorce petition in 1948, she benefited from several new legal mechanisms in place that enabled her to hope for and try to enact a different future for herself: equal access to divorce for women and men, intolerable cruelty as a legitimate basis for divorce, legal backing for the idea that individual men and women should be free to arrange their own marriages, and legal support for the idea that marriage should be companionate. These new legal mechanisms, moreover, coalesced within a new socioeconomic environment in which she could obtain independent employment at a textile factory.

The concept of legal rights may have acted as a catalyst for Cao Xiuzhen's suit, but the judicial outcome of Cao Xiuzhen's case as well as the case below make it clear that the judiciary accorded more import to the individual rights of husbands over wives. The courts, for instance, seemed to surmise that Cao Xiuzhen's motive for filing for divorce was not because of physical abuse but because of the change in the couple's economic situation. They would not grant her a divorce in order to improve her economic outlook. The courts held that a husband's poverty or inability to provide for his wife should not justify a divorce (even when accompanied by physical abuse).

HUSBAND DEFENSES: MARRIAGE FINANCE, ECONOMIC HARDSHIP, AND SOCIOECONOMIC INTERPRETATIONS OF RIGHTS

Husbands' defenses to intolerable cruelty suits suggest an understanding of legal rights that emphasized demographic and economic considerations. Demarcating the major ways in which Chinese conceptions of rights differ from modern Western understandings, political scientist Elizabeth Perry stresses the historic priority assigned to collective socioeconomic security and subsistence concerns in Chinese conceptions of justice and rights (2008a). Bringing Perry's notion of the socioeconomic Chinese variation on rights-thinking together with what demographer Ted Telford identifies as a "marriage crunch" during the Qing Dynasty that persisted, if not worsened, during the Republican period (1992) helps to illuminate the material considerations that underpinned many of the arguments regarding intolerable cruelty lawsuits. For example, husbands often understood their marital rights in relation to the economic pressures created by the marriage finance market. For poor men, the "marriage crunch" made financing a marriage extremely onerous. Such men argued, often quite successfully, that it would be unjust to permit divorce because of their poverty.

In response to cruelty allegations, many husbands mostly sidestepped the topic of cruelty altogether and stressed instead the economic stakes of the marriage. Husbands often emphasized the unfairness and economic harm they would suffer if after very substantial financial outlays, their marriages were to be dissolved. Poor husbands constructed their sense of justice around the issue of economic hardship. For men of the lower classes, marriage represented an expensive proposition. The gender ratio imbalance (as high as 156.9 males per 100 females in Beijing in 1940) certainly curtailed the opportunities available for poor men to marry.[17] In addition to gender population disparities, marriage practices continued in the Republic to allow upper-class men to have one wife as well as several concubines, which further exacerbated the scarcity of available wives for poor men. Marriage customs that required prospective grooms to bestow a bride's family with betrothal gifts also persisted, making marriage unaffordable for men barely able to sustain their own livelihoods. Once they were married, poor men confronted dismal financial prospects. If anything, their economic hardships were likely to increase with the addition of one more mouth to feed, body to clothe, and person to house. And if the men had borrowed to cover the costs of the betrothal gift and wedding ceremony, then they owed an additional and often substantial debt. A husband who could demonstrate the financial burden he bore for the sake of marriage and the impossibility of remarriage because of his poverty stood a good chance of keeping his current marriage intact. The expenses incurred did not necessarily justify any domestic abuse, but they did effectively demonstrate the husband's commitment to the marriage in the eyes of the men and apparently in the eyes of the courts.

Most litigants in intolerable cruelty cases came from lower-class backgrounds. The husbands who defended themselves against cruelty allegations worked as coopers, tofu vendors, pancake peddlers, shoemakers, and peasant laborers, or lacked steady employment. These occupations offered little chance of economic advancement. Table 5.4 illustrates the occupations of divorce litigants from 1936.[18]

In addition, monetary inflation and high unemployment, persistent problems that spiraled during the War of Resistance and intensified further during the Civil War years, turned bleak prospects even gloomier.[19] In other words, marriage signified an exorbitantly expensive undertaking for poor men in the late Republican era. The difficulty poor men encountered in trying to marry contributed to the expectation that once married, the marriage would be permanent. This economic understanding of poor men's rights contributed in turn to affirming a modern, conjugal form of patriarchy, in which rights helped to confirm existing hierarchies.

As Ding Maotou in the case below explained, he was willing to work hard and spend (and borrow) a great deal of money in order to get married because he believed and expected that his marriage would be a lifetime endeavor. Where was the justice, argued men like Ding, for him to work hard and save all his life to get married, only to have his wife leave him after barely forty days even if he had argued with his wife and perhaps even hit her a couple of times. Like the majority of husbands involved in cruelty litigation, Ding believed that "occasional" abuse, arguments, and violence were acceptable in marriage. To him occasional violence and discord constituted too flimsy a reason to dissolve a marriage arranged after substantial and excruciating financial sacrifices. Poverty gave rise to a fair share of marital disputes. For poor men like Ding Maotou the increased availability of divorce under the Republican Civil Code gave rise to the fear that their wives were trying to divorce them because of their poverty.

Table 5.4. Occupation of Litigants in 774 Divorce Cases, 1936

Occupation	*Male*	*Female*
Agriculture	295	285
Mining	4	1
Industry	77	82
Business	117	27
Transportation	13	3
Public affairs/official business	36	15
Self-employed	39	38
Service	33	36
Unemployed/lost job	60	18
Never employed/jobless	93	264
Not clear	7	5

Source: *Sifa tongji 1936*

For women too, the marriage crunch and material considerations also shaped their views on individual rights in marriage. It appears from the case records that some women were driven to marry for security and livelihood. Some, like the woman in the case below, seem to have interpreted "rights consciousness" as an exit option allowing them to escape marriages with men who could barely support them. The gender ratio imbalance operated in their favor, making remarriage a much more viable option for poor women than poor men. Husbands complained that the main motivation for their wives' lawsuits stemmed from wives' "detesting poverty and loving wealth." Husbands accused their wives of contriving to use domestic squabbles as an excuse to escape marriage to poor husbands. Husbands expressed anxieties over their financial standing or lack of financial means in cruelty suits. In other words, husbands based their explanations for their own actions and the behaviors of their wives on primarily economic motives. These preoccupations reflected prevailing social practices that made marriage an expensive undertaking for lower-class men and a means of support for women.

"MONEY AND MARRIAGE ARE NOT EASY MATTERS": LÜ LINGER VS. DING MAOTOU

The following case illustrates the contestation between a wife's grievances and her husband's economic defenses. In arguing to keep the marriage intact, the husband stressed his stakes in the marriage. Lü Linger, twenty-four *sui,* sued for divorce in Hang County, Zhejiang Province, in 1947, less than a year after being married. She claimed intolerable cruelty, describing her marriage as one full of abuse and ill treatment. She counted at least five separate incidents involving physical violence during the short period in which she lived with her husband, Ding Maotou, thirty-four *sui*. The abusive treatment began almost immediately after her entrance into her husband's home. The couple engaged in their first dispute on their wedding night, when her husband slapped her across the face and told her that she was not well behaved. The second dispute that resulted in physical violence erupted three days after their wedding, over the expenses incurred for their wedding celebration. Pressed by his creditors to repay the money he had borrowed for the wedding, Ding Maotou asked his wife for the gold bracelet he had recently given her as a betrothal gift. She refused to hand over the bracelet, and he beat her with his fists. He took the bracelet anyway, and used some of the proceeds from the sale to repay his debts and gambled away the rest of the money. Lü Linger was dismayed to learn shortly after being married that her husband had borrowed most of the wedding expenses and "had not one cent in his hands." The third, fourth, and fifth disputes that allegedly ended in Ding Maotou physically injuring his wife also stemmed from the couple's need for money. One night Ding Maotou wanted more gambling money and so he tried to sell a ring that his wife's mother had given to her before the marriage. Again he beat her (this time slapping her across the face two times and hitting her with his fists) when she would not give him her ring. Burdened yet again by his financial obligations two weeks later, Ding Maotou sent his wife out to borrow money. When she was unable to obtain any money, he beat her again to the point of injury. Finally, less than a month later, short on cash yet again, Ding Maotou attempted to persuade his wife to go and work outside the home. According to his wife, he urged her to prostitute herself in order to earn her keep. When she rejected his plan, he beat her. Ding Maotou administered this last beating with a wooden stick and caused severe injuries to Lü Linger's leg and eye. After this beating, she moved back into her natal family home. It was only forty days after her wedding. Lü Linger decided that the life of economic hardship and domestic violence that she experienced as a wife was not for her. After a few months of living with her natal family, she sued for divorce. Later she moved to Shanghai and found employment at a tobacco factory.[20] Like Cao Xiuzhen in the case previously described, Lü Linger was able to imagine an alternative life for herself when confronted with abuse. The first step toward realizing this new vision for herself required a legal break from her husband.

Ding Maotou opposed his wife's suit for divorce, denying that he had ever abused her and claiming that her motivations stemmed from greed rather than injuries that amounted to intolerable cruelty. Ding Maotou worked as a wooden-barrel maker in Hangzhou. As he described his life as a craftsman to the trial court, he worked long hours for little pay. For years he struggled just to get by on his own, not certain that he would ever be able to afford to marry. Ding Maotou had already reached his early thirties when he finally managed to obtain a wife for himself. "I am just a craftsman," Ding Maotou explained. "Both money and marriage are not easy matters." Ding Maotou's marriage fulfilled one of his most cherished wishes even though his financial situation barely allowed him to afford the expenses involved with getting married. He estimated the financial costs of his marriage to be about 3,000,000 *yuan.* He gave his wife's family about 160,000 *yuan* and a gold bracelet weighing five *qian* as a betrothal gift. He spent the rest of the money on feting guests at a formal wedding banquet. He saved up part of that money, but he had to borrow the rest, paying for the betrothal gifts and wedding banquet expenses on credit. Apparently his wife did not have a clear idea of her husband's financial situation. When she entered his home she was not impressed by what she saw. "What shabby furniture you have," she apparently remarked. "Your rooms are so small. And your financial wherewithal is so limited." Ding Maotou's humble living arrangement, his poverty, and his indebtedness disappointed his new wife, and according to Ding Maotou, constituted the root cause of her divorce suit. Despite the staggering financial setback that marriage required, Ding Maotou considered himself fortunate to marry and to find a relatively young wife at that. "It ate up a huge amount of money . . . [I] expected to be married from then on." His expectation that marriage was a permanent state derived not only from his financial investment in the marriage, but also from his emotional attachment to his wife. According to his testimony, he "only had time to cherish her, not abuse her." It was preposterous to ever think that he would beat her. She represented his most cherished, prized possession. The marriage was a serious financial and emotional investment for him. When, for instance, two million *yuan* (two-thirds of his original three million *yuan* outlay) was offered to him as an inducement to agree to divorce during an attempt at mediation at the appeals level, he replied, "I am not willing to divorce her. I don't want the money."[21]

In this case, the courts' rulings demonstrated sympathy toward Ding Maotou's economic hardships and suspicion of Lü Linger's economic motivations. The courts' skepticism toward Lü Linger's claims was evident in the line of questioning posed to her and her witness. The questions were ostensibly intended to ascertain whether the wooden stick used to beat her was round or square. When asked, Lü Linger told the court that the wooden stick used to hit her was round. When the court asked her witness the same question, he answered square. It was a tricky question, and her answer and that of her witness contradicted each other. The question seemed prompted by the suspicion that she had an ulterior motive in seeking a divorce on the ground of intolerable cruelty after living with her husband for only forty days. The court held, moreover, that Lü Linger's injuries could not be proven even though she presented a prescription for the medicine she took to recover from eye and leg injuries. Overall, her lack of adequate proof coupled with her husband's denials convinced the courts that the beatings did not amount to intolerable cruelty that merited a divorce. The Hang County District Court reinforced Ding Maotou's expectation that the marriage be maintained and denied his wife's petition for divorce. Upon appeal, the Zhejiang Superior Court affirmed the rejection of her petition. Lü Linger appealed one more time to the Supreme Court, but the outcome had not yet been determined when the 1949 Revolution interrupted the Supreme Court's operations.

Lü Linger's behavior and testimony illustrate some of the expectations that she held for her marriage as well. After receiving betrothal gifts of 160,000 *yuan* and a gold bracelet weighing five *qian* and being feted at a proper wedding banquet, she probably expected her husband to be a man of some financial means. She evidently believed that married life entitled her to a comfortable material existence. In that regard, she expected her husband to provide her with adequate living quarters, to supply the household with daily necessities like food and other provisions, and basically to support the two of them financially. She was upset about the deception used by her husband to marry her. She did not expect to have to go and look for a job in order for the two of them to make ends meet. She was absolutely dismayed when her husband tried to take back the gold bracelet that had been one of her betrothal gifts only a few days after the wedding. She was even more horrified when he took away a ring that her own mother had given her before marriage a few weeks later to boot. Not only did her husband demand that she contribute to the couple's funds, he used force and violence to do so, injuring her, she claimed, on at least five occasions. This life of poverty and abuse was not the life she expected and was not the life she was going to meekly accept as her fate.

Obviously disgruntled with marriage, Lü Linger bemoaned her "cruel fate" and "gulped down her sobs" (Supreme Court 16(5)161 petition 1947.7). She cried and took pity upon herself to be sure, but she did not simply resign herself to her fate. She took steps to find a way out of her marriage. In Chinese cities by the late 1940s, acceptance of one's marital fate was no longer near compulsory. Lü Linger lived in a society that afforded her greater choices in the realm of marriage and divorce. The available alternatives to marriage were not all that great, but at least some existed. It did not take Lü Linger very long to figure out a plan to escape her marriage. After only forty days of marriage, she went first to her natal family. A few months later, she picked up and moved to Shanghai, where she was perhaps more free from traditional constraints on a wife's behavior. There she managed to find work and housing for herself at the Shanghai Tobacco Company, establishing a viable exit option from the marriage system.

Although the final outcome of the case is not known, it is likely that even if the Supreme Court denied her appeal for divorce, her husband would probably have had a very hard time convincing her to move back in with him. By moving to the city and supporting herself, she seems to have found a way to escape her husband's control. Like Cao Xiuzhen in the previous case, rights consciousness plus the availability of women's employment enabled the wife to seek an alternative future for herself. The judicial outcomes, however, show the opposition women faced in bringing their rights claims to court, namely the interests husbands had in keeping a marriage together. The courts substantiated husbands' desires to maintain marriages. Nevertheless, for Lü Linger, who did not obtain relief from her disappointment through the court system, new opportunities to work in urban areas offered another escape route from her marriage.

"HOW CAN SUCH TRIVIAL REASONS BE ALLOWED TO SPLIT US UP?": MRS. ZHU-XU VS. ZHU ER

A case from the Hebei Superior Court in 1936, like the case between Lü Linger vs. Ding Maotou, illustrates how wife-litigant interests in asserting individual rights were pitted against husband-litigant views of intolerable cruelty through an economic lens. Mrs. Zhu-Xu,[22] residing with her natal family in Beijing, sued her husband, Zhu Er, living in a village in Tong County, for divorce on the ground of intolerable cruelty. Like Ding Maotou, the husband countered by invoking a sense of justice rooted in economic considerations, fearing divorce for "minor" or "trivial" reasons, and defending against divorce by pointing to the financial outlay he incurred in order to marry. After the Tong County government rejected her suit she appealed to the Hebei Superior Court. There she reiterated her abuse allegations against her husband, explaining that shortly after their wedding, her husband beat her because she would not engage in an illegal sexual act with him (the exact act is not specified).[23] Another night, he beat her again, this time leaving wounds all over her body. An injury report submitted to the lower court verified these injuries. She escaped to her natal home and filed suit for divorce because as she put it, her husband has a "barbarous temper and behaves inhumanely," which made it impossible for her to live with him. She could not stand to live with such a man any longer. Like many other wives who sued for cruelty, Mrs. Zhu-Xu listed the various beating incidents she endured. Since the beatings took place in their home, Mrs. Zhu-Xu was not able to present any eyewitnesses.

Zhu Er, in response, placed the beatings within the context of the couple's domestic squabbles over their daily provisions. He described how his wife often squandered the couple's fuel and rice. Because of her exorbitance, one night he felt compelled to urge her to economize. She would not listen, and they quarreled and beat each other. Zhu Er also claimed to have sustained injuries (scratches on the back of his hands). He did not usually mistreat her, he asserted. In further support of why the couple should not divorce, Zhu Er called attention to the large financial expenditures he undertook to marry her in the first place. According to his answer, "At the time I married, I shelled out 100 *yuan* as a betrothal gift and another 100 *yuan* in expenses. How can such trivial reasons be allowed to split us up?"[24]

The Hebei Superior Court judges affirmed the lower-court decision to deny Mrs. Zhu-Xu's request for a divorce. The judges recognized that Mrs. Zhu-Xu suffered from genuine physical injuries, as proven by the lower court's examination. But the judges also used the injury report to diminish the significance of the injuries, labeling them only "scratches and bites." Besides, didn't Zhu Er have scratch marks too? The marks on his body proved to the court's satisfaction that the two parties engaged in a mutual spat, with each suffering only a minor injury. The court also held that Mrs. Zhu-Xu had no proof that it was the usual practice for her husband to abuse her. It was not that Mrs. Zhu-Xu could not be believed, said the court, but rather it was just that "occasional arguments between husbands and wives that lead to physical injuries cannot be hastily pointed to as suffering cruelty which makes living together intolerable."[25]

Although Mrs. Zhu-Xu suffered physical injuries at the hands of her husband (as proven by an injury report), she was not able to obtain a divorce. The courts justified their decision by distinguishing between occasional as opposed to habitual cruelty. The courts were not willing to grant a divorce when the abuse was "only" occasional because occasional abuse was deemed to be an ordinary part of married life, illustrating the limitations of social expectations about the inevitability of conflict between married couples and the expectation that husbands would on occasion physically discipline wives who did not satisfy their desires, despite the emergence of women's consciousness of rights to protection from unequal force through the court system. Zhu Er too believed that physical abuse was not a serious enough reason to justify divorce. He argued that the couple's domestic disputes were "trivial." By contrast, Zhu Er referred to the serious and substantial financial investment that he had made in the marriage. His statements reveal the great extent to which his sense of justice related to his sense of economic sacrifice.

STATE VALIDATION FOR WOMEN'S GRIEVANCES NARROWLY CONSTRUED

Intolerable cruelty provided a relatively flexible legal standard, which was not simply imposed or dictated from above, but rather determined according to a complex process of interaction between state and society. The meaning of intolerable cruelty was shaped according to a combination of everyday social and economic realities, abstract liberal theory, and judicial intervention. The contest over the legal definition of intolerable cruelty suggests a model of state-society relations in which litigants and judges negotiated the dimensions of the conjugal bond in a complex process in which the common values, ordinary everyday senses of justice, and personal and practical interpretations of individual rights offered by wife- and husband-litigants contended with judicial standards and the state's interest in the preservation of marriage. But judicial decisions should be read with caution—they indicate that whatever negotiation took place, the state still came down mostly on the side of husbands and husbands' rights. Despite the GMD's intent to promote the principle of gender equality and despite the mobilization of a new rights discourse by wife-litigants who sued for divorce, the results were limited—judicial outcomes largely upheld the primacy of the conjugal relationship and reinforced men's individual rights over women's within these conjugal relationships.

Though the Republican Civil Code provided for individual rights and promised gender equality, only a minority of women succeeded in convincing judges of their right to divorce on the basis of intolerable cruelty. For the most part judges exhibited a low level of concern for such cases. This next section explores the multiple obstacles that made obtaining a divorce on the basis of intolerable cruelty extremely difficult. The state's validation of women's domestic grievances was limited. The instances in which the state upheld a wife's right to divorce involved narrowly construed forms of marital distress. In general, wives who successfully prevailed in their lawsuits for divorce managed to prove a form of "extreme" cruelty. The circumstances varied from case to case, but the case records show certain patterns. First, the severity, degree, and frequency of physical abuse served as important considerations. The more serious and severe the physical injury was, the higher the likelihood of winning a divorce.[26] The courts in the cases in which women succeeded focused on the nature of the beatings and the physical injuries to the wives. They did not entertain competing narratives about the wives' economic motivations for seeking divorce. Second, the burden of proving abuse rested with wives and was quite high. Documentary evidence of physical abuse helped to substantiate a wife's allegations. Injury reports (*shangdan*) taken at hospitals, police stations, and procurator offices helped too to show proof of injury. And witnesses played an important role in determining the outcome of cases as well. Eyewitnesses were particularly valuable. The more impartial the witness, the more weight judges accorded to the testimony. Finally, the existence of prior litigation or mediation agreements helped to demonstrate a pattern of repeated abuse.

Judges could draw upon several other factors to discount a wife's allegations. Unfortunately for women litigants, the "catch-all" nature of *nüedai,* or "abuse," blunted the power of their legal claims. Judges complained about the overly general citing of *nüedai*. As if female litigants lacked the language to discuss something with which they were intimately familiar, they often struggled to articulate their cruelty charges. Wives pressed by judges to explain the circumstances and details of cruelty incidents could only reply to the effect that "it is too hard to express all of my suffering" or "the pain is indescribable." Over and over again we see how litigants possessed a limited vocabulary through which they could verbally communicate their experience of cruelty.[27] Often they were only able to describe their physical reaction to the cruelty—tears, sobs, and bodily injury. In other cases litigants fell back upon repetitive claims about one beating after another.

Operating in the formal realm of the law courts, judges demanded specific incidents and witnesses or records to document them. The law was not designed to redress general oppressions, no matter how pervasive. It was difficult to address abuse as a generic complaint in the formal legal system, which generally approached complicated, messy domestic problems and turned them into standardized forms, leading to a sort of pancake effect, flattening individual circumstances. The repetitive and generalized language used to describe the experience of cruelty, for example, gave rise to judicial findings that cruelty claims were fabricated because the woman claiming cruelty could not provide a detailed account of what she experienced. So judges could regularly rule that a wife's cruelty allegations were without merit because she spoke "too generally" (*longtong*) about them. An example is the case of He Ke Dongming, who sued for divorce in 1936, accusing her husband and his parents of abusing her. To prove her case, He Ke Dongming provided the court with a copy of her husband's criminal conviction and offered her mother and a servant as witnesses. The Beijing District Court rejected her divorce petition because she failed to convince the court that she had suffered cruelty to the degree that made living together impossible. He Ke Dongming then hired a lawyer and appealed to the Hebei Superior Court. The superior court also dismissed her abuse allegations, labeling their nature "too general and sweeping" (*longtong*).[28]

The timeliness of a cruelty divorce suit also factored into the outcome of the case. A long time lapse between the incidents of alleged cruelty and the initiation of a lawsuit for divorce worked against a woman's petition for divorce on the basis of cruelty. Judges, in other words, were less willing to grant a divorce after the passage of time. The passage of time made the status quo harder to change. A wife who was married over ten years and had been living with her natal family for the last six years was questioned by the trial court about her motives. The court wondered, why divorce now after so many years had passed? From the court's point of view, the passage of time made the wife's grievance significantly less urgent and compelling. The superior court also wondered whether the wife had a hidden motive. And after the wife appealed to the Supreme Court, she was told that after an incident has been patched up, it was no longer considered a matter of intolerable cruelty.[29]

SEVERITY AND PROOF: MRS. GUO-ZHOU GRANTED DIVORCE AFTER NEARLY BEING BEATEN TO DEATH

In general, the degree of physical injury stood out as an important factor in determining the outcome of an intolerable cruelty case. A wife who suffered serious bodily harm had a better chance of prevailing than a wife whose injuries were deemed minor. A wife whose injuries were characterized as "merely scratches and bites" did not obtain a divorce, nor did a wife whose injuries left no visible scars.[30] A wife whose ears were injured when her husband hit her with a glass kerosene lamp was told that her injury was "isolated" since only her ears were injured and the rest of her body was unhurt.[31]

The wife in the next case managed to obtain her freedom from an abusive husband after her bandit husband beat her nearly to death. Mrs. Guo-Zhou from Pinggu County, Hebei Province, sued her husband, Guo Pinsan, for divorce in 1936, before the Pinggu County Government Office. Mrs. Guo-Zhou claimed she was coerced into marriage in 1933 by her husband, who was a bandit. During the marriage, he regularly beat her (*baiban nüedai*). In May 1936, he used a leather whip to viciously beat and kick her (*duda*). Luckily, a neighbor from the same courtyard intervened to save her. At the time, the village head and others feared another mishap, so they reported the incident to the Pinggu County Police. Guo Pinsan was criminally convicted and sentenced to two months in prison for the injuries he inflicted on his wife. The criminal case record also stated that Mrs. Guo-Zhou's injuries were extensive—her body was covered all over with cuts and purplish bruises. With the criminal conviction and the neighbor's testimony as evidence of extreme abuse, the Pinggu County Government granted a divorce. Although Guo Pinsan appealed the decision to the Hebei Superior Court, that court rejected his appeal, finding that "this type of abusive behavior obviously constitutes cruelty to the degree that makes living together intolerable."[32]

The facts in this case proved extreme abuse in the eyes of the court. Mrs. Guo-Zhou's severe injuries were verified by a police and injury report. The criminal conviction against Guo Pinsan for the injuries he inflicted on his wife helped convince the judges that the abuse was real. Luckily for her, a neighbor intervened to stop the beating and testified on her behalf during the trial. Her village head also intervened, bringing her case to the attention of the county authorities and helping to secure a criminal conviction for the abuse. Mrs. Guo-Zhou's husband, moreover, did not come across as a sympathetic figure. He was referred to as a bandit, and Republican courts ostracized bandits and used extraordinary legal measures like summary execution against them (Xu 2007 and 2008, 286–290). Mrs. Guo-Zhou benefited from the new framework of individual rights. Although she suffered serious bodily harm, she did not necessarily break a bone or tooth, which was the requirement during the Qing. She might have been able to claim attempted murder, which was a justification for divorce under both Qing and Republican law, but she would have needed the support and representation of her natal family (not always available), and the outcome would not have been guaranteed.

The burden of proving the existence of intolerable cruelty in a marriage fell to the party seeking a divorce, usually the wife. Mrs. Guo-Zhou was fortunate to have irrefutable proof of her injuries based upon the physical evidence of the injuries still visible on her body and the testimony of her neighbor and village headman. Another wife whose face bore the scars of knife wounds inflicted by her husband was able to obtain a divorce.[33] Wives who could not point to marks of physical injury had a more difficult time in court. Judges commonly cited inadequate proof as grounds for rejecting a wife's petition for divorce on the grounds of intolerable cruelty. Courts admonished wife-plaintiffs who were unable to submit "concrete proof," "lacked scars that could be publicly examined," or "lacked witnesses to prove their contentions."[34] Courts dismissed cruelty charges because they "lacked any tiny bit of evidence" or were only "fabrications."[35] Judges characterized one wife's allegations as "empty boasts."[36] In short, women encountered great difficulty convincing judges that the injuries they suffered amounted to intolerable cruelty.

The proof women did manage to produce was often systematically dismantled by judges. The testimony of a wife's witnesses could be invalidated as "hearsay." If a witness was the wife's mother or other relative, then her testimony could be discounted as "biased." If the testimony of cruelty came from a maidservant, it could be dismissed as "mere gossip." Also, the testimony of witnesses who did not see the abuse firsthand could be discounted and dismissed.[37] Judges provided no leeway for the fact that virilocal marriage patterns meant that the only eyewitnesses to an act of domestic cruelty would likely be a member of the husband's family or possibly a neighbor who would be reluctant to testify against a neighboring family in its dispute with a daughter-in-law.

Documents helped a wife's case but did not guarantee a divorce. In cases where a complaining wife presented written documentation of her injuries in the form of a medical report, the complaining wife raised her chances of success. There were instances, however, in which judges used such medical reports against complaining wives. Take, for example, the judge who examined a medical report and concluded that the report simply proved that the wife in question suffered only "minor injuries," because her bruises were described as the size of a flea and the bloodstains on her clothing were described as "tiny dots" (Hebei 634-1-128). Similarly, evidence in the form of a criminal complaint against an abusive husband slightly improved a wife's chances of success but did not guarantee a successful outcome in the divorce proceedings. A criminal complaint or conviction, like a medical report, could be held against the wife who presented it. Judges obviously could not refute the proof of cruelty that had been verified by another court and resulted in a criminal conviction. Judges could and did, however, interpret the presence of a single criminal conviction as proof that the cruelty was not out of the ordinary. Judges reasoned that one incident of cruelty did not amount to "intolerable" cruelty. Courts also questioned wives about why they only reported one particular incident of cruelty to the authorities if the cruelty was as pervasive as they claimed.[38] Or in instances when a complaint was filed with the police but not prosecuted in criminal court, judges construed a woman's reluctance to press charges as an admission that the allegations were not as serious as contended.

HABITUAL ABUSE: LI YOURONG RECEIVES A DIVORCE AFTER REPEATED ABUSE

In one of its earliest guidelines on intolerable cruelty after the implementation of the Republican Civil Code, the Supreme Court ruled that "habitual abuse" (*guanxing nüedai*) constituted sufficient grounds for divorce (Fu and Zhou 1964, 1931 interpretation no. 371). The flipside of this interpretation meant that "occasional beatings" (*ouer ouda*) did not constitute sufficient grounds for divorce. This distinction between occasional beatings and habitual abuse raised the burden of proof for women seeking divorce. Not only did they have to prove abuse, but they also had to prove that the abuse was habitual, not just occasional. So in cases in which the courts found the women's claims of being beaten believable, the courts could still rule against divorce if they deemed the abuse to be occasional beatings that did not amount to intolerable cruelty. A few years later, in 1938, the Supreme Court provided more guidance on the issue of frequency, holding that a husband who beat his wife to the point that she sustained injuries three times in three months could be divorced.[39]

In the next case, the husband was a repeat offender, having previously agreed through mediation to stop beating his wife. When he broke his agreement and beat her again, the courts sided with his wife and granted her a divorce. The previous legal proceeding was important in validating her complaint and demonstrating a pattern of habitual abuse. In Li Yourong's case, her injuries were not extremely egregious in comparison to many other intolerable cruelty cases. However, she had already complained to a court about her abusive husband a year earlier. At that time, she agreed to withdraw her suit for divorce because her husband promised that he would refrain from beating her. Because her husband violated their prior agreement, the courts regarded his behavior more severely.

Li Yourong sued her husband, Wang Shangfa, for a divorce in Ningyuan County, Hunan Province, in 1942, after he beat her to the point that she suffered serious injury. A year earlier, in 1941, Li Yourong had brought suit for divorce, but through the mediation of friends and neighbors, she withdrew her suit. When her husband beat her again the following year, she brought suit again and obtained a divorce. The trial court determined that the abuse in this case—Wang Shangfa beat Li Yourong with a wooden board, kicked her, ripped her clothing, and locked her up—was serious enough to merit a divorce on the basis of intolerable cruelty. Her husband appealed to the Hunan Superior Court, which affirmed the granting of a divorce. The husband appealed again to the Supreme Court, denying that he had abused his wife to the point that amounted to intolerable cruelty. The Supreme Court rejected his appeal in 1944, holding that there was ample evidence of intolerable cruelty.[40]

Unlike most wives who sued for divorce, Li Yourong had her previous suit and mediation efforts to support her version of the marriage. In most cruelty cases that involved a single incident of physical abuse, the decision was against divorce. Here, however, the husband disregarded the court's prior admonitions and his own pledge to refrain from abusing his wife. Perhaps the courts upheld the wife's rights and judged Wang Shangfa more severely because he was a multiple, repeat offender.

The cases analyzed above illuminate how the new set of legal mechanisms provided by Republican divorce law supported select wives in their attempts to escape abusive marriages when the abuse was deemed "extreme" or out of the ordinary. The state validated these women's grievances and enabled them to break free from the marriage and family system that they experienced as intolerable. Judicial interpretations of intolerable cruelty, however, were narrowly tailored so that most wives did not obtain the judicial relief they sought.

The state's validation of women's grievances under the lens of rights and liabilities was rather circumscribed. Judges weighed the conflicting interests of individual litigants and exercised caution in the validation of cruelty claims. Despite wife-litigants' willingness and resourcefulness in invoking the cruelty provisions, judges devoted much of their opinions to clarifying what types of behavior mostly did not constitute intolerable cruelty. Judges narrowly tailored the intolerable cruelty provision to fit only a small set of circumstances demonstrating a strong reluctance to grant divorce on the basis of cruelty. Judges classified many of the injuries women complained about as "minor" or "occasional" and held that they did not amount to intolerable cruelty. A high percentage of cruelty petitions also met with dismissal on the grounds that there was insufficient evidence to support the accusations. These opinions upheld traditional patriarchal attitudes, but did so on the nontraditional basis of individual rights and duties and in the context of the conjugal rather than patrilineal family.

INDIVIDUAL RIGHTS AND THE IRONIC AFFIRMATION OF MODERN CONJUGAL PATRIARCHY

This study, based on extensive archival research, reveals both the emergence and the limits of rights thinking. The emergence of rights consciousness can be located in the large number of divorce petitions filed by wife-litigants named, blamed, and claimed in accordance with the Republican Civil Code's provisions on intolerable cruelty. The framework of individual rights furnished individuals, mostly wives, with the means to turn previously inchoate dissatisfactions into legally actionable claims. These women deployed the discourse of rights to transform their ordinary, familiar grievances into newly meaningful legal actions. Their petitions demonstrate a new willingness to engage the law.

At the same time, the emergence of rights consciousness in the petitions filed by wife-litigants met with considerable resistance from husbands and judges. Husband-litigants drew upon socioeconomic concerns to counter their wives' claims and to argue against divorce. They were acutely aware of the socioeconomic realities of the "marriage crunch," accusing their wives of economic motivations and outlined their own economic suffering. Judges too grounded their understandings of individual rights in the context of socioeconomic justice. Judges evaluated the claims of wives and husbands, and in most cases affirmed the arguments of husbands to keep a marriage intact. The state's validation of women's grievances was partial to be sure, with relief from extreme forms of domestic tyranny and the denial of relief in cases in which the oppression was deemed by judges to be an ordinary part of marriage. The high rate of divorce suits disallowed by judges suggests that individual rights could be curtailed by more general concerns about social stability.

An archival case-based approach to the question of rights suggests both that the emergence of rights consciousness in Republican China offered ways for individuals to transform their sense of self and views of marriage (and these transformations should not be overlooked) but also that rights were ultimately an unstable and unreliable means to achieving gender equality. Instead, the courts promoted a modern form of conjugal patriarchy that had much in common with Qing legal practices. The judicial outcomes of these cases lend a certain economic and patriarchal cast to the meaning of individual rights. Wife-litigants' right to divorce and to bodily freedom was circumscribed while poor husband-litigants' right to maintain their costly marriages was upheld. Judicial reluctance to privilege women's right to divorce in the case of intolerable cruelty (except in instances of egregious abuse) suggests that in the context in which these rights were adjudged a certain degree of domestic abuse was deemed "acceptable." Indeed, the individual rights framework of the Republican Civil Code ironically helped to consolidate a modern, liberal form of conjugal patriarchy.

NOTES

1. For a useful primer on the various types of rights and rights theory, see Jones 1994.
2. West 2001 discusses various critiques of rights in American legal scholarship including Marxist views that deride rights as individual, bourgeois, detrimental, diversionary, and illuso-

ry, capable of token change but incapable of bringing about revolution; Critical Legal Studies views that blame rights for reinforcing existing hierarchies (Mark Tushnet); and the views of other rights skeptics who dismiss rights claims as "much ado about nothing" (Gerald Rosenberg).

3. Glosser 2003 argues that the rise of the conjugal family idea helped perpetuate the subordination of individual rights in twentieth-century China. I agree with her view that conjugal patriarchy represented the dominant trend, but I also see pockets where individual women succeeded in deploying rights discourse to transform the circumstances of their lives.

4. This chapter focuses on judicial divorce, which involved a spouse bringing a formal lawsuit for divorce against the other spouse, who opposed the divorce. In contrast, when both spouses agreed to divorce, simple procedures for divorce by mutual consent allowed the couple to divorce without seeking the approval of the state.

5. I can only suggest, not argue conclusively, that cruelty cases multiplied in the Republican period in contrast to, say, bigamy cases or incurable disease cases and offer a possible explanation for the high number of cruelty cases because the statistics about the number of Qing divorce cases that would be needed to make such a comparison are not at hand.

6. Civil Code, Article 1052, Subsection 3. Civil Code, Article 1052, Subsection 4 covered in-law abuse.

7. Though some might object to the use of theories drawn from other legal traditions, I think it is possible to borrow concepts and models that fit the circumstances and illustrate similar phenomena without necessarily equating the two legal systems or overlooking the many historical and cultural differences.

8. The work of political theorist Judith Shklar has been useful in thinking about how people develop a sense of injustice. See Shklar 1984 (discussing cruelty and the rise of liberal thinking) and Ibid. 1990 (discussing the distinctions between misfortune and injustice).

9. Lawyers played an important role in helping women turn their domestic grievances into legal complaints, serving as conduits of sort, framing disparate ordinary gripes into judicially recognizable terms. As such, lawyers were key agents in the shift that took place in which people came to view previously ordinary conflicts in terms of legal rights and duties. The importance of lawyers, however, does not diminish the agency of the women in their legal actions. The interaction between Republican lawyers and their women clients is an interesting question that requires additional research.

10. Supreme Court 16(7) 545 petition to the Xi'an District Court 1948.10.15, response 1948.10.23, oral interrogations 1948.10.25 and 1948.12.8, Xi'an District Court decision 1948.12.13; appeal to the Shaanxi Superior Court 1948.12.29, oral interrogation 1949.2.21, Shaanxi Superior Court decision 1949.2.23; appeal to the Supreme Court 1949.3.11, response 1949.3.24, additional appeal to the Supreme Court 1949.4.5.

11. Supreme Court 16(7)545 Xi'an District Court hearing 1948.10.25.

12. Supreme Court 16(7) 545 Xi'an District Court decision 1948.12.13.

13. Supreme Court 16(7)545 appeal to the Shaanxi Superior Court 1948.12.29 and additional appeal 1949.2.18.

14. Supreme Court 16(7)545 Shaanxi Superior Court oral interrogation 1949.2.21 and decision 1949.2.23.

15. Supreme Court 16(7)545 appeal to the Supreme Court 1949.3.11 and additional appeal to the Supreme Court 1949.4.5.

16. Legal scholar Stuart Scheingold, for instance, has explored the ways in which rights have helped to challenge repressive practices (1974/2004). Other sociology of law scholars have credited rights-thinking with helping to spark social movements (McCann 1994) and serving as powerful symbolic tools for justice (Epps 1998, Ewick and Silbey 1998, Merry 2006). Critical race theorists like Patricia Williams, moreover, have rebutted the arguments of Critical Legal Studies scholars (see supra note 3) and endorsed rights as vital tools for empowerment and the securing of human dignity (1991).

17. For statistics on urban gender ratios, see Esherick 2001, 21, table 1. Although Esherick's purpose in charting urban gender ratios is to demonstrate a decline in the imbalance in male to female ratios, the figures still indicate a significantly larger population of males in relation to females. Shapiro 1998, fn 114 also refers to the gender imbalance in Republican

Beijing, though the figures he cites are not as disproportionate as Esherick's. "In the early 1920s, about 64 percent of the city's population was male. See Sidney Gamble assisted by John S. Burgess, *Peking: A Social Survey* (New York: George H. Doran Co., 1921), 99."

18. Bernhardt 1994, 1999, table 7.5 indicates that divorcing couples in general (not just those involved in abuse litigation) were mostly working class or unemployed.

19. As an indication of the magnitude of inflation during the late 1930s and 1940s, price levels increased by more than 2,000 times. Pepper (1978) 1999, 95, 126–131. See also Eastman 1984, 173–177. On unemployment, see Pepper 1999, 108–109.

20. Supreme Court 16(5)161 petition 1947.7 and oral argument 1947.8.9.

21. Supreme Court 16(5)161 answer 1947.8.9.

22. There were several ways of rendering female names in Republican China. A woman could be referred to by her husband and father's surnames followed by the honorific *shi* (similar to Madame or Mrs.) or simply by her surname and a given name. I generally follow the form of the name used in the court documents. Here I translate Zhu Xu *shi* into "Mrs. Zhu-Xu," which has the same meaning as "Mrs. Zhu *neé* Xu."

23. Hebei 634-1-128 decision dated 1936.9.1.

24. Hebei 634-1-128 decision dated 1936.9.1.

25. Hebei 634-1-128 decision dated 1936.9.1.

26. See also Supreme Court 16(6) 5-1 Supreme Court decision 1937.10.7. The Supreme Court affirmed the Guangxi Superior Court's decision to grant a divorce to a wife who had suffered injuries to more than ten different parts of her body from the spousal abuse.

27. Contrast the limited vocabulary available to women in the Republican period to the radicalized vocabulary that emerged in the post-1949 period with the various political campaigns designed to popularize the 1950 Marriage Law. See Diamant 2000, 104–105, 141, and 144. See also Liu 2010.

28. Hebei 634-1-249. In this case, the court also discounted the testimony of He Ke Dongming's mother because they claimed she was biased and dismissed the testimony of the servant as "gossip" (*xushuo*) that works its way among the female servants. As for the criminal conviction, the court determined that the beating had occurred, but that it was an isolated incident, causing only minor injury. The court reasoned that if He Ke Dongming had been beaten constantly as she claimed, then she should have had injuries all over her body, not just to her ears as the injury report indicated. Besides, the court stated, disputes between a new daughter-in-law and her husband and mother-in-law were quite common in traditional families.

29. Hebei 634-1-1054.

30. Hebei 634-1-128 and Hebei 634-1-1016.

31. Hebei 634-1-755.

32. Hebei 634-1-391, Pinggu County Government decision 1936.6.9 and Hebei Superior Court decision 1936.10.13.

33. Supreme Court 16(7)2987-9 1944.2.29.

34. Hebei 634-1-1016 decision 1937.7.6. A wife's suit for divorce was rejected because she had no concrete evidence of the abuse, no visible scars, and no witnesses. Husband denied the abuse.

35. Hebei 634-1-1016.

36. Hebei 634-1-189.

37. Hebei 634-1-338: Husband denied the abuse. Wife's witness could not say with certainty that husband abused wife. Hebei 634-1-884: Wife's witnesses testified that they tried to mediate between husband and wife. Court ruled that just because husband and his stepmother occasionally beat the wife and third parties have to intervene to mediate doesn't constitute proof of intolerable cruelty.

38. See also Hebei 634-1-755 in which Mrs. Lu-Song lost her suit for divorce even after her husband was convicted of a criminal offense and fined 20 *yuan* for his behavior.

39. Fu and Zhou 1964, 82: Supreme Court 1938 interpretation no. 2111: If a husband hits his wife to the point that she sustains injuries three times in three months, then this constitutes intolerable cruelty.

40. Supreme Court 16(7)2987-9 Supreme Court decision 1944.2.29.

Chapter Six

Running Away

Cohabitation Litigation and the Reconfiguration of Husband Patriarchy

Jonathan Spence's classic account of *The Death of Woman Wang* portrays the miserable plight of one woman Wang who ran away from her husband in seventeenth-century Shandong Province. Woman Wang's family origins were not recorded and her lack of natal family relations suggested she likely had been orphaned as a child. She lived in a one-room house with her husband, Jen, a hired laborer. The two of them got along poorly. With the help of another man, woman Wang fled her home in 1671. After a short time on the road together, however, her companion changed his mind and left her on her own. A lone fugitive, woman Wang gave up and returned to her village, taking refuge at a local temple, where she was eventually discovered by her husband. Woman Wang's act of running away subjected her to a host of potentially dire legal consequences. Under the Qing Code, she could be criminally punished by one hundred blows of the heavy bamboo for "forsaking" her husband (*beifu taohun* or *beifu zaitao*). Her husband also had the power to marry her off to another man if he so desired. Of course the ultimate consequence of woman Wang's return to her husband, conjugal homicide (her husband stabbed her to death), was even more severe than the punishments prescribed under the law.[1]

Compare the predicament of woman Wang to the situation of Mrs. Feng-Zhao who ran away from her husband in Beijing in February 1936. Finding herself under constant abuse since the beginning of her marriage in 1931, Mrs. Feng-Zhao made her escape to the city of Tianjin, where she obtained employment as a maidservant. Her husband pursued her, and when she refused to return, he filed a petition with the Beijing District Court requesting cohabitation. In response, Mrs. Feng-Zhao told the court that life with this abusive husband was no longer tolerable. The court ignored her pleas, ruling that she lacked any evidence of abuse. Therefore, the court ordered Mrs. Feng-Zhao to return to live with her husband. But Mrs. Feng-Zhao did not submit to the court order, refusing to move back and filing an appeal to the Hebei Superior Court, which in its turn, rejected her appeal and affirmed the cohabitation order.[2] It is not clear from the case file if Mrs. Feng-Zhao ever obeyed the multiple court cohabitation orders. Though whatever the final resolution of this case, Mrs. Feng-Zhao's fate was to be very different from woman Wang's. Unlike the Qing Code, the civil law framework for marriage during the Republic required a basic respect for individual freedom that did not provide for any criminal penalties or other forms of force to compel a runaway wife to live anywhere against her will.

As this case and many others demonstrate, in the 1930s and 1940s, the legal consequences of a wife's running away from her marital home differed markedly from those of the late imperial period. The marriage provisions of the Republican Civil Code unequivocally defined marriage as a civil contract between an individual man and an individual woman for the purpose of living together for the rest of their lives.[3] Even though the Republican state generally exercised expanded powers over marriage and family matters, the nature of the state's intervention changed. As marriage came to be viewed as a civil contract between individuals, a set of mutual rights and duties (as distinct from criminal punishments and penalties) governed marital relations. Following the model of Germany, Switzerland, and other European countries, Chinese legislators included a provision for the mutual obligation of spouses to live together as a cornerstone of marriage.[4] This civil law framework for cohabitation (*tongju*) indirectly imposed an important limitation on a husband's right to possess his wife in the Republican period. A wife who violated the duty to cohabit by running away could not be physically forced by a court to return. Thus while husbands had the right to sue for cohabitation in a civil court, runaway wives were not considered fugitives and did not face criminal punishment or forcible relocation. The enforcement of the duty of cohabitation could only be carried out by summoning the errant wife to court, where Republican judges generally weighed concerns about conjugal feelings, abuse allegations, and the family's overall well-being in the context of civil litigation, rather than a criminal prosecution. The only recourse open to the judges was to either persuade the woman to resume cohabitation or to issue a civil judgment ordering her to return home. As a result, truly determined runaway wives could ignore orders to live with their husbands without having to face heavy state-sanctioned punishment.[5]

Such cases not only reveal the transformations in women's lives wrought by Republican-era family law, but they also illuminate the dynamics driving wives to abandon their husbands and their husbands' motives in refusing to accept the dissolution of their marriages in the 1930s and 1940s. Wives usually asserted their hope that marriage would be harmonious and that they would be entitled to a basic standard of living, receive fair treatment from their husbands and in-laws, and live free from physical abuse. Taking flight was a venerable way of coping with marital distress. Republican wives ran away for similar reasons motivating their flight in the Qing and earlier periods. By running away, wives sought to escape physical and verbal abuse, to "cool off" after disputes with their husbands, to seek refuge from their in-laws, to satisfy lingering attachments to natal (birth) family members, to relieve boredom, and to gain relief from dissatisfaction with married life in general. The most commonly cited reason was abuse at the hands of husbands or in-laws, indicating that abuse was even more common than intolerable cruelty divorce cases suggest. The adjustments in domestic relationships required by a wife's relocation demanded great interpersonal skills on the wife's part, varied with the politics within the husband's family, and could result in terrible discord.[6] As the cases examined below demonstrate, young, newly married women were particularly vulnerable to abuse (perhaps until they gave birth to a son) and faced numerous difficulties after moving into their husbands' or in-laws' homes. The court records make clear that a common source of anguish for young brides and discord among young couples was the woman's continued attachment to and interactions with her natal family despite social proscriptions against such behaviors.

BETWEEN NATAL AND MARITAL RESIDENCES

Typically, husbands of runaway wives first searched for their wives in the homes of relatives, friends, and neighbors. If their wives refused to return with them after the application of familial pressure, husbands turned to the courts to obtain cohabitation orders. The cases they brought offer insight into the men's understanding of marriage, their expectations, and their disappointments. Husbands expressed several forms of objections to their wives' attempts at escaping from cohabitation. Some of them considered their abandonment as a moral outrage, their wives having disregarded the "wifely way" (*fudao*) and failing to abide by the Three Obediences and Four Virtues (*sancong side*). Many husbands explained their unwillingness to give up cohabitation even when they acknowledged that they lived in conflict because they considered the perpetuation of a marriage an economic obligation (for more on these considerations see chapter 5 on divorce in this era) and a lifelong commitment that permanently redefined the wife's loyalties to his home and family.

Indeed, in an ideal marriage, a woman shifted her primary allegiance from her natal family to her marital family on her wedding day or even earlier. This shift in priorities was symbolized by numerous customs and rituals like the spilling of water during the marriage ceremony, which illustrated her distancing from her natal family; the placement of her husband's surname before her own surname, which demonstrated the priority accorded to a woman's marital family; changes in a wife's mourning obligations that made her obligations to her in-laws greater than her obligations to her natal family members; and of course the physical move from her natal family home to her marital family home. Despite popular beliefs about the impermanence of a daughter's ties to her natal family, scholarship on the late imperial period demonstrates that a daughter's ties to her natal family were never really severed, even after marriage. Past scholarship tells us that there was a substantial gap between the official discourse of impermanence and the actual practice of enduring natal family ties. Scholarship on contemporary China also points to the importance of enduring natal family ties (Judd 1989). This gap indicates the limitations of official prescriptions regarding a woman's relationship with her natal family. Indeed in the late imperial period, the proper boundaries of a woman's relationship with her natal family lacked specificity and were subject to variations in interpretation. During the Song Dynasty, there were many cases of husbands who encouraged wives to maintain natal family ties and even resided with their wives' natal kin on an "ad hoc" and "temporary" basis (Bossler 2000). Natal families, moreover, could serve as a daughter's allies when confronted with a "disgraceful matter," though they could just as often serve as her husband's allies (Theiss 2004). In the absence of clear and definite norms for how a woman should behave toward her natal family and what kind of attitude she should hold toward them, social practice played an important role. What constituted a proper relationship between a wife and her natal family at times had to be negotiated on an individual basis. The lack of clarity concerning a married woman's obligations toward her natal family versus her marital family contributed to making this a controversial social issue throughout the late imperial period and early twentieth century.

Enduring natal families played an important role in Republican cohabitation cases, complicating the question of marital residence for young couples and offering wives an alternative residence. A traditional refuge for women (especially newer, younger wives) in times of marital crisis was to return to one's natal family (*hui niangjia*). These visits were generally temporary, lasting a few days, after which they were accompanied back to their marital families. As long as it was on a temporary basis, the practice of taking refuge with one's natal family seems to have been quite common and more or less acceptable. Disputes arose when wives prolonged their stays, defying their husbands' wishes for them to return. Some of the cohabitation disputes also arose when a wife's natal family wanted to persuade her husband to move in with them rather than reside with his family.

In many ways, cohabitation suits represented a type of litigation that was unique to Republican China. Like judicial separations, cohabitation suits arguably exemplified the transitional nature of the 1930s and 1940s. The prevalence of cohabitation suits in the 1930s and 1940s (as indicated in chapter 4, cohabitation suits were frequently litigated marital disputes, trailing only divorce and engagement dissolution) suggests tensions surrounding marital residence were particularly fraught and that married couples did not conform to strict practices of residing with the husband's kin group (patrilocality). Cohabitation lawsuits helped to resolve the awkward tensions that arose between traditional and modern expectations of marriage, between patrilineal and conjugal notions of marriage, between a wife's natal and marital families, and over patrilocal, matrilocal, or neolocal marriage, without necessarily resorting to divorce. The weakening of patrilineal ideology under the law corresponded to changing patterns of marital residence, with numerous challenges to patrilocality. Legal and social changes facilitated a wife's enduring natal family ties as kinship relations were reclassified to place natal family relations on par with marital family ties, traditional natal family visits continued and gained judicial recognition through court-mediated settlements, and urbanization increased the proximity between wives and their natal family homes. The rise of neolocality, moreover, especially in urban areas, and other tensions over marital residence were also at the root of many of the domestic disputes that ended up as cohabitation lawsuits in Republican courts.

"SHE WAS RATHER FOND OF GLAMOUR": LIU XUESHAN VS. MRS. LIU-YANG

The mounting desirability of neolocality, at least in urban areas, is evident in the case of Liu Xueshan vs. Mrs. Liu-Yang. Toward the end of 1945, Liu Xueshan, twenty, petitioned the Beijing District Court to order his wife, Mrs. Liu-Yang, also twenty, to return to live with him. His suit named Mrs. Liu-Yang and her older brother, Yang Wensheng, as codefendants (Mr. Liu requested that her brother carry out the responsibility of turning her over). According to Mr. Liu's petition, the couple had been married two years at the instigation of their parents and a matchmaker. He characterized Mrs. Liu-Yang as being rather fond of glamour and therefore not content with the simplicity of country living (the couple resided in the outskirts of Beijing). Mr. Liu complained that she preferred to spend her days riding a bicycle around the city for enjoyment. When even slightly admonished, Mrs. Liu-Yang would threaten to commit suicide and made a habit of taking shelter at her mother's house. Mr. Liu calculated that in the two years they had been married, she had already run away three times and jumped into a well once.

Despite this pattern of behavior, Mr. Liu claimed to have been shocked to discover that on the night of July 9, 1945, Mrs. Liu-Yang absconded with a bundle of clothing. Before setting off, she made sure to deflate his bicycle tires, keeping him from immediately giving chase. Mr. Liu eventually managed to pursue his runaway wife, first heading to her mother's house, but en route he recalled that Mrs. Liu-Yang often visited her maternal aunt's house as well and so went there instead. Although at first he was told his wife was not on the premises, the persistent Mr. Liu was able to discover that indeed his wife was being hidden by her aunt. He filed a report against the aunt at the police substation, and once the police were involved they compelled Mrs. Liu-Yang's relatives to reveal her location. Once Mrs. Liu-Yang was brought before them, the police had no recourse other than to urge her to rejoin her husband. At first she absolutely refused, but then she promised to return to her husband in three to five days. Her brother, Mr. Yang, promised to accompany her back. Five days passed, and Mrs. Liu-Yang still had not returned. Finally, Mr. Liu filed suit under the law requiring husbands and wives to live together.[7]

The court accepted his petition and summoned the parties to an interrogation and mediation session. In one of the courtroom sessions, Mrs. Liu-Yang explained that she was more than willing to live with her husband, but could not live with his parents because she feared they would abuse her.[8] Under the court's guidance, the parties reached a settlement. The settlement permitted Mrs. Liu-Yang to continue to reside at her natal home for a period of three months, after which she agreed to resume her residency with her husband and marital family. Over the next few months, Mr. Liu tried several times to persuade her to return in accordance with the settlement agreement; he even filed another lawsuit to try to enforce the terms of the agreement, all without success. Mrs. Liu-Yang engaged with the law only indirectly. She ran away from home, to be sure, but she did not petition the court for a separation or divorce. It was her husband who initiated legal proceedings against her, going to court because he especially objected to the turmoil his family experienced because of Mrs. Liu-Yang's frequent natal family visits.[9] Eventually, Mr. Liu seemed to give up. The couple divorced by mutual consent after private mediation, transforming the usually temporary nature of the natal family refuge into a permanent breakup.[10]

As was common in cohabitation cases, the young wife complained about abuse from her in-laws. In this case, she feared the sexual predations of her father-in-law. On one occasion she chose to recount to the court how he tied her to a table and beat her when she refused his advances.[11] Mrs. Liu-Yang, however, was not a hapless, foot-bound, housebound woman. In fact, her husband described how she rode around the suburbs of Beijing on a bicycle and seemed to travel freely between her natal and marital homes. To escape her vulnerability as a daughter-in-law, Mrs. Liu-Yang wanted her husband to set up a small nuclear family apart from his parents and other family members. In a small family, Mrs. Liu-Yang could primarily occupy the role of wife rather than daughter-in-law.

As a young bride who had not yet given birth to a male heir, Mrs. Liu-Yang occupied a vulnerable position in her marital home, and she was subjected to a number of abuses. Her residential, emotional, and financial survival seemingly depended upon her ability to maintain her ties to her natal family and return frequently to visit them. Clearly, her natal ties remained important, even if her mother and brother beseeched her to return to her marital home. Perhaps the fact that Mrs. Liu-Yang resided in the suburbs of Beijing, close to the city's communication and transportation networks, facilitated the escape she made from her marital home. Proximity to her natal family helped her preserve those ties. In a marriage where a wife was sent to live in a faraway village, escape would have been more difficult and natal family bonds harder to maintain.

Like many other cohabitation and marriage-related suits, the outcome of the case was a court-mediated settlement. The Beijing District Court brought the parties together and reached a settlement that permitted Mrs. Liu-Yang to continue living at her natal family home for a period of three months. The judge who conducted the mediation acted to persuade her family members to intervene, chiding her brother for not resolving the situation and instructing him to try to patch things up as well.[12] The court-mediated agreement held that Mrs. Liu-Yang should return to live with her husband. But a key component of that agreement was the right Mrs. Liu-Yang won to live with her mother for three months. Perhaps a little time spent away from her husband and in-laws was all Mrs. Liu-Yang was looking for when she ran away. Her persistence in running away from her husband on several past occasions, her refusal to comply with the police command to return, and her overall determination not to reside with her in-laws must have made it apparent to the judge that any order for her to return immediately would not have been observed. The court seemingly reasoned that three months of separation would provide time to let tempers subside and allow the parties to recover their conjugal feelings (*ganqing huifu*) or establish a permanent state of separation as the case turned out.[13]

"A THORN IN HER FLESH": LI SHULIN VS. LI ZHAO XIUPIN

Like the couple in the case above, twenty-two-year-old Li Shulin and nineteen-year-old Li Zhao Xiupin also argued over the wife's natal family visits and attempts by the wife and her parents to persuade her husband to move in together with them. These types of requests for relocating a couple's place of residence were both possible escape routes from abusive living situations and also sources of marital discord in and of themselves. The story from this case also reveals the anxieties of a mother fearing the loss of her son's allegiance and affection and the older woman's resolve to prevent his separation from the patrilocal unit by, in the words of the new wife, the "cunning and fierce"[14] woman who never allowed him "to get along with me"[15] and treated her son's new bride as a "thorn in her flesh."[16]

In 1946, Li Shulin earned a steady income as an iron factory worker in Beijing. The couple had no children. His wife of less than one year, Li Zhao Xiupin, suffered daily abuse and humiliation from her mother-in-law. The various cruelties she recounted began shortly after she moved into the Li household. According to Mrs. Li-Zhao's testimony, from the first day of her married life,

> There has been no affection or any conjugal bond of which to speak of. Father-in-law and Mother-in-law are both of abnormal dispositions. They praise their son and disdain his wife. Sometimes [Father-in-law and Mother-in-law] collude to spread perverted rumors about dubious relations between Father-in-law and Daughter-in-law . . . . Furthermore, everyday at dinner, they refuse to provide enough to eat. Even more, during every meal [Mother-in-law] throws food on the floor and makes [Daughter-in-law] pick it up and eat it. She disregards hygiene. And [Mother-in-law] is always inciting her son to tyrannize [Daughter-in-law], and to hit [Daughter-in-law] for no reason. So the environment is really too difficult to endure . . . . [M]other and son have used various tortures to cause me mental distress and have made me lose any enjoyment in life . . . [17]

Unable to bear this torrent of abuse, initially Mrs. Li-Zhao tried to convince her husband that they would be better off if they moved in with her parents. Mr. Li interpreted her request as a demand that he "break off relations" (*tuoli guanxi*) with his own family. But he absolutely refused to abandon his parents and siblings, who relied upon his wages for their sole means of livelihood. The conflict over where to live was at the root of their discord from the point of view of Mr. Li. He explained that in 1945 when the young couple married,

> After the wedding, conjugal feelings could be called "harmonious (*hemu*)." Abruptly, however, the defendant [Mrs. Li-Zhao] requested that I break off relations with my family, follow her and move in with her [natal] family, and use my monthly salary to pay her entire family's expenses. I refused. My parents need me to provide for them too. If I followed her plan, my whole family would certainly have to worry about suffering from cold and hunger.[18]

Mr. Li's obligations to his family apparently trumped any obligations to provide a harmonious home life for his new bride. The situation for the wife went from bad to worse. Mr. Li was so enraged by the mere suggestion of moving away from his family that he attacked the young woman with a pair of shears, stabbing her multiple times. The attack required ten days of hospitalization for Mrs. Li-Zhao. When she was well enough to move about, she did not return to her husband's family home, taking refuge instead with her natal family for the next several months. Mr. Li paid them several visits trying to convince her to return, but she refused. Eventually he brought suit, citing the cohabitation obligation. At first he won a judgment from the Beijing District Court. Ultimately this judgment was overturned when his wife was able to present convincing evidence of abuse to the Hebei Superior Court.

This case demonstrates the resilience of Mrs. Li-Zhao's natal family ties. In the retelling of her story, we see that members of her natal family continued to be regularly involved in her life and to support her efforts to escape an unhappy marriage. For example, her younger sister was apparently present during the stabbing incident and was able to find help during the attack, probably saving her life. Mrs. Li-Zhao's father testified on her behalf during a court hearing. The case also reveals the efforts of the mother-in-law to resist the intrusion of new marital norms. Having lived to see her grown son get married, elevating her own standing in the family, the mother-in-law probably experienced the challenge to patrilocality as a personal assault. Her plight illustrates the coexistence of different notions of marriage (not just between men and women, but among women depending on generation and social status) and the complicated motivations fueling litigations in this era.

Upon receipt of Mr. Li's petition and Mrs. Li-Zhao's countersuit, the Beijing District Court summoned both parties to a mediation session and conducted an oral interrogation. In this first level of litigation husband and wife appeared alone and represented themselves before the court. The judge used the first session to verify that Mr. Li and Mrs. Li-Zhao were in fact legally married (they were) and to ascertain the demands and positions of each party (Mr. Li requested the return of Mrs. Li-Zhao, Mrs. Li-Zhao refused; Mrs. Li-Zhao countersued for divorce, Mr. Li opposed divorce). During the second session, the judge inquired into the circumstances surrounding Mrs. Li-Zhao's final departure from her marital home. He asked Mr. Li why his wife had left him. Mr. Li replied, "Because we fought. She was wounded and went to the hospital to receive treatment. I went to get her, but she wouldn't return." The court then turned to Mrs. Li-Zhao and asked her why she requested divorce. Mrs. Li-Zhao replied, "He abused me."[19] To this reply, the judge asked what proof she had. Mrs. Li-Zhao stated that there was a witness, but she could not produce the person. The judge then asked whether a conviction had been obtained in the criminal suit stemming from the stabbing incident, but there was no conviction. Taking a recess to consider the facts, the judge returned to rule in favor of Mr. Li. The court determined that Mrs. Li-Zhao did not produce solid evidence to prove the alleged abuse.

The court pointed to the fact that even the procurator's disposition submitted by the wife concluded that no criminal charges should be filed against Mr. Li. Therefore, the court saw no grounds for divorce. Since Mr. Li and Mrs. Li-Zhao were found to be legally married, they both had the obligation, ruled the court, to live together. Hence, Mrs. Li-Zhao was ordered to return to Mr. Li.[20]

Mrs. Li-Zhao declined to accept the district court's cohabitation judgment and just a week later submitted an appeal to the Hebei Superior Court. Mrs. Li-Zhao had clearly paid attention to the reasoning used by the court in its decision to reject her case. Having learned important lessons about what the court considered compelling evidence, she apparently resolved to come better prepared for the next round of litigation. Although Mrs. Li-Zhao again claimed that conjugal relations were "abominable," her appeal focused on the serious harm she suffered when her husband stabbed her rather than on the insults of her "fierce" mother-in-law. In her appeal, the stabbing incident, which previously garnered only a brief one-sentence mention in her testimony to the lower court, evolved into a dramatic recounting of an attempted murder intended to draw attention to the mortal danger she faced at the hands of her husband:

> This year on the twelfth day of the first lunar month, [Mr. Li] lured me into . . . an abandoned house, where he furiously stabbed my head, my left hand, my back, and other places with a pair of shears. I am weak and fragile and could not defend myself in time and I had no strength to fight back. So the wounds I suffered were very serious injuries. At the time I fainted for a long spell. The medical report by the Beijing No. 4 Hospital (where I stayed for over 10 days) can serve as proof. If one was to say this was not premeditated murder, who would believe it?[21]

Mrs. Li-Zhao in her appeal complained about the dual cruelty she suffered. The combination of physical brutality from her husband and mental anguish and damage to her reputation caused by her mother-in-law compelled Mrs. Li-Zhao to run away and countersue for divorce.[22] Her accusations focused on the mental anguish inflicted by her mother-in-law and the great emotional distress she suffered because of her mother-in-law. And this time, her father came to her aid and represented her before the Hebei Superior Court.[23] During the oral interrogation before the court, her father confirmed the details of the stabbing incident. Her father also testified that relations between Mr. Li and Mrs. Li-Zhao were not all that bad and he also blamed the mother-in-law, concluding that in his opinion "It was her mother-in-law that forced them apart."[24]

Just to be sure, Mrs. Li-Zhao filed yet another supplemental appeal summarizing (in even more dramatic terms) the treatment she received as a wife and daughter-in-law in the Li family.

> [Mr. Li] regarded me just like a slave. For every trifling reason, he would either call me names or beat me. I usually just bore this—there was nothing I could do. Every time I saw his face, it was like seeing the King of Hell, I trembled with fear . . . As for his mother, her abuse was extreme. Everyday she went out of her way to find some fault with me. When she opened her mouth, out came an insult. When she raised her hand, down came a blow. Mr. Li and his mother believed that the situation was as it should be, abuse that a daughter-in-law ought to endure.[25]

Again, she saw her plight as one meted out by both her husband and her mother-in-law.

Mrs. Li-Zhao's greater sophistication in pleading her case upon appeal paid off. In a reversal of the lower court's cohabitation order, the three-judge panel of the Hebei Superior Court announced that:

> It is known that for married couples eking out an existence, to quarrel and bicker is, as a matter of course, impossible to avoid. However, to wield a knife and cruelly wound [a spouse] in reality makes it difficult to maintain the safety of cohabitation. In this case [Mr. Li] took a pair of shears and plunged them into various places on [Mrs. Li-Zhao's] body and head. Not only the vivid words of [Mrs. Li-Zhao], but also the bloody clothing, the written diagnosis of the Beijing No. 4 Hospital, the disciplinary report of this Court's procurator all substantiate this [incident]. And [Mr. Li] does not deny it.

Having been provided with compelling evidence of extreme abuse and mortal danger of cohabitation, the court assessed the emotional state of the Li's marriage: "Conjugal feelings in this case have already reached the condition where 'affections are irreparably severed (*enduan yijue zhi jing*).' If we try to forcibly maintain them, not only will the happiness of the family not be promoted, but the well-being of the individual will also be difficult to protect."[26]

The court reached its decision to grant a divorce in the interests of both the Li family's welfare (without explicitly mentioning the mother-in-law of whom Mrs. Li-Zhao had complained so vociferously) and Mrs. Li-Zhao's individual safety. In its opinion, the judges abided by the legislators' notion of marriage as a union of two individuals and emphasized the severed bonds between the marital couple, not the wife's disputes with her in-laws. The court, therefore, took into account the happiness of the family, the condition of the conjugal unit, and the well-being of the individuals.

As shown in the litigation overview chapter, the right to appeal a marital dispute was an important Republican-era development. Courts could disagree with each other over how to judge a marital dispute, revealing a state that was "uneven," "multiple," and "disaggregated" (Theiss 2004, Xu 2008, and Diamant 2000). Here, the trial court rejected Mrs. Li-Zhao's suit for divorce (not enough evidence of intolerable cruelty), and granted Mr. Li's request for cohabitation. Upon appeal, the Hebei Superior Court reversed the judgment. It agreed with the Beijing District Court that domestic quarrels were a matter of course, and to be expected. But it determined that wielding a sharp object in order to wound a spouse exceeded the bounds of ordinary abuse.

A few additional factors serve to explain the different outcomes in the lower and superior courts. First, the representation by Mrs. Li-Zhao's father in the second case probably strengthened her case. She was no longer just the helpless daughter-in-law of the Li family, but could count on the support of her natal Zhao family to take on her husband. Her father's testimony confirmed almost everything that she had said before. And his appearance on her behalf must have reinforced the notion that Mrs. Li-Zhao would be welcomed back at her natal home in the event of divorce. Natal families did not always serve as a wife's allies, but when they did, they could be very helpful. Another possible reason for her success in the second round of litigation was the additional evidence she presented to verify the seriousness of the stabbing incident. In addition to the procurator's report given to the first court, Mrs. Li-Zhao submitted the physical evidence of her bloody clothing and the hospital's written diagnosis detailing the injuries she suffered. Thus, Mrs. Li-Zhao demonstrated significant resourcefulness in securing her father's support, procuring physical and written evidence, and skillfully portraying the abuses she suffered. In the end, a wife who had simply taken temporary leave of her marital family survived two rounds of litigation and managed to secure a judgment for judicial divorce.

WANG QIAN FENGYIN'S THREE ANNUAL VISITS: NEGOTIATING NATAL FAMILY VISITS

Wives faced conflicting pressures to live with their in-laws even as they desired to return to their natal families. By running away, the young wife in the case of Wang Jun vs. Wang Qian Fengyin was able to negotiate the right to visit her parents on a regular basis. Married in 1943, Wang Jun, twenty-three, a Beijing policeman, and his wife, Wang Qian Fengyin, twenty-one, frequently quarreled over her visits to her parents. She spent so much time at her parents' house that Wang Jun had to petition the Beijing District Court in 1945 to seek her return under the cohabitation obligation. The court, acting as a mediator in the case, helped the parties reach a settlement. The wife's elderly parents agreed to return their daughter to her husband on the condition that he promise never to abuse her and that he allow her to make at least three annual visits to her natal family. The parties agreed that the wife was entitled to three annual visits with her natal family during the traditional holidays as well as in cases of emergency or for other important matters (weddings, funerals, etc.). The husband also pledged not to abuse his wife. In return, the wife promised not to make visits to her parents beyond the terms of the agreement.[27]

The terms of this settlement spelled out the parameters under which the wife could visit her natal family. The court-mediated settlement seemed to fill the void in formal regulation over a wife's natal family ties that were typically fueling numerous disputes between the couple. The wife and her parents thus managed to negotiate a court-endorsed agreement that guaranteed the preservation of their natal family ties. In mediating this case and the case above, the state intervened to define what a married woman could expect with respect to her relationship with her natal family. It is important to note that the state did not simply order wives to reside with their husbands but rather, in the course of court-mediated settlements and judgments, courts acknowledged that married women were entitled to spend time living with their natal families. By establishing these parameters, the state validated the customary expectation that a married woman was entitled to certain "visitation" rights with her natal family.

RUNNING AWAY AS A PRELUDE TO DIVORCE

Settlements could result in divorce as well as in reconciliation. A wife's running away could sometimes serve as the first step toward divorce as in the case of Gu Wenxiu vs. Mrs. Gu-Zhang. In 1942, Gu Wenxiu sued his wife Mrs. Gu-Zhang for cohabitation after she left him. The Beijing District Court mediated an agreement in which Mr. Gu agreed to withdraw his cohabitation suit and to divorce Mrs. Gu-Zhang. Mrs. Gu-Zhang agreed to give Mr. Gu 100 *yuan* to find another wife.[28] By insisting that Mr. Gu receive 100 *yuan* as a condition of the divorce, the court explicitly recognized and addressed the socioeconomic difficulties men faced with respect to marriage. The terms of the settlement enabled Mrs. Gu-Zhang to exercise her right to divorce and, by supplying Mr. Gu with 100 *yuan,* which he might be able to use to remarry, to prevent turning her former husband into a permanent bachelor (and thus a potential problem for social stability). Thus for a woman with some means, perhaps funds from her still-close natal family or savings from paid wage labor in an urban area, divorce became a real possibility.

CONCLUSION

Cohabitation lawsuits stand out as the one category of marital litigation in which more husbands than wives consistently initiated legal proceedings. In English and Chinese, "cohabitation" is an awkward term which generally connotes couples living together without the benefit (or detriment) of being married. In Republican China, however, cohabitation had a different meaning for married couples and was one of the most common categories of civil litigation. The Republican Civil Code's cohabitation obligation required husbands and wives to live together, and cohabitation lawsuits involved informal separations or other violations of this duty. In contrast to the wives who sought a formal divorce, judicial separation, or annulment in the other litigation chapters, the wives discussed in this chapter took the informal, extrajudicial action of running away. Runaway wives did not initially turn to the courts for help in resolving their marital conflicts; they simply sought refuge away from the marital homes, usually with the help of their natal families, relatives, or neighbors. It was their husbands who initiated legal proceedings in these cases, enlisting the courts' help in securing the return of their wives by bringing suit under the cohabitation provision. Once sued by their husbands and thus brought into the formal legal system, though, wives could and did countersue for separation or divorce.

The commonplace nature of these cohabitation suits reflected tensions over changing patterns of marital residence in society in general. Modern ideas of marriage stressed the principle of gender equality. Expectations regarding the balance between a wife's duties and loyalties to her marital family versus her natal family were becoming less one-sided. Expectations over how a wife should respond to abusive situations in her marital home shifted from dutiful tolerance to opening up possibilities for alternative arrangements like separation or divorce. The situation surrounding the question of marital residence was more complicated than the custom of patrilocality would suggest. Expectations regarding marital residence also shifted as increased urbanization combined with the weakening of patriarchal ideology under the law undermined the norm of patrilocality. Legal recognition accorded to natal families, the proximity of natal families to married daughters, and women's traditional recourse of seeking refuge in their natal families challenged patrilocality. In an era of changing social norms, the law's abandonment of patrilineal ideology coupled with the persistence of patrilocal marriage generated various tensions and drove a sharp rise in the number of lawsuits over these matters.

Records of cohabitation suits from the 1930s and the 1940s demonstrate that a married woman's relationship to her natal family continued to be a controversial social issue, though the contours of the balance between her natal and marital families were changing. In determining what the proper boundaries were for this relationship, married women's own behavior helped shape the norms in significant ways. In litigation over the cohabitation obligation, married women most often pressed for a closer relationship with their natal families, one that included extended natal family visits on a more frequent basis. Their behavior points toward a shift in popular understandings of the nature and character of the married woman–natal family relationship. With the waning of patrilineal norms in other areas and the equalization of marital and affinal ties in the area of kinship classification under the law, the status of natal families was elevated formally, which may have bolstered closer natal family ties at the level of social practice as well.

NOTES

1. Spence 1978; Qing Code, statute 116, Xue 1970, vol. 2, 311–312; Bernhardt 1994, 190; Huang 2001, 161.

2. Hebei 634-1-321 Beijing District Court decision dated 1936.7.16 and Hebei Superior Court decision dated 1936.12.12.

3. Civil Code, Article 972; Hu 1931, 4.

4. Civil Code, Article 1001: Husband and wife are under mutual obligation to live together, unless for good reason they cannot live together. Article 1002: A wife takes the domicile of the husband as her domicile; a "chui-fu [*zhuifu*]" takes the domicile of the wife as his domicile. These two articles remained in force in the Republic of China, Taiwan, until 1998 when Article 1002 was revised to allow both spouses the right to determine their place of residence. See Chen Qiyan, et al., eds. 1999, 132, n. 72.

In the interim period from the fall of the Qing to the promulgation and enactment of the Republican Civil Code in 1929–1931, the Daliyuan (the former Supreme Court) introduced the notion that husbands and wives had a civil obligation to live together. See *Daliyuan panjueli quanshu* 1972, 211, 228-229: 1920 ruling no. 201; 1920 ruling no. 59; 1919 ruling no. 1354; 1918 ruling no.1009; 1918 ruling no. 863; 1916 ruling no. 444. Although the Daliyuan's vision of marriage centered upon the individual husband and wife, it still afforded substantial rights to the husband's parents and grandparents. For instance, a husband had the right to determine the residence of the married couple, but with the significant limitation that his decision had to meet the approval of his grandparents and parents. See *Daliyuan panjueli quanshu* 1972, 211 and 228: 1917 ruling no. 259 (a husband needs parental permission to reside apart from his parents or grandparents); 1918 ruling no. 303 (a wife cannot compel a husband to live apart from her father-in-law); 1918 ruling no. 1418 (a wife needs the permission of her mother-in-law to live apart from her).

5. Hu 1931, 160, 163–164, quoting the Daliyuan 1916, explanation no. 510. See also Huang 2001, 195–196. For examples of disobedient wives who perplexed local judges who appealed to the Ministry of Justice for guidance, see *Sifayuan jieshi huibian,* vol. 1, 89, no. 93 (1929), vol. 2, 84–85, no. 476 (1931). The case files contain numerous examples of husbands who had to repeatedly sue for cohabitation and enforcement to try to persuade their wives to return to them.

6. Excellent descriptions of the domestic quarrels that arise in these situations are found in the anthropological accounts by Wolf 1968, 1972, and 1974.

7. Beijing J65-22-13 petition dated 1945.11.18. The address listed on the petition indicated that the Lius resided in the western suburbs of Beijing. See also the related case Beijing J65-22-643.

8. Beijing J65-22-13 oral interrogation dated 1946.1.11.

9. Beijing J65-22-13 petition dated 1945.11.18.

10. Beijing J65-22-643 oral interrogation dated 1946.5.4.

11. Beijing J65-22-13 oral interrogation dated 1946.1.11.

12. Beijing J65-22-13 oral interrogation dated 1946.1.11.

13. Beijing J65-22-643 oral interrogation dated 1946.5.4.

14. Beijing J65-22-880(2) supplemental appeal dated 1946.7.17.

15. Beijing J65-22-880(2) oral argument dated 1946.9.23.

16. Beijing J65-22-880(2) supplemental appeal dated 1946.7.17.

17. Beijing J65-22-880(1) answer dated 1946.5.14.

18. Beijing J65-22-880(1) petition dated 1946.4.13.

19. Beijing J65-22-880(1) oral argument dated 1946.5.24.

20. Beijing J65-22-880(1) Beijing District Court decision dated 1946.5.24.
21. Beijing J65-22-880(2) appeal to the Hebei Superior Court dated 1946.6.2.
22. Beijing J65-22-880(2) supplemental appeal dated 1946.7.17.
23. Beijing J65-22-880(2) certificate of representation filed on 1946.7.17.
24. Beijing J65-22-880(2) oral interrogation dated 1946.7.22.
25. Beijing J65-22-880(2) supplemental petition dated 1946.9.24.
26. Beijing J65-22-880(2) Hebei Superior Court decision dated 1946.9.27.
27. Beijing J65-21-1542 settlement dated 1945.1.22.
28. Beijing J65-19-378 mediated agreement dated 1942.4.18.

Chapter Seven

Bourgeois Affairs

Separation and Support Litigation and Injury to Reputation

The marriage principles embodied in Nationalist family law made possible a greater range of choices for wives confronted with their husbands' infidelities. With the overall shift from patrilineal notions of marriage to conjugal ones, a husband's violation of the mutual duty of sexual fidelity came to represent a grave threat to the harmony of the conjugal bond. As noted in chapter 5, a husband's adultery or taking of a concubine constituted a ground for divorce under the Republican Civil Code. A wife could not obtain a divorce, however, if her husband had taken the concubine before the effective date of the Republican Civil Code (May 5, 1931) or if more than six months had passed since she discovered her husband's adultery. After a successful campaign by women's groups to revise the criminal code in 1934–1935, a husband's adultery could lead to criminal prosecution.[1] For a wife who did not wish to or could not divorce or pursue a criminal prosecution, however, the remedy of judicial separation (*bieju*) presented an attractive option.[2] A judicial separation enabled a wife who had suffered the indignity of a husband's infidelity to escape from having to live under the same roof as her husband and his concubine. Filing suit for a separation, moreover, enabled a wife to avoid the stigma of divorce. Even though attitudes toward divorce had changed considerably by the 1930s, divorce was still generally regarded as undesirable. A judicial separation allowed a wife to maintain her married status in name and in law but excused her from the duty of living with her husband and freed her of messy domestic entanglements. If a wife could prove that a separation was justified, she might also obtain a financial award that would enable her to maintain a separate livelihood. With her living expenses taken care of, she would not be pressed to remarry like the wives who divorced without any provision for their maintenance. The very possibility of such legally sanctioned alternative living arrangements illustrate how shifting popular expectations of a mutual rather than one-sided duty of sexual fidelity within marriage shaped laws in the Republican era.

The lawsuits for marital separation examined in this chapter are striking examples of how Nationalist family law intersected with changing expectations of marriage. We see how pockets of bourgeois[3] wife-litigants shaped Nationalist family law to serve their interests by successfully carving out a novel remedy for marital separation and support for living expenses (*shenghuofei*) when confronted by a husband's sexual infidelity. During the 1930s and 1940s, the simultaneous waning of the late imperial cult of chastity and the rise of sexual fidelity as a mutual duty reinforced one another to alter attitudes toward cheating husbands. Wives were still expected to remain faithful to their husbands. Husbands, though, were now held to similar standards (at least in law if not in practice) and in the Republican era, a husband's taking of a concubine triggered far more social disapproval than in the late imperial era and much more serious legal consequences. The remedy of judicial separation and support served as a legal mechanism for the defense of a wife's individual interests against those of the patrilineal family. It represented a fitting option for the highly transitional 1930s and 1940s, especially for bourgeois women who created the remedy through their lawsuits, and who by doing so created a viable, socially acceptable exit option from an unhappy marriage.

A BOURGEOIS REMEDY

Unlike husband-initiated cohabitation suits under Article 1001 (discussed in chapter 6), wife-initiated separation suits under the same article tended to involve litigants from a higher socioeconomic stratum and invoked questions of support for living expenses that cohabitation suits did not. In theory a judicial separation could be granted to a wife of any class for any number of reasons. Most of the successful separation suits, though, involved similar scenarios with a bourgeois wife suing for separation after her husband had taken in a concubine, had an extramarital affair, or committed some other violation of the mutual duty of sexual fidelity. Separation lawsuits brought by wives for other reasons, such as intolerable cruelty, met with much less litigation success. In cases involving cruelty rather than adultery, wives faced the initial difficult of convincing the courts that they had a legitimate reason for living apart, before the court ever reached the question of support. Although bourgeois women obtained litigation success only on a limited basis, they did achieve novel and quite remarkable legal victories when the courts adjudicating their marital disputes recognized the harm done to them by their husbands' infidelities and sanctioned alternative living arrangements for them that included provisions for their living expenses.

The bourgeois nature of successful judicial separation suits was not all that surprising given the many complications that accompanied this type of litigation. The litigation process and procedures for judicial separation and support suits differed from other marital disputes that did not involve monetary claims. All petitioners were responsible for court fees (*caipan fei, an fei, shenpan feiyong*), but these fees varied depending upon whether mediation or adjudication was requested and also whether a suit involved a monetary claim. In general, court fees were higher for separation suits because they included claims for support and living expenses. Courts calculated such fees on a graduated basis.[4] If petitioners failed to submit their court fees in a timely manner, their petitions and appeals were dismissed. Separation suits in which the proper court fees were not paid in full could be dismissed on procedural grounds. Dismissal on the ground of nonpayment of fees was not uncommon, especially at the appeals level, which required appellants to submit another round of court fees.[5] At the appeals level, litigants were also subject to additional procedural rules that restricted the types of cases that could be appealed. Civil Procedure Code Article 463-1, for example, stipulated that a case had to involve at least 500 *yuan* for it to be heard by the Supreme Court. To keep up with inflationary trends, the minimum amount was raised to 100,000 *yuan* after 1945. Separation and support appeals that did not meet the minimum amount requirement were dismissed upon procedural grounds.[6] Bourgeois women were certainly in a better position with respect to these financial requirements, but that was not the only reason for their judicial success. Their social status too helped them gain more recognition and accommodation in the judicial system than women of other classes.

The question of which groups of women or men benefited the most from marriage law reform often hinged on the type of marital dispute at issue. Certain types of litigation benefited certain groups more than others. Although the case records do not provide complete information about the class background of litigants, the cover sheet and other court documents often impart evidence of occupation and other indications of economic status. In separation and support cases, more details about the litigants' social class emerge from the amount of money in contention, the amount and type of property possessed by the litigants (land, houses, clothing, jewelry, furniture, bedding, etc.), and the estimates of monthly living expenses. Lawsuits for judicial separation and support mostly benefited urban bourgeois women, women who hailed from natal families of some means and were married to husbands whose social standing was middle to upper class. Litigation outcomes suggest that judges accorded more sympathy to bourgeois women than any other group of female litigants in marital disputes. Social status and a wife's social reputation mattered in important ways in the adjudication process.

The section below discusses a number of successful separation and support cases through case narratives, followed by case analysis. Despite the numerous legal and procedural hurdles that stood in the way of the successful pursuit of a judicial separation, some wife-litigants managed to overcome them all and prevail in their lawsuits. Most of the cases that fit within the category of successful separation and support suits corresponded to a specific, narrow fact pattern. These suits generally involved wives from middle- to upper-class backgrounds and wealthy husbands who engaged in some form of sexual marital misconduct that courts interpreted to have irreparably damaged the wife's reputation as well as the conjugal bond. The outcomes suggest that class background mattered just as much if not more than gender in marital litigation.

MRS. LING-FAN: MENTAL DISTRESS CAUSED BY HER HUSBAND'S TAKING OF A CONCUBINE

The following case offers a glimpse into how separation and support for living expenses litigation proceeded when the parties were members of a wealthy landlord family. The case ran the full course of litigation with a trial court decision, an appeal to the superior court, and a final appeal to the Supreme Court. The case originated in the city of Suzhou in 1933 when Ling Fan Jingzhao, twenty-seven, sued her husband, Ling Guangyan, twenty-nine, and his father, sixty-two, for marital separation, living expenses, and compensation after her husband took in a concubine. At the trial court level, the Wu County District Court, which had jurisdiction over Suzhou where the parties resided, granted Mrs. Ling-Fan a separation and support in the form of the earnings from 250 *mu* of land. Neither Mrs. Ling-Fan nor Mr. Ling was satisfied with the decision, and both launched appeals to the Jiangsu Superior Court. At the appeals level the case again involved three parties: Mr. Ling, Mr. Ling's father, and Mrs. Ling-Fan. The parties, moreover, engaged a total of five lawyers, two for Mr. Ling, one for Mr. Ling's father, and two for Mrs. Ling-Fan. The outcome of the case would affect a substantial amount of money and property.

Upon appeal, the opening issue concerned the disposition of the marriage. The parties pressed opposing claims. While Mrs. Ling-Fan wanted a separation, Mr. Ling insisted on cohabitation. Since the law obligated a husband and wife to live together, the burden of proof rested on Mrs. Ling-Fan to establish a legitimate reason for living apart from her husband. Her main argument underscored the harm (mental distress and injury to reputation) she had suffered when her husband acquired a concubine in 1932. Mr. Ling, however, painted a much rosier picture of their marriage than Mrs. Ling-Fan. According to Mr. Ling, feelings between the couple were "exceptionally good (*qinggan jihao*)." He admitted he took in a concubine in 1932. But he argued that before he undertook such action, he had obtained his wife's consent. As proof, he described how on the day his concubine entered their home the concubine ritually bowed to Mrs. Ling-Fan. In addition, on his father's birthday in 1933, Mr. Ling, along with his wife and concubine, offered their congratulations to his father together. He argued that these actions on Mrs. Ling-Fan's part constituted her tacit approval of the concubine. Nevertheless, the court did not believe that Mrs. Ling-Fan's behavior constituted consent. It noted that her silence alone was not enough to prove that she agreed to her husband's taking in a concubine.[7]

Once the superior court determined that a legitimate reason for separation existed, the court turned to the monetary issues. At the level below, the district court had awarded Mrs. Ling-Fan earnings from 250 *mu* of land in support. Mr. Ling vehemently rejected this award. He argued that in 1929 his father had appointed him to manage a large amount of the family's landholdings. But before the commencement of the current litigation, his father had rescinded the arrangement and taken the land back. So that land did not even legally belong to him, maintained Mr. Ling. On the other side, Mrs. Ling maintained that she deserved payment of 65 *yuan* a month for as long as the litigation ran its course, in addition to the earnings from property already awarded to her by the lower court. The Jiangsu Superior Court held that, in general, after separation for a legitimate reason a wife's living and household expenses should be paid by her husband. In calculating the amount of money appropriate in this particular case, the court first evaluated the cost of living in Suzhou, which it deemed "not too expensive." In light of this evaluation, the court deemed Mrs. Ling-Fan's request for 65 *yuan* a month excessive. The court settled on 40 *yuan* a month as the appropriate amount of living expenses. Mr. Ling hence had to set aside 40 *yuan* a month in cash for spousal support during the months that the parties had engaged in litigation. The court also ordered Mr. Ling to cede the earnings from 160 *mu* of land (90 *mu* less than the lower court had ordered) to Mrs. Ling-Fan. This grant of the earnings from 160 *mu* represented Mrs. Ling-Fan's source of livelihood after the separation.[8]

An additional matter before the court involved Mrs. Ling-Fan's demands for compensation. This issue was not essential to determining the separation and support decision, but it does show interesting details about the couple's lifestyle. First she wished to be compensated for a set of padauk furniture and appliances that she owned before Mr. Ling pawned the items for 560 *yuan*. The lower court reasoned that if he could pawn them for 560 *yuan*, then the items must be worth at least 1,000 *yuan*. Unfortunately for Mrs. Ling-Fan, the superior court did not agree with the lower court's ruling. The superior court was persuaded by Mr. Ling's argument that he should not have to pay 1,000 *yuan* in compensation when he could simply redeem the items. Thus, it ruled that Mr. Ling could simply return the items. The second group of items for which Mrs. Ling-Fan sought compensation were two gold bracelets, valued she said at 1,200 *yuan*. The lower court had only awarded her 600 *yuan* in compensation for these items. Mr. Ling contended upon appeal that Mrs. Ling-Fan agreed to spend the money they obtained for the bracelets on a jaunt to Shanghai. Having agreed to part with the bracelets, she should not be entitled to any compensation. The superior court agreed with Mr. Ling. It held that Mrs. Ling-Fan could not ask for compensation for items with which she had willingly parted, and it vacated the lower court's order for Mr. Ling to pay 600 *yuan*. Mrs. Ling-Fan had still more luxurious articles for which she demanded compensation. The third set of items was her clothing that was stored in one of the wooden trunks Mr. Ling had pawned, as well as a *qipao* she had made out of fabric from India, which Mr. Ling took away from her to give to his concubine. The value of the clothing according to Mrs. Ling-Fan amounted to 500 *yuan*. The lower court had rejected this claim for lack of proof, and the superior court did the same. Last among her demands for compensation, Mrs. Ling-Fan brought up a 750 *yuan* loan Mr. Ling had supposedly borrowed from her father. The large sum of the loan hinted at the wealth that Mrs. Ling-Fan's natal family possessed. To have granted such a large loan they must have been of considerable financial standing. Mr. Ling argued that since his creditor was her father, not her, she was not entitled to sue for payment. Besides, he claimed that he had already repaid 500 *yuan* of the loan. But both the lower and superior courts held for Mrs. Ling-Fan and ordered him to repay the loan to her (perhaps on the theory that the money was transferred from her father to her, then to Mr. Ling).

The court then turned its attention to Mr. Ling's father. Mrs. Ling-Fan argued that he should be held jointly liable for his son's financial obligations. But the superior court held that a father-in-law was not responsible for his daughter-in-law's living expenses after she had moved out of his house. Mr. Ling's father was implicated, however, in the scheme to rescind his gift of land to Mr. Ling. The court saw through the ruse and held that Mr. Ling was the owner of the land, even though Mr. Ling's father had not registered the gift of land in accordance with the provisions of the new civil code. Since the gift was made in 1929, before the effective date of the civil code, the requirement that land transfers be registered did not apply, reasoned the court. Still not satisfied, Mr. Ling and his father appealed again, this time to the Supreme Court. The Supreme Court's 1934 decision dismissed both appeals and affirmed the Jiangsu Superior Court's rulings in all respects.

Mrs. Ling-Fan was one of the select wives who ultimately managed to successfully pursue her petition for a separation, living expenses, and compensation. She overcame her husband and father-in-law's objections and persuaded judges from three different levels of the judicial system of the merits of her claim for separation. In addition, the judges unanimously endorsed her right to a substantial amount of support, though the courts disagreed as to the exact appropriate amount. Mrs. Ling-Fan's litigation success depended upon a number of factors. First, her and her husband's class background shaped the dynamics of the case. She could afford to hire lawyers to represent her through several rounds of litigation, and her natal family was quite wealthy as evidenced by her father's loan to her husband of a substantial amount of money as well as her expensive clothing, jewelry, and furniture. Her husband, moreover, was also without question wealthy enough to provide for her living expenses. Like his father before him, her husband possessed considerable landholdings.

Mrs. Ling-Fan's reaction to her husband's taking of a concubine illustrates an important difference between late imperial and Nationalist family law. Like wives in the past, Mrs. Ling-Fan described being upset by her husband's action. Unlike wives in the past, though, Mrs. Ling-Fan was so bothered that she arranged to live apart from her husband (most likely she returned to her natal family) and turned to the courts to validate her move and obtain financial support. Perhaps wives in the past left their marital homes when their husbands took in concubines too, but they must have done so on an informal basis; they did not turn to the courts to affirm their right to live apart and seek judicial orders for financial support. In this case we see judicial intervention to protect a wife who chose to leave a husband who had taken a concubine. The wife turned to the courts to grant her a separation and living expenses, and the courts responded by affirming her right to live apart and to be supported financially in doing so.

Interestingly enough, her lawyers chose to describe the injury to Mrs. Ling-Fan caused by her husband's taking a concubine as "mental distress" and "injury to reputation" rather than adultery. Perhaps her lawyers' framing of her injury in these terms reflected the unique status of concubinage during the Nationalist era. The law did not regard it as bigamy in part because the ceremony for welcoming a concubine into the family differed from the ceremony for a bride. Concubinage also differed in nature from an adulterous affair. Though the legal status of concubinage would seem to meet the criteria for adultery, the definition of adultery under Nationalist law was certainly controversial at least before the amendment to the criminal code in 1935. Mrs. Ling-Fan's lawsuit originated in 1933 before this revision took effect. By 1933 social attitudes toward concubinage had certainly changed, with attitudes turning increasingly strong against the practice. Mrs. Ling-Fan's case seems to indicate that for women of her class and age (twenty-seven in 1933) it was no longer automatically acceptable for husbands to behave in this way. No parties disputed the fact that Mr. Ling had taken a concubine and that by doing so, he committed a morally offensive act that damaged both his marital relationship and Mrs. Ling-Fan's status and reputation.

Judicial sympathy and intervention in marital disputes during the Nationalist era seemed particularly acute and attentive when protecting the reputations of middle- to upper-class women, who were more likely to have husbands who could afford the pleasures of concubines and mistresses. These types of sexual transgressions most often led to the imposition of judicial separation and support judgments. This pattern will become clearer below when we discuss cases that involved women from a lower social class. Judges seemed to approach the marital disputes of women without much social standing in less helpful and protective ways.

For Mr. Ling, his act of taking in a concubine in 1932 had very different legal consequences than in earlier time periods. In the late imperial era, a wife would most likely have to accept her husband's taking of a concubine even if this upset her. In stark contrast, under Republican law he lost the company of his wife and incurred the obligation to provide for her financial support, though, in 1933, he was still not subject to criminal prosecution for his act (unlike after 1950).

The courts' decisions regarding Mr. Ling's father also underscore the important shift in Nationalist law from patrilineal notions of marriage and property to conjugal and individual notions. It was the conjugal unit rather than the patriline that was of primary legal significance. For instance, Mr. Ling's father did not bear legal responsibility for his daughter-in-law's living expenses; her husband alone bore that responsibility. Also, Mr. Ling's father's gift to Mr. Ling made the property Mr. Ling's individual property (subject to the conjugal unit's status rather than the patriline's claims), even as Mr. Ling tried to take refuge in the assertion that the property belonged to his father. Mrs. Ling-Fan's natal family, moreover, was not held legally responsible for her well-being even though it appeared that they could afford to provide for her living expenses in case her husband could not.

"AN UPRIGHT WOMAN": ZHENG HUAJIN VS. ZHENG ZHULING

The next case also illustrates the award of a judicial separation and living expenses to a bourgeois woman whose husband violated the mutual duty of sexual fidelity. The young daughter of a wealthy family, Zheng Huajin, twenty-one, married Zheng Zhuling, twenty-nine, in 1931.[9] Three years later, in 1934, she discovered that her husband was in love with another woman. So she sued for marital separation and support in the Zhenjiang District Court. In November 1934, the district court granted her petition for separation and awarded her 600 *yuan* in living expenses. Both Mrs. Zheng and Mr.

Zheng were dissatisfied with the decision, and both brought appeals before the Jiangsu Superior Court. Mr. Zheng appealed both the separation and the award of living expenses, whereas Mrs. Zheng only appealed for a larger sum of living expenses.

Before the Jiangsu Superior Court considered the monetary issue, it had to determine whether or not Mrs. Zheng was entitled to a separation in the first place. She based her claim on the grounds that Mr. Zheng had secretly engaged in an affair with another woman. Her main proof of the affair was a photograph of her husband in an embrace with the other woman. The woman in the photograph, countered Mr. Zheng, was simply the nurse who took care of him in the hospital before he was ever married, not his mistress. As for the alleged affair, he admitted it had taken place but claimed it had ended a while ago. The superior court rebuffed Mr. Zheng's explanation. It held that the photograph revealed a particularly close relationship between Mr. Zheng and the woman in the photo. The close embrace captured in the photograph and the inscription on the back that clearly identified Mr. Zheng and his mistress constituted sufficient proof that he had committed adultery. Since adultery represented a legitimate reason for marital separation, Mrs. Zheng was therefore entitled to a separation.[10]

As for the issue of living expenses, Mr. Zheng contested the lower court's award of 600 *yuan* and denied that he should have to pay any amount for his wife's living expenses. First, he described how he was financially strapped. He claimed that his father passed away in 1932, leaving behind his elderly mother and eight brothers. The family property had already been divided. He admitted that he had inherited the Baosheng silverware shop and 1,200 *yuan* worth of silver. But he claimed that the shop was now shut down. He had lost his job some time back and was now in financial straits. Moreover, he maintained that Mrs. Zheng was capable of supporting herself. She was young, physically strong, and had her own considerable financial holdings. Her parents, besides, were very wealthy (*po fuyou*). So even if the couple separated, Mr. Zheng should not be responsible for her living expenses. Therefore, there was no need for him to pay her 600 *yuan*.[11]

Mrs. Zheng argued the contrary: that the award of 600 *yuan* in living expenses was not enough to support her. In its place, she wanted 3,840 *yuan*, which she calculated on the basis of eight *yuan* a month over a period of forty years. In support of her demand, she argued that her husband was very wealthy. He possessed "extremely plentiful family property, of which he was inordinately conceited, and recklessly spent his money." As for herself, she had no financial prospects. She was "an upright woman, residing in an out of the way place, where the present circumstances do not provide opportunities for women's employment. And without the ability to engage in handicrafts, on the basis of what financial resources could [she] support [herself]?" True, she did possess some property. But her husband was more than capable of providing for her living expenses, and he had inherited property. His plot to shirk this responsibility clearly proved his lack of decency.[12]

Accordingly, the Jiangsu Superior Court tackled the decision of whether to award no money as Mr. Zheng requested, 3,840 *yuan* as Mrs. Zheng requested, or 600 *yuan* as the lower court ruled. The superior court rejected both Mr. and Mrs. Zheng's appeals and concurred with the figure of 600 *yuan* chosen by the lower court. The superior court first considered Mrs. Zheng's circumstances. Most importantly, the superior court cited the fact that Mrs. Zheng was only a "weak girl" (*ruo nǘzi*) (age twenty-one), who would be unable to support herself after the separation. The court did not take up Mr. Zheng's assertion that Mrs. Zheng had the youth, strength, and financial resources to provide for herself. Next, the court evaluated Mr. Zheng's circumstances. It found that the 1,200 *yuan* that Mr. Zheng had inherited demonstrated that he had ready money and would be able to make a one-time payment of 600 *yuan*.

Similar to Mrs. Ling-Fan in the case above, Mrs. Zheng hailed from a well-to-do natal family and was married to a man of some wealth. Both women were also similar in age, in their twenties, and married for about three years, with no children. When they discovered that their husbands had violated the duty of sexual fidelity, they chose to leave their marital homes and live apart. This fact pattern was repeated in several other successful support suits.[13] By the 1930s, the injury caused by a husband's infidelity (whether in the form of taking a concubine or having an affair) apparently outweighed the stigma of a judicial separation.

Nationalist courts had the most sympathy for these types of women and intervened most strongly to protect their interests. The courts granted them permission to live apart from their husbands (presumably for the rest of their lives) and ordered their husbands to hand over substantial sums of money and property to cover the expenses for their wives to live apart (the 600 *yuan* granted to Mrs. Zheng was exactly half of her husband's 1,200 *yuan* inheritance). The courts, moreover, focused upon the conjugal bond and the damage that had been done to this bond as well as the damage to the wife's reputation. Courts dismissed the husbands' various claims that their property belonged to their fathers, that their wives' families could support them, or that the husbands needed the property to support their own parents or other family members. Here, courts clearly privileged the wife's position within the conjugal unit over the interests of the husband's patriline.

For Mr. Zheng, the outcome of the case underscored that as a husband he no longer enjoyed great latitude under the law to have sexual relations outside of his marriage. The consequences of doing so could be quite serious. In his case, he lost the company of his wife and had to give up half his inheritance for his affair.

"A WOMAN FROM A TRADITIONAL-STYLE FAMILY:" SUN FAN TONGHUA VS. SUN JUNFU

In 1945, Sun Fan Tonghua, fifty-nine, originally from Zhejiang Province, but residing in Beijing at the time she initiated her lawsuit, demanded a judicial separation and living expenses from her husband, Sun Junfu, fifty-eight, also originally from Zhejiang.[14] Mrs. Sun-Fan belonged to a wealthy, landowning family and lived among many servants. She was represented by a lawyer in all of her legal proceedings. And she maintained a strong network of family members and friends who supported her case against her husband.

Her plea for a marital separation before the Beijing District Court included a demand for a one-time monetary payment of 8,000,000 *yuan*, title to the house where she currently resided, and payment of her litigation fees and expenses.[15] To support her claim, she provided the court with a highly damaging description of her husband. In order to solidify her position as the "innocent" party, Mrs. Sun-Fan illustrated the various ways in which she had been victimized by her husband. According to her petition, Mr. Sun did not engage in a proper occupation, relied solely upon collecting the rents on property he inherited, and lived in a very dissolute manner. Moreover, since taking in a concubine fourteen years ago in 1930, Mr. Sun regarded his legitimate wife as a thorn in his eye and did not take care of her at all. In fact, he had tried to beat her to death and get rid of her. Recently, he had tried to force her to divorce. In 1944 he even sent three men to beat her into submission and force her to move out. On top of that, he had filed a lawsuit against her, falsely accusing her of theft.

As for her own disposition, Mrs. Sun-Fan maintained that she was born into a traditional-style family and therefore learned to be very tolerant of her husband. For many years she endured his abuses and never argued with him. Now she was approaching sixty, she had given birth to a son now grown and married, and she had never behaved in a way that would warrant a divorce. Because of her husband's false accusations, pressures to divorce, and increasing abusiveness, she could no longer tolerate living with him. She wanted a separation. But after separation, she had no way to support herself and nowhere to live, so she requested support for her living expenses in the form of money and property. Given the poverty of her current circumstances, moreover, she was not able to pay the litigation fees, calculated at 61,740 *yuan*, and instead submitted a request for the waiver or deferral of the fees, signed by eight friends and relatives who supported her lawsuit (one listed his occupation as a lawyer and another listed his occupation as a clerk at the Supreme Court).[16]

The Beijing District Court conducted three interrogation sessions in this case. The focus of the inquiry in each was the circumstances of Mr. Sun's taking in a concubine. Mrs. Sun-Fan's lawyer, her maidservant, her son, her daughter-in-law, and her maternal relative were all asked when Mr. Sun obtained his concubine, where the concubine resided, and whether they had met the concubine in person. It turned out that he had taken in the concubine fourteen years ago.

The outcome of the case was a court-mediated settlement in which Mrs. Sun-Fan and Mr. Sun agreed to divorce. In return for her agreement to divorce, Mrs. Sun-Fan received a payment of 4,000,000 *yuan* (half of her original request, a tidy sum even accounting for inflation) from Mr. Sun and was allowed to assume title over the house where she currently resided (real property to provide security in case of further inflation).

In terms of outcomes, Mrs. Sun-Fan was relatively successful. Even though she had resisted a divorce, she agreed to it in the end in exchange for money and property that would allow her to live independently. Most women did not possess Mrs. Sun-Fan's standing or the resources at Mrs. Sun-Fan's disposal. Mrs. Sun-Fan was not the typical wife-litigant. She was significantly older (her age may have made her a more sympathetic litigant). She came from a privileged class background. Her natal family possessed wealth, land, and servants. She could afford to hire an attorney to pursue her case. She had friends and relatives support her claim as witnesses. Her husband was also of the landlord class. Like the other successful separation and support litigants, Mrs. Sun-Fan, moreover, benefited from the shift from patrilineal to conjugal notions of marriage in at least a couple of ways. First, she was not forced to return to live with her natal family as might have been the case under late imperial law. Instead she was given money and shelter that would allow her to live independently after the dissolution of her marriage. Second, her husband's taking of a concubine, which would have been tolerated under the patrilineal family system, was now interpreted by the courts as an injury to the conjugal unit.

The court's devotion to investigating the circumstances of Mr. Sun's taking of a concubine, to the exclusion of Mrs. Sun-Fan's other claims of abuse and false accusations, suggests the significance of Mr. Sun's sexual transgression and the relative insignificance of his other transgressions accorded by the court. Proof of his sexual transgression effectively enhanced Mrs. Sun-Fan's moral standing as an innocent party before the court and increased the degree of guilt placed upon Mr. Sun. The judicial investigation of this matter also seems contrary to the weight of the law, which required a woman to raise any objections she might have to her husband's taking a concubine within six months of his doing so (if she had wanted a divorce, which was not her goal). Here, Mrs. Sun-Fan admitted that the events took place fourteen years ago. For women like Mrs. Sun-Fan whose husbands took in concubines before the effective date of the Republican Civil Code, judicial separation offered a means to escape the more stringent requirement that the wife object to her husband's taking of a concubine within six months.

For upper-class litigants, moreover, sexual transgressions involved an additional consideration, the consideration of social status and reputation. It was not simply a case of a husband's infidelity harming the conjugal bond; his sexual transgression harmed Mrs. Sun-Fan's personal status and reputation as well. Class or at least social status once more played an important role in the outcome of this lawsuit.

BEIJING DISTRICT COURT SEPARATION SUITS FROM 1945

Those wives who won judicial separations and provisions for living expenses were mostly from well-off backgrounds and represented a fortunate minority. The next section discusses a group of separation and support suits filed at the Beijing District Court in 1945 by women from lower- to middle-class backgrounds. These cases represent a sample of the separation and support suits filed in Beijing that year; they do not represent all the separation suits from that year. Most of these litigants failed to obtain an outright judgment in their favor, a common outcome in separation suits. Of the six cases, not a single one resulted in an outright successful judgment for separation and support. Unlike the successful wife-litigants discussed in the section above who charged their husbands with sexual infidelity, most of these Beijing suits involved the more common charges of physical and verbal abuse by husbands and in-laws. Below are short summaries of the cases.

Mrs. Zhao-Liu

In May 1945, Mrs. Zhao-Liu, twenty, filed a petition against her husband, Zhao Deshou, thirty-one, for a separation and 2,400 *yuan* a month in living expenses. The couple married the year before through a matchmaker arrangement. Mrs. Zhao-Liu complained of physical and verbal abuse by her mother-in-law and sister-in-law, which drove her to leave her marital home. Ten days after the date of her petition, the court called the parties to an interrogation hearing. At the hearing, Mrs. Zhao-Liu changed her mind about the lawsuit and agreed to return to live with her husband and his family. The court drew up a settlement agreement in which Mrs. Zhao-Liu expressed her willingness to return to cohabit with her husband, and both parties agreed to pay their own litigation fees.[17]

Mrs. Zhao-Liu was married for less than a year when she brought her lawsuit before the court. Although she eventually agreed to drop her suit, she had taken the formal step of bringing her domestic disputes before the state authorities. She complained to the court about her in-laws and their treatment of her, perhaps thinking that some sort of judicial intervention might bring about a positive change in her living situation. Perhaps she calculated that her mother-in-law and sister-in-law would not be so bold in their abuse after she had alerted the authorities to their behavior.

Mrs. Fu-Xing

In February 1945, Mrs. Fu-Xing, twenty-one, along with her mother Mrs. Xing-Hai, forty-one, filed a petition against her husband, Fu Jianzhong, twenty-three. The couple married in 1942 through a matchmaker arrangement and had two daughters. Mrs. Fu-Xing requested a judicial separation and asked the court to order her husband to find a place to live for her and her two young daughters. She listed her occupation as jobless and her husband's occupation as service worker in the examination department at the Tongren Hospital. Mrs. Fu-Xing's mother represented her in all court proceedings because Mrs. Fu-Xing was too ill to appear in court herself, having become incapacitated after being beaten by her mother-in-law and sister-in-law during her second pregnancy.[18]

Mrs. Fu-Xing's petition complained about abuse by her husband, her mother-in-law, and her sister-in-law. She explained that they felt free to frequently insult and abuse her because of the poverty of Mrs. Fu-Xing's natal family. Mrs. Fu-Xing's natal family was of the petty merchant class (*xiaobenying*) and could not afford to give her a fancy dowry. She was an old-fashioned country girl (*xiangxia nü*) with no education, and her husband's family thought that she was not good enough for them (*menhu budang*). Her mother- and sister-in-law's abuse was extreme; they beat and scolded her for no good reason. Her husband sided with his mother and sister and also abused Mrs. Fu-Xing, unleashing unspeakable cruelties. One day, her husband accompanied a pregnant Mrs. Fu-Xing and their daughter back to her natal family's home, saying he would pick her up in a few days. He never came back. Mrs. Fu-Xing's mother (who was also pregnant) tried several times to bring Mrs. Fu-Xing back to her marital family, but each time the mother-in-law and sister-in-law met them in their courtyard and would beat her daughter. The last time, when Mrs. Fu-Xing and Mrs. Fu-Xing's mother were both late in their pregnancies, the mother-in-law and sister-in-law assaulted both of them. Mrs. Fu-Xing fell ill for a long period of time. It had been over six months since Mrs. Fu-Xing was returned to her natal family. Mrs. Fu-Xing's mother explained that there were ten members of her family, and they could not afford to continue supporting their married daughter and two granddaughters (during her stay with her natal family Mrs. Fu-Xing had given birth to another girl).

Mrs. Fu-Xing's husband sided with his mother and sister against his wife in their domestic quarrels. According to her husband, the couple's disputes originated with his wife's pestering of him to move out of his family's home. She wanted the couple to establish a separate residence, but he refused. He was a filial son who wanted to remain living with his parents and siblings. He offered 80 *jin* of food and grains to Mrs. Fu-Xing's father, if his wife would agree to a divorce. Fed up with his wife's pleas to set up a separate household, he escorted his pregnant wife and young daughter back to her natal home and never returned to pick them up. He also filed a separate, criminal complaint against his wife and her mother stemming from a physical altercation between the women. The case file does not contain a record of any decision in this case. Perhaps the parties reached some sort of private mediation to divorce along the terms suggested by the husband.

The court documents and letters filed in this case describing Mrs. Fu-Xing's complaints of abuse, beatings, and scoldings underscore the complexity of domestic relations otherwise disguised by the commonplace nature of these complaints. The two families, the Fus and the Xings, were entangled in a stormy relationship, trading insults and injuries. Social class prejudice seemed to be at the root of the abusive treatment directed at Mrs. Fu-Xing. The marriage failed to pair a bride and groom from "matching doors." The records make it clear that the husband's family's social class was far above that of the wife's. The wife's family described themselves as "petty merchants" who could only afford a meager dowry for their daughter, making her subject to insult and ridicule. Mrs. Fu-Xing also described herself as an uneducated "country bumpkin," while we know that her husband was employed at a city hospital.

Like the cohabitation suits examined in chapter 6, separation suits pointed to the importance of physical residence and the complexities of human relations generated by living together under one roof. These lawsuits allow a glimpse into the marital tensions between the traditional practice of patrilocality, where a wife lived with her husband's family, the traditional alternative of periodic visits to a wife's natal family home, and modern ideas of neolocality. Mrs. Fu-Xing apparently tried to convince her husband to set up an independent household for the two of them and their daughters. She did not enjoying living with her abusive mother- and sister-in-law, who showered her with contempt. While she was pregnant, her husband returned her and her daughter to her natal family and never went back to pick them up. She was shuttled back and forth a number of times, as her mother tried to return her to her husband's family.

Mrs. Fu-Xing's natal family was itself a complicated unit. The family was a large one with ten members ranging from an elderly grandmother to two new infants. The family struggled to support its existing members, and it could not afford to take on the support of Mrs. Fu-Xing and her two young daughters. Mrs. Fu-Xing's mother, Mrs. Xing-Hai (who was also pregnant), attempted numerous times to escort her pregnant daughter back to her marital home. Each time, she witnessed her daughter being refused entry and enduring beating by the mother- and sister-in-law. Usually, she let them beat her daughter, thinking that a beating might help their anger to subside. The last time, though, she could not stand watching them beat her heavily pregnant daughter and intervened to stop them (even though she herself was pregnant).

Mrs. Bi-Shi

In July 1945, Mrs. Bi-Shi, eighteen, sued for a separation and support of 6,000 *yuan* a month. She married only the year before. Her main complaint was about an abusive father-in-law. Her father-in-law, forty-seven, a peasant, filed a response describing the various faults of his daughter-in-law. The court did not record a decision in this case perhaps because the parties were able to resolve their differences. This case seems similar to Mrs. Zhao-Liu's above, involving a newly married couple whose disputes seemed to indicate the difficulties of living with an extended family rather than serious problems with the conjugal relationship itself. Judicial intervention took the form of encouraging the parties to resolve their difficulties through mediation.[19]

Mrs. Bai-Liu

In July 1945, Mrs. Bai-Liu, twenty-four, sued for a separation and support of 10,000 *yuan* a month. She accused her husband, Bai Dashen, forty-one, of not only having a mistress, but also of moving his mistress into their home to eat and sleep together. The couple married in 1938 through a matchmaker and had one daughter. At first her husband treated her well. Then as time passed, he grew to disdain her and became more and more abusive. Mrs. Bai-Liu claimed that she was from a good family and therefore tried to tolerate and be patient with her husband, but as she thought about her and her daughter's situation she realized that this abuse could go on for a very long time. She would most likely be abused to death. Therefore, she appealed to the court to try to mediate an agreement by which she could live apart from her husband and his mistress. If mediation did not work, then she wanted a formal adjudication. Less than a month after the date of her original petition, Mrs. Bai-Liu changed her mind and submitted another petition to the court to withdraw her original petition. According to this petition, the parties reached a settlement through private mediation. The terms were not revealed, but the parties were no longer in dispute. In the event that an out-of-court settlement had not been reached, Mrs. Bai-Lu, like the bourgeois women whose husbands took in concubines, would likely have had a strong case for a judicial separation, assuming she could prove her allegations about her husband's mistress.[20]

Mrs. Guan-Wang

In June 1945, Mrs. Guan-Wang, thirty-six, filed a petition against her husband Guan Huating, for a separation and support of 3,000 *yuan* a month. The couple married in 1939 through a matchmaker arrangement. Her husband had two children from a previous marriage and owned 60 to 70 *mu* of land. Mrs. Guan-Wang cared for these children and helped her husband with the household business. After marriage she discovered that her husband cavorted with "bad people" (*feiren*). Her husband spoiled his children and told them to abuse Mrs. Guan-Wang. At first she tolerated the abuse, hoping that her husband would change. But the abuse got worse, with her husband eventually kicking her out of the house and even refusing to let her gather up her clothing and belongings. Mrs. Guan-Wang finally reached the point where she had no choice but to request a separation. She was living with relatives who could not afford to support her. A month later, the Beijing District Court dismissed Mrs. Guan-Wang's petition, stating that she had not filed the fees of 122.5 *yuan*.[21]

Had Mrs. Guan-Wang submitted the required court fees, the outcome of her case is difficult to discern. Her husband owned a substantial amount of land, but her allegations against him were primarily about his abusive behavior, rather than sexual misconduct. In general, abuse allegations were harder to prove, and she most likely would have had a difficult time convincing the court to grant a separation and support.

Mrs. Shi-Zhang

In September 1945, Mrs. Shi-Zhang, thirty-three, a widow, petitioned for separation and support against Shi Yuzheng, her father-in-law, and Shi Yunting, her stepson. She specifically requested court mediation. She accused them of cruelty that made living together intolerable. Mrs. Shi-Zhang requested 8 *mu* of the family's total landholding of 24 *mu* and two rooms of the family's six-room house. Mrs. Shi-Zhang married in 1932, and the couple got along well. Her husband had a son, eleven, from a previous marriage. Unfortunately, Mrs. Shi-Zhang's husband fell ill and passed away in 1934. At the time of his death, Mrs. Shi-Zhang was pregnant and later gave birth to a daughter. As a widow, Mrs. Shi-Zhang continued to live with her daughter, stepson, and father-in-law. When her stepson was seventeen, she arranged for him to be married. Shortly after the stepson married, he and his new wife began to abuse Mrs. Shi-Zhang and her daughter. Mrs. Shi-Zhang's father-in-law, too, favored his grandson's wife over his deceased son's widow and grew abusive toward Mrs. Shi-Zhang.[22]

The case file does not contain a decision by the court. The facts in this case highlight the complications of the marriage and property law in force during the Republican period. The widow's case draws attention to just some of the legal uncertainties that arose during this transitional period. First of all, Mrs. Shi-Zhang brought her separation and support petition against her father-in-law and stepson. The provision for judicial separation, however, only applied to a wife and husband. So if her suit was formally adjudicated it most likely would have been dismissed on this ground. However, her petition stressed that she sought the court's help through mediation. In mediation, the more technical legal requirements of standing could be set aside. The remedy of judicial separation and support, in this case, served Mrs. Shi-Zhang's interest in getting her a hearing before the court.

Her property claims were even more complicated than the question of who could be sued under the judicial separation provision. Ownership of the family's twenty-four *mu* of land and six-room house was the key issue to be determined. One interpretation favored the father-in-law. If the property was regarded as his individual property, he could not be compelled by the court to hand over any part of it to his widowed daughter-in-law. Another interpretation was more favorable to Mrs. Shi-Zhang. If the property was determined to belong to her deceased husband, then Mrs. Shi-Zhang and her daughter were entitled to a substantial part of it. The property would have been divided among her and her husband's children on an equal basis at the time of his death (assuming he did not have a will). Hence, Mrs. Shi-Zhang, her daughter, and her stepson would have each inherited eight *mu* of land and two rooms of the house.[23] Mediation by the court seemed to represent the best way of resolving this dispute in a fair and just manner, allowing the court to take into account the competing property law regimes. This case also reveals the irony of a judicial "separation," which would leave Mrs. Shi-Zhang and her daughter still living in the same house as her father-in-law and stepson, though with separate arrangements for living and cooking.[24]

CONCLUSION

Bourgeois women who successfully sued for judicial separation and support pushed the litigation envelope to create a legal remedy that served their individual interests. On the one hand, the findings in this chapter confirm past interpretations that charge Nationalist family law with catering to the interests of the well-to-do, like the CCP claim that Nationalist law was "bourgeois" law. Bourgeois women certainly possessed advantages in the litigation process and were afforded a stake in their social status that was not granted to other types of women. On the other hand, the findings give rise to an interpretation of the GMD state as quite paternalistic, with judges who extended significant sympathy and protection to wives, defending wives' individual interests against those of the patrilineal family.

Nationalist family law endowed the husband-wife relationship with greater legal significance, and Nationalist courts took the mutual duty of sexual fidelity between husband and wife quite seriously. Instead of an outright ban on concubinage, like the one adopted under the Communist Marriage Law, one way Nationalist family law treated the problem was through the intermediate option of judicial separation and support for living expenses. The separation suits demonstrate a distinct change in the law's stance on concubinage and other forms of adultery and bear witness to the great lengths to which Republican courts went to protect the bourgeois women whose husbands violated their duty of sexual fidelity. Nationalist-era separation suits also reveal certain cracks in the belief in the permanency of marriage. Marriage was still viewed as a permanent, lifelong union. However, when the marriage failed to meet the parties' expectations in certain ways, there were viable alternative arrangements. Without requiring women to divorce, judicial separation could free a wife from the entanglements of having to live with a husband and his concubine or to endure extramarital affairs. Such arrangements were perhaps not new, but the courts' sanctioning of these alternatives through judgments for judicial separation and support was a novel and transitory development in urban pockets of Repulican China.

NOTES

1. One of the most successful campaigns of the Chinese women's movement in the 1920s and 1930s targeted the practice of concubinage. The eradication of concubinage was an issue that affected bourgeois women more than others to be sure, and these women spearheaded the attack on concubinage in social attitudes and legal consequences. Lisa Tran has discussed the changing sexual morality reflected in Republican law, especially the changing legal status of concubines (2009).

2. The same provision under which husbands sued when their wives refused to live with them (examined in the cohabitation chapter), Republican Civil Code Article 1001, which obliged a husband and wife to live together unless a legitimate reason prevented them from doing so, also served as the basis for litigation initiated by wives for a judicial separation.

3. Although the term *bourgeois* carries ideological weight and may be an imperfect fit for describing Chinese society, the term is nonetheless useful for describing women of a certain wealth and status.

4. As a point of comparison, Kathryn Bernhardt has estimated that for divorce suits from the 1940s, only 19 percent of female plaintiffs requested alimony (1994, 198).
There was some relief available to a woman could not afford to pay the fees. She could submit an additional petition to request the waiver of the fees on the grounds of impoverishment. See Beijing J65-22-1714.

5. See Supreme Court 16-2956-7 (1942) for an example of a suit dismissed because of the nonpayment of fees and Supreme Court 16-495-2 (1943) and Supreme Court 16-495-6 (1940) for separation and living expenses appeals dismissed because of unpaid fees.

6. See Supreme Court 16-2956-3 (1938) and Supreme Court 16-2956-11 (1937) for suits originating from Hunan Province that were dismissed because the amounts in contention did not meet the minimum requirements. Separation and support appeals that failed to meet the minimum amount requirement from Yunnan Province include Supreme Court 16-495-16 (1948) and Supreme Court 16-495-28 (1941).

7. Jiangsu 1047-38-1443 decision dated 1934.5.25.

8. Jiangsu 1047-38-1443 decision dated 1934.5.25. The court reached the figure of 160 *mu* by taking the estimate that one *mu* of land yielded three *yuan* profit per year. Thus the yearly profits from 160 *mu* totaled 480 *yuan*, which covered the 40 *yuan* per month the court ordered Mr. Ling to pay to Mrs. Ling-Fan.

9. Jiangsu 1047-38-1472 decision dated 1935.3.4.

10. Jiangsu 1047-38-1472 decision dated 1935.3.4.

11. Jiangsu 1047-38-1472 decision dated 1935.3.4.

12. Jiangsu 1047-38-1472 decision dated 1935.3.4.

13. For other cases involving similar fact patterns, see Jiangsu 1047-38-1869 (an adulterous husband ordered to pay a monetary award of 400 *yuan* in 1930); Supreme Court 16-2702-3 (husband who took a concubine was ordered to pay 15,000 *yuan* in support to his wife, decision dated 1945.9.17); Supreme Court 16-495-11 (1943 case in which a wife from Yunnan Province received a separation and 3,000 *yuan* in household living expenses after her husband took in a concubine); and Supreme Court 16-1319-2 (1938 case in which the Supreme Court upheld the Fujian Superior Court's granting of living expenses for a wife whose husband committed adultery).

14. Beijing J65-22-1714 petition dated 1945.5.25.

15. On currency inflation see Pepper 1999, 95–96; Eastman 1984; Yick 1995; and Chang 1958.

16. Beijing J65-22-1714 request to defer fees dated 1945.8.2.

17. Beijing J65-21-1241 petition, dated 1945.5.25 and settlement agreement dated 1945.6.5.

18. Beijing J65-21-1641 petition dated 1945.2.5.

19. Beijing J65-21-1875 petition dated 1945.7.17 and response dated 1945.7.25.

20. Beijing J65-21-1878 petitions dated 1945.7.2 and 1945.7.30.

21. Beijing J65-21-2045 petition dated 1945.6.7.

22. Beijing J65-22-1572 petition dated 1945.9.4.

23. Bernhardt 1999, 118–121, examines the property and inheritance rights of widows under the Republican Civil Code.

24. In my research, I also came across fourteen cases from a different province that confirm the findings of this chapter (Supreme Court 16-495). An examination of fourteen separation and support appeals filed with the Supreme Court between the years 1937 and 1948 that originated from Yunnan Province, which included Kunming, a major wartime city for the GMD, reveals the different treatment courts at all three levels of the judicial system accorded to the social damage and individual mental distress caused by a husband's taking of a concubine compared to the distress and hurt generated by a wife's living with an abusive husband or abusive in-laws. In the latter cases, judicial intervention was not as forthcoming or accommodating. A wife who was unhappy about the physical and verbal abuse she received at her marital home had a much harder time convincing the judges to intervene on her behalf than a wife who suffered the social humiliation of a husband taking in a concubine or engaging in an extramarital affair. Judges treated physical and verbal abuse as an ordinary part of married life that had to be more or less tolerated. Judges rejected the notion that physical abuse was significant enough to merit a judicial separation judgment.

Of the fourteen separation and support cases included in this Supreme Court file, the only ones that resulted in a judgment in favor of the wife's petition for separation and support involved a husband who had taken a concubine. Of the fourteen Supreme Court separation and support suits, nine were appeals initiated by husbands who opposed the judgments for separation and support by the lower courts, four were appeals by wives who opposed the denial of their separation and support claims by the lower courts, and one was an appeal initiated by a stepson against his widowed stepmother. The Supreme Court dismissed six appeals for nonpayment of fees. The Supreme Court dismissed two appeals because the minimum amount of money or property in contention was not met.

Chapter Eight

Natural Eunuchs

Husband Impotence Annulment Litigation and Legal Opportunism

The previous litigation-based chapters have examined the means available to Republican Chinese women to escape their marital obligations through judicial divorce, judicial separation, and extrajudicial action like running away. Chinese women steadily tested the limits of the law by experimenting with litigation over novel provisions of the Republican Civil Code. For women who wanted to break free from their marriages but found that none of the provisions for divorce or separation applied, aside from running away, another possibility was to sue for an annulment. Wives who sought to escape undesirable marriages grasped for legal tools to help them and some latched onto the impotence provision to pursue their interests. At the same time, of all the grounds for annulment or any other kind of marital dissolution contained in the Republican Civil Code, perhaps the one that upset the traditional order most conspicuously was a wife's accusation of impotence. Thus, the records from annulment lawsuits alleging impotence make possible a new perspective on women and Republican law.

The right to sue for annulment under the Republican Civil Code opened up a range of possibilities, but winning a judgment for annulment proved to be extremely problematic on the ground of sexual incapacity due to time limitations, burdens of proof, and other obstacles. Still, merely invoking the right to sue for annulment did provide women with a public venue—the courtroom—for airing domestic grievances both impotence related and unrelated complaints. It also granted women access to the investigative arm of the state. Women's access to a courtroom venue and its ensuing publicity as well as access to the investigative power of the state altered the traditional dynamics of marital disputes with an expanded range of actors, influences, and consideration. The development of a category of litigation over husband impotence increased the legal avenues and remedies available to wives, while placing restrictions upon husbands. The legal remedy for husband impotence gave wives more leverage and discretionary power within the marriage, regardless of the final outcome of the litigation.

The incorporation of this foreign concept of husband impotence into the Republican Chinese legal system triggered crosscurrents of cultural reinterpretation among legislators, lawyers, litigants, judges, and the press, creating a perfect climate for women to embrace this sort of legal experimentation. The underlying logic of impotence lodged in Christian notions of marriage had scarce precedent in Chinese law. The legal condition of husband impotence originated in medieval canon law that required physical consummation to make a marriage valid.[1] Ironically, Republican Chinese lawmakers adopted this medieval provision as part of their efforts toward legal modernization. As the prominent legal scholar Hu Changqing explained (quoting Kant), "Marriage is the union of the two sexes, man and woman, for the purpose of lifelong mutual sexual possession, its defining characteristic."[2] Hu's commentary on the idea of the conjugal debt illustrates the legal transformation in which lawmakers deprived the patriline of much of its legal significance and correspondingly raised the legal status of the conjugal unit. The idea that sexual intercourse should be a specific requirement to legitimate a marriage union placed renewed importance upon the physical union of husband and wife. By adopting this definition of marriage, legislators indirectly created a powerful legal tool for wives to pursue their individual interests.

The importation of a foreign definition of a valid marriage created a curious and anomalous legal situation indeed. The closest precedent for impotence in late imperial law was the breakup of an engagement or marriage by reason of a loathsome disease. In the case of the late imperial provision, however, fertility and continuity of the patriline supplied the underlying logic. Fertility and infertility, of course, mattered greatly in a marriage system formed around the interests of patrilineal descent. But before the Republican Civil Code, only female infertility legally existed. The rationale for the adoption of sexual incapacity (both male and female) as a cause for marital dissolution was rooted in the redefinition of marriage set forth by Republican legislators. Suits for annulment initiated by wives in urban Republican China on the ground of a husband's sexual incapacity gave rise to the creation of a new legal category, that of the impotent husband.

Republican Chinese lawmakers' incorporation of Western models coupled with the principle of gender equality (based upon a biological construction of gender) required the startling recognition that both female and male impotence constituted legal grounds for marital dissolution, which in turn spawned an area of litigation plagued by legal ambiguities. Civil Code Article 995 read: "Where one of the parties is incapable of marital intercourse at the time of marriage and such incapacity is incurable, the other party may apply to the Court for the annulment of the marriage; but such application may not be made after three years from the time of the discovery of such incurability."[3] Incapacity to engage in sexual intercourse was designated in Chinese by the term *bu neng rendao*, roughly translatable as "incapable of engaging in the way of being human."[4] The provision also left certain questions and details of definition unaddressed. Did impotence concern penetration, ejaculation, emission, or something else? How was incurable impotence to be distinguished from temporary impotence? And how was the Chinese state, through its judicial officers, to make such determinations? Ambiguities like these allowed women to air all sorts of grievances in the name of impotence. In effect, Republican legislators adopted Western legal models for marital dissolution (even the distinction between divorce and annulment, as such was absent from imperial law codes). However, they did not necessarily adopt wholesale the underlying logic of marriage that produced these laws and in particular for impotence the idea of the conjugal debt. This legislative ambiguity left judges and litigants free to interpret these provisions in light of existing Chinese norms. In the conduct of judicial proceedings, for instance, female litigants moderated the sheer audacity required to bring forth accusations of impotence against their husbands by consistently resorting to claims of feminine weakness and victimhood and couching their motivations within conventional goals of motherhood. Meanwhile male litigants, in particular, adamantly resisted the imperative that they submit to a physical examination and reiterated their desire not to dissolve the marriages they had expected to last a lifetime.

The impotence provision of the Republican Civil Code sanctioned the expanded scope of marital dissolution initiated by the Daliyuan/Supreme Court in the 1920s and created new opportunities for wives to escape undesirable marriages. The enactment of the provisions for a legal divorce or annulment unleashed a small stream of petitions for marital dissolution filed by wives who accused their husbands of impotence.[5] The number of impotence cases did not represent a statistically large area of litigation (in contrast to, say, divorce suits based on intolerable cruelty or cohabitation suits). Nor were impotence cases geographically widespread beyond the cities. Yet impotence suits were significant for other reasons. They grabbed the most public attention (though statistically important, spousal abuse cases rarely made the news). Furthermore, the notoriety that accompanied impotence cases publicized the issue well beyond the portion of the population actually afflicted by impotence in marriage, perhaps tapping into the general social anxiety about male weakness. As historian Hugh Shapiro has adroitly discussed, spermatorrhea ("involuntary emission") burst forth in the popular and medical imagination during the Republican period in part because of perceived threats to Chinese masculinity, concern for weakened male Chinese bodies, and the precariousness of urban life. Rumors surfaced, for instance, that the Guangxu emperor had died of spermatorrhea, Republican medical writers became obsessed with spermatorrhea, and for pharmaceutical companies, the more widespread the disease, the greater number of afflicted men, the greater the chances of profiting from a remedy.[6] In short, cases concerning husband impotence were statistically small but symbolically powerful.

Each impotence case to be examined in this chapter has one feature in common: the husband's impotence was never the determinative factor in the outcome of the case. For the wife-litigants making the allegations impotence more often than not served as a ruse to gain dissolution of the marriage for ulterior motives. Possible ulterior motives included a mix of spite and greed—Yan Peizhen was alleged to have been disappointed that her husband did not want to sleep with her after a hard day's work, and even more disappointed in the poor financial situation of her in-laws; money—Mrs. Liu-Zeng no longer wanted to be married to a eunuch; once he had exhausted his fortune, she could try to remarry a husband with a better financial position; fear—perhaps Ji Shuling's elaborate stories regarding her husband's impotence reflected her genuine fear that he was impotent; and love—Mrs. Fang-Pu may have wanted to leave her loveless marriage and start a new life in Shanghai with her paramour.

THE FIFTEEN-YEAR-OLD BRIDE AND HER OVERWORKED BICYCLE REPAIRMAN HUSBAND

The following case published in the Beijing newspaper *Shibao* (Truth Post) in 1936 illustrates the radical potential for upsetting marital power relations represented by the annulment provision for husband impotence.[7] As the scandal surrounding the case made clear, husband impotence as a legal category opened the door to subjecting the most intimate details of married life to public scrutiny. The public interest in the scandal may also have reflected social anxieties about changing sexual norms and anxieties regarding weak male bodies in particular.

Over a three-month period, *Shibao* provided continuous coverage of the impotence suit initiated by Yan Peizhen, fifteen, against Huang Yongkang, twenty-six, her bicycle repairman husband. The newspaper referred to it as "the natural eunuch (*tianyan*) case that's captivated the whole city."[8] Instead of the indirect language of "incapable of being human" in the Republican Civil Code, the newspaper referred to the husband impotence case with the more colorful moniker of "the natural eunuch case" (the usage favored by the judge and litigants as well). The first headline announced, "Fifteen-year-old girl, Yan Peizhen, alleges her husband is a natural eunuch: district court held hearings yesterday afternoon—Huang Yongkang sent to hospital for major examination."[9] Listed immediately below the headline were the litigants' names, addresses, the identity of their matchmaker, and the name of the judge who presided over their case. Pictures of the husband and wife accompanied the article. The couple married a few months earlier in December 1935. After only a few days of living with her marital family, Yan Peizhen returned to her natal family (as was customary in Beijing) and made several more natal family visits. When summoned to return to her marital family, she repeatedly refused. In February 1936, she filed suit to dissolve her marriage.

The newspaper coverage of Yan Peizhen's lawsuit was notable for the frank, often explicit revelation of intimate marital details. The first *Shibao* article publicizing the lawsuit on March 6, 1936, for instance, included a verbatim transcription of the previous day's court proceeding in which the trial judge questioned Huang Yongkang, his matchmaker, and his lawyer about the couple's sleeping arrangements, sexual problems, and other causes of marital discord, common questions in the conduct of judicial investigations into husband impotence accusations. After ascertaining Huang Yongkang's age, place of birth, and address and establishing the couple's date of engagement and marriage, the judge promptly inquired into the couple's sleeping arrangements: "Did you and Yan Peizhen sleep in the same room?" Huang Yongkang answered yes. Later, the judge returned to the subject of the couple's bedroom arrangements and intimate activities. The judge inquired further: "You and Yan Peizhen slept in the same bed, did you 'do that thing' (*nage qingxing*)?" Huang Yongkang replied that yes the couple had done it but that Yan Peizhen denied it, insisting that she was still a virgin.[10]

Once the judge determined that the couple did indeed share a bedroom, he delved into questions about why marital feelings in this case had soured (*ganqing bu hemu*), probing yet another intimate area of their marriage. Huang Yongkang pointed to several causes for his wife's discontent related to both his physiology and his finances. "I recently recovered from an illness. There are also family problems; it is impossible for me to work in the bicycle repair trade and support a family. Yan Peizhen saw that my family's circumstances were not so good, so she was not willing to be my wife," he explained. Huang Yongkang did not elaborate upon his illness during this interrogation, but later reports revealed that the illness to which Huang Yongkang referred stemmed from a bout with spermatorrhea (*yijing*), involuntary, often nocturnal, sperm emission.[11] The other cause he mentioned, his work as a bicycle repairman, created difficulties for his marriage for at least a couple of reasons. His earnings, first of all, did not amount to enough money to support his new bride as well as his parents and siblings. Apart from the low wages, he complained that his work was also physically draining. "During the day I repair bicycles for people, and it's so exhausting that at night I was not able to satisfy her [Yan Peizhen's] sexual desires." According to Huang Yongkang, his refusal to engage in intimate relations with Yan Peizhen during the night as well as his inability to provide much for her materially constituted the two key reasons why she filed suit against him. He swore he was "absolutely not impotent/a natural eunuch," and was willing to prove the truthfulness of his words by voluntarily undergoing a medical examination.[12]

Huang Yongkang's matchmaker and lawyer also affirmed his account of the marriage. The matchmaker testified that Huang Yongkang was indeed not impotent. Huang Yongkang's lawyer asserted that the premise of the case rested upon a false accusation. He pointed out that Yan Peizhen was only a fifteen-year-old girl who, if asked, probably could not even explain the meaning of "natural eunuch" or "incapable of marital intercourse." Clearly, she must be acting at the instigation of her natal family, he claimed. Huang Yongkang's lawyer portrayed the lawsuit as a convenient ruse, devised by Yan Peizhen and her natal family in order to slip out of a marriage for which they had already received a 50 *yuan* sum, to seek additional monetary gain, and be free to make another perhaps more lucrative match for their daughter.[13]

More details about the feuding couple and their families appeared the next day when *Shibao* published an interview with Huang Yongkang's mother, Mrs. Zhang. The headline blared, "Is Yan Peizhen a virgin? (*chunü*)."[14] As the plaintiff in this case alleging husband impotence, Yan Peizhen was also subjected to public scrutiny. Was she a "virtuous," i.e., sexually pure woman? What was her family background? Why was she bringing suit? The article featured Mrs. Zhang's description of the Huang and Yan families, her views on the question of her son's reproductive capabilities, and her analysis of the couple's personalities. Mrs. Zhang began by comparing the two families' backgrounds. In her own family, there were nine children—Huang Yongkang was her oldest son. Last year, with his uncle, the famous actor Huang Zihou, as matchmaker and the payment of 50 *yuan* in betrothal fees, her family secured the marriage to Yan Peizhen.[15] Mrs. Zhang's description of the Yan family dwelt upon the Yan family's poverty and need for financial support: "[The Yan family] has six daughters, Yan Peizhen is the fifth. Her father is already over 70. Her family is poor (*jiadao pinhan*)." As concrete proof of the family's privation, the bride arrived with a dowry consisting merely of two wooden boxes. Mrs. Zhang's comments seemed to imply that the Yan family may have been driven to file their lawsuit by financial concerns. Perhaps they regretted the match once Yan Peizhen and her family realized that Huang Yongkang, with his eight siblings and parents all in need of his support, would not be an ideal son-in-law for their family of six daughters and an elderly father. To escape the match, Yan Peizhen returned to her natal family and refused to go back to the marital home, claiming one excuse after another, first an obligation to attend a funeral, then the inconvenience of her menstrual cycle. Surely, monetary considerations must have factored heavily in the Yan family decision to sue, speculated Mrs. Zhang, especially since Yan Peizhen's lawsuit demanded not just an annulment but an additional 700 *yuan* in damages. As for other potential motivations for the suit, Mrs. Zhang admitted that her son may have suffered from spermatorrhea, but she immediately proclaimed that doctors were treating the dysfunction and that it was almost completely cured. Mrs. Zhang then offered the contrast between Huang Yongkang and Yan Peizhen's personalities as another potential reason for the suit. She described Yan Peizhen as extremely lively (*huopo*), and her son as loyal, faithful, reliable, and truthful (*zhongshi*). Perhaps, she speculated, her boy was too self-conscious, modest, or embarrassed (*zixiu*) to be intimate with such a woman. Finally, Mrs. Zhang declared that she would request the court to investigate whether her daughter-in-law was a virgin. Elsewhere during the interview, Mrs. Zhang recounted her first impression of her daughter-in-law as a fourteen-*sui* girl who looked more like eighteen or nineteen. "At the time of the wedding, the Yan girl said she was fourteen *sui,* but the *qipao* she wore was over four feet, one inch in length," implying that Yan Peizhen was taller than typical for her age and possibly less innocent and more mature than one would expect a young girl to be. These were questions that Mrs. Zhang raised in an effort to discredit Yan Peizhen and therefore her lawsuit.

The next step in the lawsuit involved even more explicit revelations of personal information about Huang Yongkang in particular, with the publication of the medical report assessing whether he was impotent. The first hearing concluded with the judge ordering Huang Yongkang to pay a five *yuan* fee for a medical exam to be conducted at the Beijing Medical University within ten days. The court would summon the parties back for another hearing after receipt of the medical report. According to the newspaper, Huang Yongkang complied with the order to undergo a physical exam on March 16, 1936, at 10 a.m. After several weeks, *Shibao* reported on the findings of the medical expert's report. It seems that the medical examiner detected signs of sexual incapacity in Huang Yongkang. The medical examiner, however, attributed his sexual dysfunction to exhaustion and fatigue, rather than impotence. According to the report, Huang Yongkang's body was exhausted from excessive work (*caolao guodu*) causing a disorder in his nervous system/neurasthenia (*shenjing shuairuo*).[16] In other words, Huang Yongkang worked too hard repairing bicycles. His body could not endure the excessive strain, causing his nervous system to suffer and affecting his ability to engage in sexual relations.

In an interview with a *Shibao* reporter printed the following day, Huang Yongkang himself spoke of the case, reiterating that he was not impotent and emphasizing that he was physically weak but that his spermatorrhea was in the process of being cured. In his interview, he also underlined the importance of the marriage to his family. As a family that was not rich, he explained, getting a wife was very difficult. He added that he hoped mediation would settle the dispute and mend the rupture between him and his wife.

A couple of months later, the newspaper reported the final outcome of the case. Through the intervention of relatives and friends, the couple had "privately" agreed to a mutual-consent divorce.[17] In the end, Huang Yongkang proved to the city of Beijing that he was capable of sexual intercourse and vindicated himself in that regard, yet he agreed nonetheless to grant his wife a divorce. Although Yan Peizhen's allegations of husband impotence proved false and she did not get her annulment, she still obtained the end to her marriage she so publicly sought.

The case suggests that bringing suit under the husband impotence provision required little legal sophistication. Here, a fifteen-*sui* girl (fourteen by Western reckoning) filed suit. The taint of the allegation, however false, provided the wife with a certain amount of bargaining power. Ruse or not, she was ultimately able to dissolve her marriage. An important part of the radical potential inherent in the impotence provision was the possibility of public exposure, embarrassment, humiliation, and notoriety. Impotence cases generated substantial publicity and posed a danger to husbands' social reputations. Besides, the medical examination and the judicial interrogation into the details of Huang Yongkang and Yan Peizhen's marital arrangements marked an expansion and intensification of the state's intervention in marriage and family.

THE PALACE GIRL AND THE EUNUCH

The veracity of the wife's charge of impotence against her eunuch husband in the next case was well founded. Nonetheless, her lawsuit to dissolve her marriage could not escape the suspicion that she was manipulating the law to help her discard a husband for financial motives. Twelve years into the marriage her husband remained as impotent as he was at the beginning of the marriage. The most conspicuous change in the relationship had to do with the husband's economic woes.

In 1937, Mrs. Liu-Zeng, twenty-nine, of Beijing, sued her husband to dissolve their marriage and sought an alimony payment of 2,500 *yuan*. Mrs. Liu-Zeng claimed that her husband was a castrated eunuch incapable of marital intercourse. Nevertheless, the Beijing District Court denied her petition. She appealed to the Hebei Superior Court (with the aid of a lawyer) and levied a host of grievances against her husband. In addition to her charge of impotence, Mrs. Liu-Zeng also claimed intolerable abuse related to her husband's artificially created impotent condition (he underwent castration to become a eunuch, unlike those who were naturally impotent). Her appeal stated, "When his sexual desires spring up violently, he often forcibly oppresses [his wife] and commits various abuses. [His wife's] body is small and weak. She has no means to defend against his devastation."[18] She appealed to the court to protect her from her stronger and more powerful eunuch husband. Although the Lius married twelve years ago, Mrs. Liu-Zeng claimed she was too young (seventeen *sui*) and too afraid to publicly complain about his condition at the time of their marriage. She attributed her delay in filing suit to her feminine weakness and maintained that her powerlessness as a woman prevented her from filing suit earlier.

Mr. Liu, age not listed, also represented by a lawyer, did not deny that he was castrated. Instead, he defended himself by attributing ulterior motives to his wife. By his account, Mrs. Liu-Zeng was originally a palace girl called "Cuishun." Mr. Liu and Mrs. Liu-Zeng both worked in the palace. In 1925 when all palace dwellers were evicted, Mrs. Liu-Zeng asked someone to arrange a match for her. She knew Mr. Liu was a eunuch and she was still willing to marry him. In order to secure the marriage, Mr. Liu spent money and gifts amounting to 100 *yuan* in silver. Mrs. Liu-Zeng's father presided over the marriage. After the wedding, Mr. Liu continued to provide financial support for Mrs. Liu-Zeng's father and brothers. Mr. Liu stressed that he had been married twelve years already. In the last two years, Mr. Liu suffered financial setbacks and has not been able to provide the same level of support for his wife and in-laws. Earlier this year, Mrs. Liu-Zeng absconded with all of Mr. Liu's belongings. According to Mr. Liu, his wife was acting under the spell of her father and brothers. Mrs. Liu-Zeng's suit consisted of nothing more than lies and slander.[19]

Mr. Liu's explanation resonated with a number of tropes familiar to other types of marital litigation. For instance, he listed the amount of money he expended in order to marry, thus solidifying his claims over his wife. He also accused his wife of acting "under the spell" of someone else. In effect, Mr. Liu shifted the direction of the case away from his physical inadequacies, which he did not contest, and toward his financial support of her and her family members. He pinned the origins of the suit on his deteriorating economic position and portrayed his wife as a money-grubbing woman, as evidenced by her previous theft of all his belongings. He contended that the real cause for her lawsuit was his decline in economic status, not his sexual inadequacy. His status as a eunuch did not keep his in-laws from arranging a match for their daughter with him; how could impotence be brought up twelve years later as a reason to dissolve the union?

The Beijing District Court and the Hebei Superior Court judges sided with the eunuch husband. The judges held that twelve years of marriage was too long to wait to sue: "Appellant [wife] claims her age was just 17, and therefore she was afraid to tell anyone, but there are twelve years between now and then. Why didn't she say something sooner?"[20] The lapse of time again hurt the wife's credibility and lent support to the notion that she had an ulterior motive in filing suit. Never mind that the law stipulated three years from discovery, not length of marriage. Moreover, the court determined that Mrs. Liu-Zeng was not an innocent victim in need of the court's help in redressing a grievous situation. But rather, she was held to be a knowing participant in the marriage. As a palace girl, she should have been aware of her husband's status as a eunuch, reasoned the court. As for Mrs. Liu-Zeng's allegation of abuse, the court cited lack of proof—it was only her word without further evidence. Then the court promptly dismissed all her allegations as unsubstantiated.

The superior court's decision implied that the case involved a blatant manipulation of the law by the wife and her natal family. No one doubted that Mr. Liu the eunuch was impotent. But Mrs. Liu-Zeng turned to the law to help her escape from her marriage to a eunuch only years after her wedding. She accused him of being impotent and abusive. Her concern about her husband's impotent condition, however, seemed to arise only after he became both impotent and poor.

THE VIRGIN AND HER THREE PAIRS OF PANTS

The wife in the next case worried that she had been tricked into marriage to an impotent man. She turned to the state to help her escape this trickery and dissolve the marriage. Her lawsuit instigated a series of intrusive interrogation sessions and physical examinations that brought the power of the state into the couple's bedroom. The state's investigation into the couple's marriage helped assuage her anxieties. She only agreed to return to her husband after a hospital examination deemed him capable of engaging "in the way of being human."

In 1943, Ji Shuling, twenty-six *sui*, brought suit before the Beijing District Court, accusing her husband of impotence and demanding to dissolve their marriage. The couple was engaged through a matchmaker in December 1941 and married on December 26, 1942. Only a few weeks later, Ji Shuling petitioned to dissolve the marriage. In her petition, Ji Shuling narrated how on her wedding night (*tongfang zhi ye*) she discovered that her husband was incapable of intercourse. He explained to her that he had various troubles on his mind that prevented him from consummating the marriage that night. Ji Shuling claimed to be ignorant of such matters: "I am just a young girl, just married, of course I had no idea what was the matter." Then she described how he took some medicine, which he explained was "virility-enhancing," (*zhuangyang yao*) and how he cursed the drug for not working. She recounted how he sweated profusely, but was still unable to engage in intercourse. Her own innocence and modesty, she said, prevented her from raising her complaint sooner: "At the time I was so embarrassed that I didn't tell anyone else." When she returned to her natal family for a visit, she explained the situation to the matchmaker, who tried to intervene. Her husband refused to divorce. Therefore, Ji Shuling had to bring suit. She accused her husband and in-laws of tricking her into marriage (*qipian hunyin*). She expressed her outrage and surmised that she had been tricked because her natal family consisted only of her widowed mother and younger sister (there was no man in the house). She explained her motive for filing suit in terms of her future: "I have to think of the rest of my life, my future." In other words, she had to think of herself. When asked about her motive during a later interrogation session, Ji Shuling made it clear that her reasons for filing for a divorce were motivated not by the fact that her husband's alleged impotence deprived her of sexual pleasure, but instead by the fact that it deprived her of the opportunity to have children. When asked why she wanted to dissolve her marriage, she clung firmly to traditional values and ideas about motherhood as the key to the meaning of life. She cited the old adage, "Life is for the purpose of raising sons and daughters (*rensheng suowei shenger yangnü*)."[21] In other words, she claimed to cherish the idea of motherhood and her grievance had to do with being denied that possibility by an impotent husband.

Her husband, Cai Shizhong, twenty-five *sui*, worked as a janitor at Beijing Normal University. Cai Shizhong defended himself against the impotence charges by placing the blame for the nonperformance of his conjugal duties on his wife. Cai Shizhong denied taking any erection-enhancing drugs and refuted the claim that his sexual organs were diseased. Instead, Cai Shizhong declared that his wife refused to have sex with him. According to Cai Shizhong, his wife wore three pairs of pants to bed and rebuffed all his imploring that she take them off. It was her behavior (and bedtime attire) that prevented the newlyweds from performing their conjugal duties. Furthermore, Cai Shizhong cited the heavy financial costs he incurred in order to marry. As he told the judge, "I spent over 100 *yuan* to marry her. How can the marriage be dissolved just like that?" Finally, Cai Shizhong claimed he did not suffer from impotence and was willing to undergo a medical examination to prove his assertion. He was even willing to pay the ten *yuan* fee required for the examination.[22]

Ji Shuling's impotence allegation against her husband drew the state into the most private aspects of her life. The Beijing District Court responded to Ji Shuling's original petition by calling the parties to court to a mediation session. Since the mediation attempt failed to produce a settlement, Ji Shuling filed another petition, this time requesting adjudication. In response to this petition, the judge ordered the parties to appear at two oral interrogation sessions. During these sessions, the judge subjected both Ji Shuling and Cai Shizhong to questions about the most intimate details of their married life.

The questions posed by the judge were very explicit. How long had Ji Shuling and Cai Shizhong lived together? Ji Shuling replied that they had lived together only ten days before she returned to her natal family home. "Have you two slept together (*he fang*)?" was the next question, to which Ji Shuling replied with the story of their failed wedding night. The judge then asked Ji Shuling for a night-by-night account of the first few days after she moved into Cai Shizhong's home. Did he perform his conjugal duties? She answered no. What remarks did he make as he attempted to perform his conjugal duties? "He told me not to tell anyone . . . He said it's just that I can't get an erection and apologized." The judge inquired further into the length of her husband's penis. "It's too small [gesturing with her fingers about two inches]." Then he suggested that Ji Shuling try rubbing his privates to get an erection. She replied that she had tried, and it too had failed. The judge also delved into excruciating details about Ji Shuling's character and behavior. During the first oral interrogation, the judge pointedly asked Ji Shuling whether she was "still a girl (*guniang*)." She claimed to still be a "girl."[23] Although a wife's virginity was not strictly relevant to determining the sexual incapacity of a husband, the question was raised in a number of the impotence annulment suits.

Perhaps the most explicit example of the state's intrusion into private life pertained to the medical examination to which Cai Shizhong was subjected. The expert report (*jiandingshu*) issued by the medical examiners declared Cai Shizhong capable of engaging in sexual relations and ultimately bolstered his defense. But the price of this report was an intrusive physical examination (during which the examiner rubbed warm alcohol on Cai Shizhong's sexual organs with a cotton ball in order to stimulate an erection) and revelation of the particulars of Cai Shizhong's sexual performance during the examination, including the exact length of his penis with (ten centimeters) and without an erection (seven and a half centimeters), the length of time he was able to maintain an erection (one minute), and the presence of white mucus around the top of his member (removable according to the report).[24] This medical evaluation revealed the reach of the state's investigative arm when a wife initiated an impotence suit.

A week after the medical examination was completed, the judge summoned the parties to court once again. This time he directed his comments to Ji Shuling. The judge explained to her that the medical report conclusively determined that Cai Shizhong was not impotent. Therefore, he urged her to drop her suit. Ji Shuling admitted that she had no other grounds for a divorce, aside from her impotence allegation, and she agreed to drop her suit and return to live with her husband. The judge commended her decision to withdraw the lawsuit and advised her to go and "pass the days well" (*haohao guo rizi*). In the end, Ji Shuling failed to win an annulment. Her legal action, however, did allow her a few months' stay with her mother and sister away from her husband (quite possibly crucial to a new bride). It also cleared up for her any fears about whether her husband was truly impotent. For his part, even after his legal and medical ordeals, Cai Shizhong agreed to take her back.[25]

A *TONGYANGXI'S* ATTEMPT TO REMAKE HER LIFE

The former *tongyangxi* (adopted daughter-in-law) at the center of the next case attempted to remake her fate and turned to the Republican court system to help her.[26] She had been brought to her husband's family home as a young girl and was in her twenties when she tried to extricate herself from the marriage that her parents had arranged for her. At the time of her lawsuit, she had already left her marital home and found work as a maidservant in Shanghai.

Unlike the new brides who sued to dissolve their marriages within weeks of their weddings, this couple lived together for a very long time before the wife brought suit alleging husband impotence in 1947 before the Zhuji County District Court in Zhejiang Province. The bride, Fang Pu Meixiang, twenty-five *sui,* entered her husband's home back in 1934 as a *tongyangxi*. At that time she was only twelve *sui.* She married five years later in 1939 when she was seventeen *sui.* Mrs. Fang-Pu's lawsuit may have represented her attempt to escape her fate as a *tongyangxi* and pursue her own fortune and create new possibilities for herself. Her impotence accusation served as a kind of legal tool to fall back on when none of the other provisions for divorce applied.

In her petition (drafted with the help of a lawyer), Mrs. Fang-Pu expressed her disappointments and grievances having to do with both her general life circumstances as well as against her husband. Mrs. Fang-Pu's primary complaint was that she had been forced to endure the past thirteen years in a loveless, affectionless relationship. Back in 1934 Mrs. Fang-Pu was only twelve s*ui* and was "too young and powerless" (*nianyou wu li dikang*) to resist her parents' command that she enter her husband's home as a *tongyangxi.* Thus she claimed to have been coerced into a marriage that she had no say over. During their years together her husband never once performed his conjugal duties. At first she thought he was waiting until she was older to consummate the marriage. As the years passed, however, she realized that her husband was impotent, suffering from both mental and physical diseases. She remarked that after thirteen years of living together, Mr. Fang "has never acted in a sexual way (*bu dong chunse*), nor has he had love affairs with any mistresses." She summed up her claims with the disparaging accusation: "His behavior is completely feminine; generally speaking he is, without a doubt, a woman." In a weak position as a young bride and without the means to oppose her husband and in-laws, she was not previously able to sue for divorce. By her own account, she was the victim of circumstances not of her own making.[27]

Mrs. Fang-Pu went on to explain her motives for filing for divorce. She justified her actions in terms of her very traditional desire to have children, not a modern desire to be part of a sexually fulfilling marriage. Her grueling work as a servant forced her to think about her future livelihood. Anxious about the future, she fretted that if she had "no children—how will I be able to support myself in the future."[28] A prior attempt at mediation with her husband failed. Therefore, she implied her circumstances have left her with no choice but to embark on this current action to divorce her marriage. It was her aspiration for motherhood and the security that stems from having children that motivated her suit. Only by ending her current marriage would she be afforded the opportunity to remarry and have children of her own who would ultimately take care of her.

Mr. Fang provided a very different account of the couple's marriage. He retained a lawyer and responded to Mrs. Fang-Pu's lawsuit with a countersuit for cohabitation. He denied all of Mrs. Fang-Pu's accusations and charged her with shrewd manipulation of the law. He claimed that her allegations of his genital disorder were "utter falsehoods." He assured the court that his male organs were intact. Proof of his reproductive capabilities, he claimed, was demonstrated by his wife's birth of a daughter a few years earlier (based on the traditional assumption that any child born in wedlock must have been fathered by the husband). Their daughter passed away in infancy, but they adopted a son (now five *sui*). According to Mr. Fang, the real trouble began last year when his father-in-law brought his wife back to her natal home. Mr. Fang went to pick her up several times, but she refused to return home with him. Now she had hatched up a scheme (*ling you qitu*). She trumped up baseless impotence claims in order to disguise her ulterior motives. "Why would she wait until now to initiate a divorce? It serves to show she has an ulterior motive. So she fabricated facts to serve as grounds for divorce."[29] Indeed, according to his version of the facts, he was the victim of his wife's manipulation of the law and baseless allegations, not the other way around.

As judges were quick to perceive, impotence cases carried multiple subtexts, with often complicated sets of allegations and counterallegations. In judges' evaluations of claims and counterclaims such as those between Mrs. Fang-Pu and Mr. Fang, judges lessened the tribulations that beset husbands in impotence cases by providing a measure of judicial protection to male litigants. Although legally speaking, female and male impotence now possessed equal validity as causes for annulment, husbands and wives were not approached in an equally consistent manner by judges. Based upon the questioning and testimony in case records, judges (rightly so in some cases) viewed impotence petitions with suspicion. They shared the husbands' fear that female litigants were employing the impotence provision in an opportunistic fashion in order to disguise a desire for marital dissolution for ulterior motives. To avoid the use of impotence as a pretext for other claims and to offset the potential shame and humiliation for the husband in an impotence case, judges resorted to several practices designed to protect the interests of the husband. For example, they did not limit their investigation to the physical condition of the husband, but freely inquired into extraneous matters like whether a wife was a virgin or not, whether a wife had engaged in an extramarital affair, and the length of time a wife spent living with her natal family rather than her in-laws. Moreover, judges imposed an extremely high burden of proof for impotence claims (as they usually did for other petitions for marital dissolution as well). Usually the burden of proof fell on the wife's shoulders, not just to prove impotence as an incurable medical condition but to disprove a husband's counterallegations as well. Finally, judges upheld strict adherence to the statute of limitations on impotence claims (to be brought within three years from the time of discovery of incurability).

The judge at the Zhuji District Court did not look favorably upon Mrs. Fang-Pu. At the end of one of the oral interrogations, the judge tried to persuade Mr. Fang that "this type of woman" would only bring trouble to him and his family. The judge urged Mr. Fang to accept a payment of one hundred *yuan* from Mrs. Fang-Pu, divorce her, and use the money to find another, more suitable woman to marry. But Mr. Fang would not agree.[30]

When the trial judge interrogated Mr. Fang about his reasons for not obeying the court's order to submit to a medical examination, Mr. Fang explained that his family was impoverished and therefore could not afford to pay for such an examination. This explanation seemed to satisfy the judge. Significantly, the court did not make any sort of medical evaluation of Mr. Fang's physical condition before ruling on the case. Even though the judge had ordered Mr. Fang to undergo a medical exam, he did not compel Mr. Fang to do so and did not hold Mr. Fang's avoidance of such an exam against him.

Instead, the judge laid the burden of proof on Mrs. Fang-Pu. First the judge questioned the timing of her suit.

> Judge: Why do you want to divorce him now?
>
> Mrs. Fang-Pu: Since I arrived at his home at age twelve, I have never slept with him. He is incapable of intercourse, so I want to divorce him.
>
> Judge: Why did you not bring this up before?

Mrs. Fang-Pu: When I was young, he probably thought I was too young. I had no idea he would not sleep with me even now. I have to think of the rest of my life. I can't not bring [this problem] up.[31]

In its eventual decision, the court cited her delay in filing suit as its reason for invalidating her claim. The court emphasized that the Fangs had been married for over ten years. The statute of limitations had thus expired. The court was not persuaded that the lengthy lapse in time between marriage and lawsuit for divorce could be attributed to Mrs. Fang-Pu's youth and weaknesses as a woman and child-bride.[32] The lengthy delay generated the court's suspicion. In the court's view, the longer the passage of time, the greater the possibility that ulterior motives were at work.

Aside from the timing of her case, the judge also probed the husband's allegation that the couple had a child together.

Q: Have you given birth to any children?

A: I gave birth to a daughter. She died after just over a month.

Q: If [your husband] is impotent, then how could you have given birth?

A: The daughter I gave birth to was not necessarily [my husband's]. I was raped by the Japanese. At that time, I wasn't the only woman to be raped by the Japanese.[33]

The judge continued with questions about the date and place of Mrs. Fang-Pu's childbirth. Her testimony did not convince the court. In its decision, the court used her admission to having had a child as proof of her husband's virility and discounted her claims of rape, as she had nothing beyond her own words to corroborate her story. Mrs. Fang-Pu could not surmount the burden of disproving her husband's allegations and the presumption that any child born in wedlock had been fathered by her husband. In essence, the judge sidestepped the issue of impotence as the inability to perform sexually and avoided an actual examination of the husband's body by pointing to other evidence of his virility (the birth of a daughter). The court found the evidence of his virility, however contested, was sufficient to refute the charge of impotence.

Mrs. Fang-Pu was persistent. She hired another lawyer and filed an appeal with the Zhejiang Superior Court. In contrast to Mrs. Fang-Pu's trial court strategy, her appeal did not recount her victimhood and weaknesses as a woman but focused instead on attacking the trial court's refusal to subject her husband to a medical examination. She emphasized the trial court's faulty investigation (*qianque diaocha*) of the case. Proper procedure required a physical exam. Her appeal insisted upon a medical exam and urged the court to undertake an investigation of the bodily evidence of impotence, not the other allegations related to her behavior:

> [The allegation of the husband's impotence] is a fact that can be proven through investigation; matters must not be left unresolved. Judge Du (from the trial court) ordered him to go to the Superior Court for examination. The defendant refused to go. Then Judge Yuan ordered him to go [to] the public hospital for an exam. The hospital ordered him to be hospitalized, and he again refused. Finally, they ordered him to be examined yet again, and he stubbornly refused. The original court allowed his refusal and rejected the wife's petition. It was particularly good at not investigating evidence . . . The basic question is whether or not the husband is capable of reproduction. If his reproductive organs are not dysfunctional, then why, after repeated orders to undergo examination, did he refuse time and again?[34]

She ignored the statute of limitations issue. She simply demanded that her husband be subjected to a medical examination. Regardless of the other circumstances of the case, she was adamant that a thorough examination of her husband be conducted. Mrs. Fang-Pu's insistence on the medical examination suggests that the exam served as a kind of weapon, perhaps a legal tool that could be used to humiliate Mr. Fang. Mrs. Fang-Pu tried her best to draw the state into her marriage.

Mr. Fang's response to his wife's appeal, also drafted by a lawyer, repeated his trial court defense and added a few more unflattering details about his wife. He reiterated the fact that thirteen years had passed since Mrs. Fang-Pu entered his family's home. He also retold the fact that his wife had given birth to a daughter who died in infancy back in 1944. Next he defended his masculinity, stating: "I am strong of body and have no disease. How can one speak of any dysfunctional ability to reproduce?" Then he proceeded to introduce new evidence of his wife's immoral behavior. His answer proceeded systematically to discredit Mrs. Fang-Pu by accusing her of adultery and culminated in a request to examine her breasts in order to prove she had been breastfeeding a child conceived in the adulterous affair (not the infant daughter who had died):

> When she went back to her natal home as a guest in July 1946, her father's friend, Shi Yousheng, lured her to his house. She committed adultery with Shi Yousheng's brother-in-law, Lou Amao, and it bore fruit. She gave birth to a daughter [whom she has arranged to have adopted by another family]. You can examine her breast area, and the truth will be revealed. Now she has [made up these lies about my impotence] to demand a divorce . . . . Her various claims and appeals are all just empty words . . .[35]

His response deflected attention from his physical condition and put her sexual behavior and physical condition squarely at issue. Since she pressed so hard for an examination of him, she should undergo examination herself to prove her adulterous behavior. Despite the fact that the law contained no provision that made a wife's impotence claim void in case of her own adultery, the taint from the adultery allegation raised suspicions about the veracity or validity of the wife's claims.

Unlike the trial court's wide inquiry into the various allegations listed in the pleadings, the Zhejiang Superior Court focused more narrowly on making a legal determination about whether the husband was impotent and inquiring into whether the wife had met the statute of limitations. First, the superior court ordered an actual examination of Mr. Fang. The medical examination reported that Mr. Fang was "lacking in sexual desire." But the report was deemed inconclusive. The court determined that his deficient sexual desire did not necessarily mean that he would never be able to perform sexually. Perhaps he was incapable, but not incurable. Moreover, the court emphasized the fact that the parties had been married for over ten years, and thus the time within which Mrs. Fang-Pu should have filed for marital dissolution had expired long ago. Like the lower court, it sided with the husband.[36]

Regardless of how weak willed Mrs. Fang-Pu claimed to have been in the past, she did not allow two unfavorable judgments to deter her from her goal of ending her marriage. She persisted once again and hired yet another (her third) lawyer to draft an appeal to the Supreme Court. This appeal stressed the fact that the lower two courts had refused to examine the evidence in the case. The report by one doctor that her husband's "sexual desire was imperfect, but that it was not impossible for him to ever engage in intercourse" was not satisfactory. The case file does not record the outcome of Mrs. Fang-Pu's appeal to the Supreme Court. The documents in the case file do attest to Mrs. Fang-Pu's persistent engagement with the law. This former *tongyangxi* was determined to find a solution to her marital woes, drawing upon a range of legal tools at her disposal, since the implementation of the Republican Civil Code in 1931. Perhaps she really did have another lover. That might plausibly explain her ability to hire a lawyer, submit court fees, and keep filing suit.

CONCLUSION

Republican impotence law inspired crosscurrents of cultural reinterpretation. Litigants who brought suit under the new provision for husband impotence had little, if any, guidance in their actions. The imprecisely understood law contributed to the practice of wife-litigants adopting the impotence provision in an enterprising manner. The idea of a conjugal debt to be paid did not gain much traction, but the foreign definition of marriage from which the impotence provision derived helped open the door to litigant manipulation and resistance, judicial improvisation, and public curiosity. It armed wives with a substantial, radical tool with which they could push the litigation envelope in order to shape the outcomes of their marriages and their future economic survival regardless of the ultimate judgment. Even though most wives failed to obtain a divorce from the courts, they did use the publicity, fear of scandal, threat of a medical examination, acrimonious recriminations, and other litigation-related effects to their advantage. In some cases, wives managed to satisfy their interests without the benefit of a favorable judgment. Nevertheless, in contrast to the bold actions wives took in manipulating the law for their own devices, most legal actions taken in the name of impotence were justified by personal and familial goals expressed in wholly conventional terms.

At face value, impotence claims represented direct challenges to the masculinity of the husbands accused. Yet the legal determination of impotence in marital dissolution proceedings involved a web of sexual, economic, and moral issues that could not be solved by a purely medical determination of a husband's physical condition. Lawsuits brought forth under these provisions veered off in tumultuous directions, with demands for physical examinations made by both parties. Often, attacks on a husband's masculinity were refracted back to a focus on the behavior of his wife and her economic and other motivations. The scarcity of legal precedent, customary practice, clear legislative principles, and conclusive medical reports left plenty of room for judicial discretion in the outcome of impotence proceedings. The imprecise legislative language further enlarged the scope of judicial improvisation. The judicial decisions that resulted, moreover, tended to be conservative in nature and protective of husbands. The burden of proof placed upon wives proved insurmountable in almost every case. Yet judges took the impotence charges seriously enough to order husbands to undergo intrusive, potentially humiliating medical examinations. So no matter how much protection high standards of proof afforded husbands, husbands could not always avoid the necessity of a medical examination. In the end, a husband's physical condition was largely immaterial to the legal determination of whether he could or could not "engage in the way of being human."

NOTES

1. On the ecclesiastical origins of the physical consummation requirement see Darmon 1985, 6–9; and on the conjugal debt see McLaren 2007, 29–32.

2. Hu 1931, 11, n. 6.

3. Civil Code, Book IV, Family, 10. Female impotence generally referred to "stone maidens" (*shinü*), for which under imperial law, the marriage could be called off—on grounds that the groom's family was not informed of the situation during betrothal negotiations. See Shi 2000, 250.

4. McLaren 2007 points out that despite its ancient origins "impotence" was a modern term. In English the usage of impotence dates from the seventeenth century (xiii).

5. Civil Code Articles 995 and 1052-7 overlapped. The condition of husband impotence gave rise to a claim for annulment, not divorce. Many litigants and their lawyers, however, used divorce and annulment interchangeably. The cause of action that impotence gave rise to in Western law differed from country to country as well. Shi 2000, 249–250.

6. Shapiro 1998 provides a fascinating account of the disproportionate prominence accorded to spermatorrhea during the Republican period, which was explained in part by a general social anxiety about Chinese masculinity and the weakened male body.

7. The reporting on this sensational legal case may be read alongside the studies that analyze the way newspapers in Republican China contributed to the formation of public opinion, social attitudes, and individual subjectivity and sexuality. See Goodman 2006 and Lean 2007 on the sensationalist tastes of a new reading public.

8. *Shibao* 1936.3.31, 1936.4.28, 1936.5.10.

9. *Shibao* 1936.3.6.

10. *Shibao* 1936.3.6.

11. Huang Yongkang's circumstances fit Hugh Shapiro's description of the disease of spermatorrhea becoming a concern for working-class men during the Republican period. See Shapiro 1998, especially pp. 574–580.

12. *Shibao* 1936.3.6.

13. *Shibao* 1936.3.6.

14. *Shibao* 1936.3.7.

15. *Shibao* 1936.3.7.

16. *Shibao* 1936.3.17.

17. *Shibao* 1936.5.10.

18. Hebei 634-2-179 Hebei Superior Court decision dated 1937.12.21. Appeal from Beijing District Court decision dated 1937.6.25.

19. Hebei 634-2-179 decision dated 1937.12.21.

20. Hebei 634-2-179 decision dated 1937.12.21.

21. Beijing J65-19-235 petition dated 1943.1.23.

22. Beijing J65-19-235 oral argument dated 1943.1.29.

23. Beijing J65-19-235 oral interrogation dated 1943.1.29.

24. Beijing J65-19-235 medical report dated 1943.2.11.

25. Beijing J65-19-235 oral argument dated 1943.2.19.

26. *Tongyangxi* or *sim-pua* refers to "adopted daughters-in-law." *Tongyangxi* entered their future husbands' households as young girls as part of a minor form of marriage practiced by families who could not afford the expenses of the major form of marriage. See Wolf and Huang 1980, 82–84 and ch. 17.

27. Supreme Court, 16(5)-755-2 petition to Zhuji District Court, Zhejiang Province dated 1947.3.24.

28. Supreme Court 16(5)-755-2 petition to Zhuji District Court, Zhejiang Province dated 1947.3.24.

29. Supreme Court 16(5)-755-2 answer dated 1947.5.1.

30. Supreme Court 16(5)-755-3 oral argument dated 1947.10.20.

31. Supreme Court 16(5)-755-3 oral argument dated 1947.10.20.

32. Supreme Court 16(5)-755-3 decision dated 1948.2.28.

33. Supreme Court 16(5)-755-3 oral argument dated 1947.10.20.

34. Supreme Court 16(5)-755-2 appeal to Zhejiang Superior Court dated 1948.3.25.

35. Supreme Court 16(5)-755-2 answer to appeal dated 1948.4.26.

36. Supreme Court 16(5)-755-2 opinion dated 1948.4.30.

Chapter Nine

Conclusion

Departing from depictions of Republican law as an elite pursuit that failed to exert much influence, this study demonstrates the growing importance of law in Republican China and the myriad ways in which Republican law came to serve the purposes of a wide cross-section of society. A close reading of archival sources that have preserved the voices of ordinary Chinese women and men has made it possible to trace the ways the Republican Civil Code in particular came to both reflect and drive social transformations in this period. The emergence of a formal civil law system in early-twentieth-century China changed the nature of law and made "law" a more prominent and increasingly accessible component of daily life. In formally separating civil from criminal law, Chinese lawmakers made it possible for ordinary people to move from viewing the totality of law and judicial processes in terms of a repressive system of punishment for crimes against the public order. Instead, civil law, embodied by the remarkably modern and liberal Republican Civil Code, endowed individuals with legal rights and duties, embraced a capitalist logic over Confucian ideology and played a central role in the regulation of private disputes. The emergence of this civil law framework contributed to the reformulation of the relationship between law and society, enabling individuals to engage the legal system in new ways. The mounting rates of civil litigation attest to the fact that more and more people sought legal solutions to their disputes and that Republican litigants looked toward the juridical system as a possible source of justice. Female litigants, especially, engaged the law in enterprising ways and made creative use of provisions of the Republican Civil Code to press their interests.

The deepening of the relationship between law and society corresponded to the increasingly complex negotiations, sophisticated transactions, and conflicts involved in modern Chinese society and economy. Marriage, that most central of social institutions, was redefined, "modernized," in fundamental ways. Changes in the legal regulation of marriage corresponded to shifts in popular perceptions of marriage, especially in the new urban cultures. Lawmakers envisioned that the custom of arranged marriage would give way to individual consent and freedom to marry. The practice of concubinage would gradually disappear to allow for a stricter interpretation of the principle of monogamy. Legal and social trends suggested that marriage would serve the interests of the conjugal couple rather than the larger patrilineal family. A married woman's surname and domicile could be negotiated rather than assumed to follow that of her husband. Most fundamentally, the expansion of women's access to divorce as well as other means of marital dissolution gave rise to the perception that marriage was not simply a permanent fate to be endured until death; marriage could be and perhaps should be dissolved under certain legally delineated circumstances.

Throughout the 1930s and 1940s, husband and wife litigants wrangled over questions of marital status, marital residence, property, and sexuality. As divorce lawsuits attest, marital status mattered greatly to the identity of men and women. For many men, poverty and imbalances in the ratio of marriageable men to women continued to make marriage a costly undertaking. Husbands expressed distress over the heavy financial burden placed upon them by the costs of marrying and consistently asserted their expectation that marriage was a lifelong commitment requiring the cohabitation of husband and wife. For women, growing opportunities for employment outside of the family home made marital status less absolutely necessary as a means to secure their livelihood. Wives no longer had to tolerate egregious acts of cruelty, as insults and violence could amount to legally actionable claims for divorce. Just as new legal options gave wives hope that they could escape an unhappy marriage, husbands too engaged the law, especially through cohabitation suits. Cohabitation disputes reflected tensions over changing patterns of marital residence as a result of increased urbanization and the weakening of patrilineal ideology. The law posed serious challenges to the norm of patrilocality. New laws allowed for more choice over the issue of marital residence, recognized the conjugal family ideal, and granted women's relationships with their natal families greater legal standing. The novel separation and support lawsuits brought by upper-class women, furthermore, reveal the drawing of a new relationship between gender and property. Modern marriage and property laws enabled women to separate from their husbands and still continue to receive material support in various forms, including housing, rent, grain, monthly stipends, and one-time lump sum payments of money or property. Husband impotence annulment suits, finally, coincided with a growing preoccupation with male sexual anxieties.

Though not overtly political acts, the power struggles that ensued in the course of litigation over marital discord reflected larger political struggles that accompanied China's transition from empire to republic. At the heart of the relationship between Republican law, state, and society lay a deep contradiction: a liberal, modernizing legal system stood at odds with the GMD's authoritarian political regime. The Republican Civil Code was an integral part of a new civil law system that represented an important exception to the GMD's general authoritarianism. Nowhere was this contradiction more in evidence than in the code's provisions for a legal system based upon rights and duties and the equality of persons under the law. These principles resulted in the creation of new legal mechanisms for the defense of individual interests. The resulting lawsuits suggest that there were possibilities for negotiating individual rights and duties even under an authoritarian political system.

The process of modern rights creation in Republican China involved legal elites, lawmakers, scholars, and judges, to be sure. The implementation of these new rights and remedies, however, depended upon the interplay of written laws, judicial procedures, and most importantly, individual grievances and various other pressures from below. Framing marital disputes in terms of rights encouraged people to conceive of their concerns in new ways. The records of thousands of marital disputes from the 1930s and 1940s attest to the fact that Republican marriage and divorce laws were not dead letters. Litigants appropriated Republican legal mechanisms and the lens of rights and duties to shape their marital disputes. Litigant "rights consciousness" not only helped to transform the way individual husbands and wives thought about what oppressed them but also gave form to their feelings of injury and injustice. Litigants forged various meanings of rights that often had little to do with lawmaker concerns with liberal modernity and much more to do with individual experiences with poverty, injustice, and grievance against family tyranny. It was through this process of reinterpretation and transformation that individual rights and equality came to be understood and rendered meaningful to ordinary people in the contexts of both family and state.

As in the Qing era, Republican law courts served as a primary site of interaction between state and society. Thus court records offer clues about the link between litigation and adjudication of marital disputes and state formation. Despite chronic budget shortfalls and mounting caseloads, the administration of justice in the Republican period was fairly commendable. Court costs were relatively moderate, proceedings handled quickly, and outcomes reasonably reliable. Republican courts were accessible to litigants. Individual wives gained the same access to the court system as their husbands enjoyed. The state through its judicial officials continued to validate husbands' claims over their wives, but the civil law framework for these disputes limited husbands' means of enforcement. As for women's grievances, the state's validation of them was limited and selective. Judicial separation and support cases reveal the courts' sympathetic treatment of bourgeois women, while intolerable cruelty divorce cases show the courts to be quite lenient regarding physical abuse. Yet the courts went to great lengths to investigate accusations of husband impotence, even when they suspected the claims to be spurious. All of these cases make clear that the Republican civil law system handled marital disputes not as "minor matters" but as formal matters to be litigated, investigated, mediated, adjudicated, or appealed in their own right.

The findings of this work also stimulate a rethinking on questions of periodization and change pertaining to Chinese women's history. The history of marriage law and practice during the late Republican era compels us to stop thinking of the 1930s and 1940s as "dark years." In terms of women, marriage, and the law, these two decades marked an important transitional period that reflected the project of liberal modernity. The changes in marriage law and practice in this transitional period were certainly not as radical as the period after the 1949 Revolution, but they were believed to have ushered in a "bloodless social revolution" in their own time. Every year between 1931 and 1949, thousands of Chinese women took legal action to improve the conditions of their marital and family lives. These women initiated lawsuits to transform their marital relationships for diverse reasons that varied by location, class background, and individual circumstance. In some cases, female litigants acted in accordance with a long tradition of women venting their domestic grievances to local officials. But by filing formal lawsuits, women in the 1930s and 1940s were also insistently moving beyond conventional practices. They were asserting newly minted legal rights often in defiance of the wishes of husbands, in-laws, natal families, and prevailing gender norms. Women as legal actors mobilized resources to mount legal challenges to their marriages and attempted to deploy the law to serve their interests. As this study has made clear, attempted social change in the 1930s and 1940s differed from the mass movements of the 1920s and 1950s in its nature, agents, and scale. Individual litigants made incremental, selective progress on a case-by-case basis, more appropriately measured by the cumulative effect of thousands of individual legal actions directed at personal domestic situations. These legal actions may be harder to detect, but in the history of Chinese women, it is perhaps the changes in marital and family life that most directly affected the lives of the majority of women.

At the same time, the book points to the ways in which women's engagement with the law and their anticipated emancipation through law were constrained throughout the 1930s and 1940s by socieconomic considerations. Not all litigants succeeded in obtaining legal relief for their domestic conflicts, as judicial records of marital disputes from these years illustrate. The exercise of women's legal rights was often circumscribed by prevailing patterns of entrenched patriarchy and pervasive poverty. The persistence of these deeply rooted problems of patriarchy and poverty reveal the limits of

Republican liberal modernity. Women continued for the most part to occupy a precarious economic position. In addition, class background, education level, natal family status, marital residence patterns, and other socioeconomic conditions continued to factor into the outcomes of Republican marriage litigation, limiting the beneficiaries to a select group of women.

When we integrate the study of gender and law, we gain a new understanding of both. This integration makes it possible to understand the Republican paradigm of liberal modernity as an important transitional period that was crucial to consolidating both legal and social trends. The Republican Civil Code, as an embodiment of GMD liberal modernity, represents a case of what I have called "legal exceptionalism." This legal exceptionalism is clear in the various developments described in this book. First, the major overhaul of Chinese law represented by the Republican Civil Code marked a liberal triumph promoting a socially progressive agenda in the context of an indisputably authoritarian regime. The creation of that liberal, modern legal regime launched a series of changes that transformed the nature of Chinese marriage, law, and society in the 1930s and beyond. For instance, in its pursuit of modernity the GMD fostered a shift from patrilineal to conjugal notions of marriage that dated back to the mid-Qing and paved the way for socialist notions of radical gender equality. Second, Republican legal exceptionalism was evident in the building of a reliable modern judicial organization. Third, the social impact of the code was widespread, with popular engagement with the law reaching new levels. This engagement is palpable in the cases of marital disputes from the period, which reveal a growing rights consciousness and an adaptation of the lens of rights and duties by ordinary women and men to interpret marital discord.

It is a truism that Chinese women have long suffered from the cruel tyrannies of domestic life. During the Qing Dynasty, the state rarely took notice of women's domestic circumstances unless they resulted in extreme violence, as in the tragic demise of woman Wang. Women also garnered the attention of the Qing state when they took their own lives to protest against their treatment. By the early twentieth century, however, the minimally invasive Qing state had given way to a more intrusive Republican state, and women gained new pathways out of desperate situations. The twentieth century marked the end of state-sanctioned domestic cruelty. During the Republican period, women's domestic plights increasingly became a matter of state concern, while women learned to contemplate their conditions in new ways. Through the emergence of rights consciousness, individual women gained a new way of thinking about their domestic oppressions. They responded to the modernizing drive of the state in the realms of marriage and family reform by embracing a new legal language of rights and duties that they then used to frame their domestic grievances into formal legal complaints. Many reached for an expanded set of legal tools (divorce, annulment, and separation and support) to resolve their disputes or at least obtain state intervention. The legal system proved ready to listen even to young brides, like Yan Peizhen of "natural eunuch" fame, who could now invoke the power of the state to redirect the course of her marriage. More changes were to come in the twentieth century. State-society relations underwent further transformation in the Socialist period, when an even more energetic state led by the Communist Party made combating domestic abuse a central part of its political program at least in the early 1950s. These changes in state-society relations illuminate the Republican period as an era when modern liberal ideas of individual rights and gender equality animated marriage, law, and society against the weight of authoritarian politics.

References

ARCHIVES

Beijing Municipal Archives (cases cited as "Beijing" followed by the file number)
Hebei Provincial Archives (cases cited as "Hebei" followed by the file number)
Jiangsu Provincial Archives (cases cited as "Jiangsu" followed by the file number)
Second Historical Archives, Nanjing (cases cited as "Supreme Court" followed by the file number; judicial files cited as "No.2A" followed by the file number)

BOOKS AND ARTICLES

Alford, William P. 1997. "Law, Law, What Law? Why Western Scholars of Chinese History and Society Have Not Had More to Say about Its Law." *Modern China* 23:4 (Oct.): 398–419.

Alford, William P., and Shen Yuanyuan. 1993. "'Law Is My Idol': John C.H. Wu and the Role of Legality and Spirituality in the Effort to 'Modernise' China." In *Essays in Honour of Wang Tieya*, edited by Ronald St. John Macdonald, 43–53. Dordretch, Netherlands: Martinus Nijhoff.

Alford, William P., and Shen Yuanyuan. 2004. "Have You Eaten? Have You Divorced? Debating the Meaning of Freedom in Marriage in China." In *Realms of Freedom in Modern China*, edited by William C. Kirby, 234–263. Stanford, CA: Stanford University Press.

Allee, Mark A. 1994. *Law and Local Society in Late Imperial China: Northern Taiwan in the Nineteenth Century*. Stanford, CA: Stanford University Press.

Andors, Phyllis. 1975. *The Unfinished Liberation of Chinese Women, 1949–1980*. Bloomington: Indiana University Press.

Angle, Stephen C. 2002. *Human Rights and Chinese Thought: A Cross-Cultural Inquiry*. New York: Cambridge University Press.

Angle, Stephen C. and Marina Svensson, eds. 2001. *The Chinese Human Rights Reader: Documents and Commentary, 1900–2000*. Armonk, NY: M. E. Sharpe.

Antony, Robert J. 1995. "Scourges on the People: Perceptions of Robbery, Snatching, and Theft in the Mid-Qing Period." *Late Imperial China* 16:2 (Dec.):98–132.

Baker, Hugh D.R. 1979. *Chinese Family and Kinship*. New York: Columbia University Press.

Barlow, Tani E. 1991. "Theorizing Woman: *Funü, Guojia, Jiating* [Chinese Women, Chinese State, Chinese Family]." *Genders* 10 (Spring): 132–160.

Barlow, Tani E. 2004. *The Question of Women in Chinese Feminism.* Durham, NC: Duke University Press.

Beahan, Charlotte. 1975. "Feminism and Nationalism in the Chinese Women's Press, 1902–1911." *Modern China* 1:4 (Oct.): 379–416.

Bergère, Marie-Claire. 1997. "Civil Society and Urban Change in Republican China." *China Quarterly* 150 (June): 309–328.

Bergère, Marie-Claire. 1989. *The Golden Age of the Chinese Bourgeoisie, 1911–1937.* Translated by Janet Lloyd. New York: Cambridge University Press.

Bernhardt, Kathryn. 1994. "Women and the Law: Divorce in the Republican Period." In Bernhardt and Huang 1994, 187–214.

Bernhardt, Kathryn. 1996. "A Ming-Qing Transition in Chinese Women's History? The Perspective from Law." In *Remapping China: Fissures in Historical Terrain*, edited by Gail Hershatter, Emily Honig, Jonathan N. Lipman, and Randall Stross, 42–58. Stanford, CA: Stanford University Press.

Bernhardt, Kathryn. 1999. *Women and Property in China, 960–1949*. Stanford, CA: Stanford University Press.

Bernhardt, Kathryn, and Philip C.C. Huang, eds. 1994. *Civil Law in Qing and Republican China*. Stanford, CA: Stanford University Press.

Birge, Bettine. 2002. *Women, Property, and Confucian Reaction in Sung and Yuan China, 960–1368.* Cambridge: Cambridge University Press.

Bodde, Derk, and Clarence Morris. 1967. *Law in Imperial China, Exemplified by 190 Ch'ing Dynasty Cases.* Cambridge, MA: Harvard University Press.

Boorman, Howard L., and Richard C. Howard, eds. 1967–1979. *Biographical Dictionary of Republican China*. 5 vols. New York: Columbia University Press.

Bossler, Beverly. 2000. "'A Daughter Is a Daughter All Her Life': Affinal Relations and Women's Networks in Song and Late Imperial China." *Late Imperial China* 21:1(June): 77–106.

Bourgon, Jérôme. 2002. "Uncivil Dialogue: Law and Custom Were Not to Merge into Civil Law under the Qing." *Late Imperial China* 23:1 (June): 50–90.

Bourgon, Jérôme. 2004. "Rights, Freedoms, and Customs in the Making of Chinese Civil Law, 1900–1936." In *Realms of Freedom in Modern China*, edited by William C. Kirby, 84–112. Stanford, CA: Stanford University Press.

Bouye, Thomas M. 2000. *Manslaughter, Markets, and Moral Economy: Violent Disputes over Property Rights in Eighteenth-Century China.* Cambridge: Cambridge University Press.

Brødsgaard, Kjeld Erik, and David Strand, eds. 1998. *Reconstructing Twentieth-Century China: State Control, Civil Society, and National Identity.* New York: Oxford University Press.

Brownell, Susan, and Jeffrey N. Wasserstrom, eds. 2002. *Chinese Femininities, Chinese Masculinities: A Reader*. Berkeley: University of California Press.

Buxbaum, David C. 1971. "Some Aspects of Civil Procedure and Practice at the Trial Level in Tanshui and Hsinchu from 1789 to 1895." *Journal of Asian Studies* 30:2 (Feb.): 255–279.

Buxbaum, David C. 1978. "A Case Study of the Dynamics of Family Law and Social Change in Rural China." In Buxbaum 1978, 217–260.

Buxbaum, David C., ed. 1978. *Chinese Family Law and Social Change in Historical and Comparative Perspective*. Seattle: University of Washington Press.

Cai Yuanpei. (1904) 1984. "Xinnian meng (New year's dream)." Reprinted in *Wuzhengfu zhuyi sixiang ziliao xuan* (Selected materials on anarchist thought), edited by Ge Maochun, Jiang Jun, and Li Xingzhi. 2 vols. Beijing: Beijing daxue chubanshe.

Chan, Sinn Yee. 2004. "The Personal Is Political: Confucianism and Liberal Feminism." In *The Politics of Affective Relations: East Asia and Beyond,* edited by Daniel A. Bell and Hahm Chaihark, 97–118. Lanham, MD: Lexington Books.

Chang, C.H., Y.L. Liang, and John C.H. Wu. 1925. "Persons in Chinese Law." *China Law Review* 2:6 (Oct.): 257–279.

Chang, Kia-ngau. 1958. *The Inflationary Spiral: The Experience in China, 1939–1950.* Cambridge, MA: Technology Press of Massachusetts Institute of Technology.

Chen Changheng. 1930. "Duiyu minfa qinshu jicheng liangbian yuanze shang ying xianjue gedian zhi yijian (Opinion on the preliminary principles to be resolved in the civil code family and inheritance books)." *Falü pinglun* (Law Weekly) 347–348 (June 8 and 15): 30–32, 25–30. Reprinted in slightly different form in *Zhongyang ribao* (Central Daily News) (July 3–5).

Chen Dongyuan. (1928) 1994. *Zhongguo funü shenghuo shi* (History of the lives of women in China). Taipei: Shangwu.

Chen Ganyi. 1930. "Wo duiyu suowei 'Minfa shang de san ge wenti' de yijian (My opinion on the so-called 'Three questions about the civil code')." *Dagongbao* (L'impartial) (May 9).

Chen Guyuan. (1925) 1933. *Zhongguo gudai hunyin shi* (A history of marriage in traditional China). Shanghai: Shangwu.

Chen Guyuan. (1935) 1989. *Zhongguo fazhi shi* (A history of the Chinese legal system). Shanghai: Shanghai shudian.

Chen Hengzhe. 1936. "Chuan xing suoji (Sundry anecdotes from traveling through Sichuan)." *Duli pinglun* (Independent critic) 190 (Mar. 1): 14–20.

Chen Liren. 1930. "Minfa qinshubian ji ge wenti (A few questions about the civil code family book)." *Dagongbao* (May 22–24).

Chen Qiyan, Huang Zongle, and Guo Zhengong, eds. 1999. *Minfa qinshu xin lun* (New treatise on the civil code family book). Taipei: Sanmin shuju.

Chen Tingzhen. 1940. "Xin jiating zhidu zhi shangque (Discussion of the new family system)." *Zhongguo nü qingnian* 1:3 (June): 4–7.

Cheng, F.T. [Zheng Tianxi]. 1930. "Recent Legislation in China." *China Law Review* 4:5 (July): 117–120.

Cheng, Joseph Kai Huan. 1976. "Chinese Law in Transition: The Late Ch'ing Law Reform, 1901-1911." PhD diss., Brown University.

Cheng Taisheng. 1981. *Hu Hanmin de zhengzhi sixiang* (The political thought of Hu Hanmin). Taipei: Liming wenhua shiye gongsi.

Cheng, Tien-hsi [Zheng Tianxi]. 1948. "The Development and Reform of Chinese Law." *Current Legal Problems* 1:170–187.

Chiang Yung-ching [Jiang Yongjing]. 1977. "Hu Han-min's Ideas on Women's Rights and His Achievements." Translated by K.C. Ma. *Chinese Studies in History* 10:4 (Summer): 34–72.

Ch'ien, Tuan-sheng. 1950. *The Government and Politics of China.* Cambridge, MA: Harvard University Press.

China Year Book 1929–1930. 1929. Edited by H.G.W. Woodhead. Tianjin: Tientsin Press.

Chu, Boyer P.H. [Zhu Baoxian]. 1935. *Commentaries on the Chinese Civil Code Book 1, General Principles.* Shanghai: Shanghai Law Book Publishing Society.

Ch'ü T'ung-tsu [Qu Tongzu]. 1961. *Law and Society in Traditional China.* Paris: Mouton.

Civil Code of the Republic of China. (1930–1931) 1976. Translated by Ching-lin Hsia [Xia Jinlin], James L.E. Chow [Zhou Fuqing], Liu Chieh, and Yukon Chang. Arlington, VA: University Publications of America.

Cohen, Paul A. 2002. "Reflections on a Watershed Date: The 1949 Divide in Chinese History." In *Twentieth-Century China: New Approaches,* edited by Jeffrey N. Wasserstrom, 27–36. London: Routledge.

Collins, Leslie E. 1976. "The New Women: A Psychohistorical Study of the Chinese Feminist Movement from 1900 to the Present." PhD diss., Yale University.

Cong, Xiaoping. 2007. *Teachers' Schools and the Making of the Modern Chinese Nation-State, 1897-1937.* Vancouver: University of British Columbia Press.

Conner, Alison W. 1994. "Lawyers and the Legal Profession during the Republican Period." In Bernhardt and Huang 1994, 215–248.

Conner, Alison W. 2003. "The Comparative Law School of China," pp. 210–273 in C. Stephen Hsu, ed., *Understanding China's Legal System.* New York: New York University Press.

Cott, Nancy F. 2000. *Public Vows: A History of Marriage and the Nation.* Cambridge, MA: Harvard University Press.

Croll, Elisabeth J. 1980. *Feminism and Socialism in China.* New York: Schocken Books.

Dai Yanhui. (1955) 1965. *Zhongguo qinshu fa* (Chinese family law). Taipei: Taida faxueyuan shiwu zu.

Daliyuan panjueli quanshu (Complete edition of the Daliyuan's written opinions). (1931) 1972, edited by Guo Wei. Taipei: Chengwen chubanshe.

Darmon, Pierre. 1985. *Trial by Impotence: Virility and Marriage in Pre-Revolutionary France*. Translated by Paul Keegan. London: Chatto and Windus.

Davin, Delia. 1976. *Woman-Work: Women and the Party in Revolutionary China*. Oxford: Clarendon Press.

Davis, Natalie Zemon. 1983. *The Return of Martin Guerre*. Cambridge, MA: Harvard University Press.

Deng Jixing. 1933. "Xiugai minfa qinshubian zhi jianyi (Suggestions on the revision of the civil code family book)." *Funü gongming* (Women's Echo) 2: (Aug. 1): 5–9.

Deng Jixing. 1935. "Minfa qinshu bian nannü bu pingdeng ge tiao yanjiu (Research on the provisions of the Civil Code Family Book that are not gender equal)." *Funü gongming* 4: (Jan. 20): 33–37.

Desan, Suzanne. 2004. *The Family on Trial in Revolutionary France*. Berkeley: University of California Press.

Diamant, Neil J. 2000. *Revolutionizing the Family: Politics, Love, and Divorce in Urban and Rural China, 1949–1968*. Berkeley: University of California Press.

Diamant, Neil J., Stanley B. Lubman, and Kevin J. O'Brien, eds. 2005. *Engaging the Law in China: State, Society, and Possibilities for Justice*. Stanford, CA: Stanford University Press.

Diamond, Norma. 1975. "Women under Kuomintang Rule: Variations on the Feminine Mystique." *Modern China* 1:1 (Jan.): 3–45.

Dikötter, Frank. 2002. *Crime, Punishment, and the Prison in Modern China, 1895–1949*. New York: Columbia University Press.

Dirlik, Arif. 1991. *Anarchism in the Chinese Revolution*. Berkeley: University of California Press.

Dirlik, Arif. 1996. "Reversals, Ironies, Hegemonies: Notes on the Contemporary Historiography of Modern China." *Modern China* 22:3 (July): 243–284.

Eastman, Lloyd E. 1974. *The Abortive Revolution: China under Nationalist Rule, 1927–1937*. Cambridge, MA: Harvard University Press.

Eastman, Lloyd E. 1984. *Seeds of Destruction: Nationalist China in War and Revolution 1937–1949*. Stanford, CA: Stanford University Press.

Edwards, Louise P. 2008. *Gender, Politics, and Democracy: Women's Suffrage in China*. Stanford, CA: Stanford University Press.

Eisenstein, Zillah R. (1981) 1993. *The Radical Future of Liberal Feminism*. Boston: Northeastern University Press.

Engels, Friedrich. (1891) 1972. *The Origin of the Family, Private Property, and the State*. New York: Pathfinder Press.

Epps, Charles R. 1998. *The Rights Revolution: Lawyers, Activists, and Supreme Courts in Comparative Perspective*. Chicago: University of Chicago Press.

Escarra, Jean. (1936) 1961. *Chinese Law: Conception and Evolution, Legislative and Judicial Institutions, Science and Teaching*. Translated by Gertrude R. Browne. Seattle: University of Washington.

Esherick, Joseph W. 1995. "Ten Theses on the Chinese Revolution." *Modern China* 21:1 (Jan.): 45–76.

Esherick, Joseph W. 2001. "War and Revolution: Chinese Society during the 1940s." *Twentieth-Century China* 27:1 (Nov.): 1–37.

Ewick, Patricia and Susan Silbey. 1998. *The Common Place of Law: Stories from Everyday Life*. Chicago: University of Chicago Press.

Falü cao'an huibian (Compilation of draft laws). (1926) 1973. Compiled by Xiuding falü guan. Taipei: Chengwen chubanshe.

Falü da cidian (A complete law dictionary). 1934. Edited by Wang Hanzhang, Dong Kang, et al. Shanghai: Datong shuju yinxing.

Fei'e [pseud.]. 1933. "Ta yinggai xing sheme (What should she be surnamed?)." *Nüsheng* 1:10 (Feb. 15): 18–19.

Felstiner, William L.F., Richard L. Abel, and Austin Sarat. 1980–1981. "The Emergence and Transformation of Disputes: Naming, Blaming, Claiming . . ." *Law and Society Review* 15:3-4: 631–54.

Fitzgerald, John. 1996. *Awakening China: Politics, Culture, and Class in the Nationalist Revolution.* Stanford, CA: Stanford University Press.
Fitzgerald, John. 2002. "Conclusion" to *Defining Modernity: Guomindang Rhetorics of a New China, 1920-1970*, edited by Terry D. Bodenhorn, 263–276. Ann Arbor: Center for Chinese Studies, University of Michigan.
Fogel, Joshua A., and Peter G. Zarrow, eds. 1997. *Imagining the People: Chinese Intellectuals and the Concept of Citizenship, 1890–1920*. Armonk, NY: M.E. Sharpe.
Freeze, ChaeRan Y. 2002. *Jewish Marriage and Divorce in Imperial Russia.* Hanover, NH: University Press of New England for Brandeis University Press.
Fu Bingchang. 1930a. "Qinshu jicheng liang bian gezhong zhongyao wenti (Various important issues regarding the family and inheritance books)." Speech to the Legislative Yuan reprinted in *Zhongyang ribao* (Apr. 20–21), as "Qinshu jicheng qicao de kunnan, yuanze yi chengqing Zhongzhenghui heding: Fu Bingchang zai Lifayuan zhi yanjiang (Difficulties with the family and inheritance books, CPC requested to set the principles: Fu Bingchang's speech to the Legislative Yuan)," *Dagongbao* (Apr. 28), and as "Qinshu jicheng fa shang de ji ge zhongyao wenti (A few important issues regarding family and inheritance law)," *Falü pinglun* 342 (May 4): 15–19.
Fu Bingchang [Foo Ping-sheung]. 1930b. Introduction to *The Civil Code of the Republic of China, Books I–III*, p. xx–xxi. Translated by Ching-lin Hsia [Xia Jinlin], James L.E. Chow [Zhou Fuqing], Liu Chieh, and Yukon Chang. Arlington, VA: University Publications of America.
Fu Bingchang [Foo Ping-sheung]. 1930c. Introduction to *The Civil Code of the Republic of China, Books IV–V*. Translated by Ching-lin Hsia [Xia Jinlin], James L.E. Chow [Zhou Fuqing], Liu Chieh, and Yukon Chang. Arlington, VA: University Publications of America.
Fu Bingchang and Zhou Dingyu, eds. 1964. *Zhonghua minguo liu fa liyou pan jie huibian* (Compendium of rationales, judgments, and explanations of the six laws of the Republic of China), vol. 2 (Civil Law). Taipei: Xin lu shudian.
Furth, Charlotte, Judith T. Zeitlin, and Ping-chen Hsiung, eds. 2007. *Thinking with Cases: Specialist Knowledge in Chinese Cultural History*. Honolulu: University of Hawaii Press.
Gallagher, Mary E. 2005. *Contagious Capitalism: Globalization and the Politics of Labor in China*. Princeton, NJ: Princeton University Press.
Gallagher, Mary E. 2006. "Mobilizing the Law in China: 'Informed Disenchantment' and the Development of Legal Consciousness." *Law and Society Review* 40: 4 (Dec.): 783–816.
German Civil Code. 1907. Translated by Chung Hui Wang [Wang Chonghui]. London: Stevens and Sons.
Giddens, Anthony. 1979. *Central Problems in Social Theory: Action, Structure, and Contradiction in Social Analysis*. Berkeley: University of California Press.
Gilmartin, Christina K. 1990. "Violence against Women in Contemporary China." In *Violence in China: Essays in Culture and Counterculture,* edited by Jonathan N. Lipman and Stevan Harrell, 203–221. Albany: State University of New York Press.
Gilmartin, Christina K. 1995. *Engendering the Chinese Revolution: Radical Women, Communist Politics, and Mass Movements in the 1920s*. Berkeley: University of California Press.
Gilmartin, Christina K., Gail Hershatter, Lisa Rofel, and Tyrene White, eds. 1994. *Engendering China: Women, Culture, and the State*. Cambridge, MA: Harvard University Press.
Glosser, Susan L. 2003. *Chinese Visions of Family and State, 1915–1953.* Berkeley: University of California Press.
Goldman, Wendy Z. 1993. *Women, the State and Revolution: Soviet Family Policy and Social Life, 1917–1936.* Cambridge: Cambridge University Press.
Goodman, Bryna. 2006. "Appealing to the Public: Newspaper Presentation and the Adjudication of Emotion," *Twentieth-Century China* 31: 2 (Apr.): 32–69.
Goodman, Bryna. 2005. "The New Woman Commits Suicide: The Press, Cultural Memory and the New Republic." *Journal of Asian Studies* 64:1(Feb.): 67-101.
Goodman, Bryna. 1995. *Native Place, City and Nation: Regional Networks and Identities in Shanghai, 1853–1937.* Berkeley: University of California Press.

Goodman, David S. G. 2000. "Revolutionary Women and Women in the Revolution: The Chinese Communist Party and Women in the War of Resistance to Japan, 1937–1945." *China Quarterly* 164 (Dec.): 915–942.
Greiff, Thomas E. 1985. "The Principle of Human Rights in Nationalist China: John C.H. Wu and the Ideological Origins of the 1946 Constitution." *China Quarterly* 103 (Sept.): 441–461.
Hanawalt, Barbara A. 2007. *The Wealth of Wives: Women, Law, and Economy in Late Medieval London.* New York: Oxford University Press.
Hardwick, Julie. 2009. *Family Business: Litigation and the Political Economies of Daily Life in Early Modern France.* Oxford: Oxford University Press.
Harrison, Henrietta. 2000. *The Making of the Republican Citizen: Political Ceremonies and Symbols in China, 1911–1929.* Oxford: Oxford University Press.
Hartog, Hendrik. 2000. *Man and Wife in America: A History.* Cambridge, MA: Harvard University Press.
Hegel, Robert E., and Katherine Carlitz, eds. 2007. *Writing and Law in Late Imperial China: Crime, Conflict, and Judgment.* Seattle: University of Washington Press.
Hershatter, Gail. 1986. *The Workers of Tianjin, 1900–1949.* Stanford, CA: Stanford University Press.
Hershatter, Gail. 1997. *Dangerous Pleasures: Prostitution and Modernity in Twentieth-Century Shanghai.* Berkeley: University of California Press.
Hershatter, Gail. 2007. *Women in China's Long Twentieth Century.* Berkeley: University of California Press.
Hobsbawm, Eric J. 1994. *Age of Extremes: The Short Twentieth Century, 1914–1991.* London: Abacus.
Hsia, Ching-lin [Xia Jinlin]. 1977. *My Five Incursions into Diplomacy and Some Personal Reminiscences.* New York.
Hu Changqing. 1929. "Mingyu quan zhi benzhi (The essence of the right of reputation)." *Falü pinglun* 274 (Jan.13): 1–6.
Hu Changqing. 1930. "Du Chen Changheng shi 'Duiyu minfa qinshu jicheng liangbian ying xianjue gedian zhi yijian' (Reading Mr. Chen Changheng's 'Opinion on the preliminary principles to be resolved in the civil code family and inheritance books')." *Falü pinglun* 352 (July 13): 9–13.
Hu Changqing. 1931. *Zhongguo hunyin fa lun* (Treatise on Chinese marriage law). Nanjing: Falű pinglun she.
Hu Changqing. 1997. *Zhongguo minfa zonglun* (General discussion of Chinese civil law). Reprint. Beijing: Zhongguo zhengfa daxue chubanshe.
Hu, Chi-hsi. 1974. "The Sexual Revolution in the Kiangsi Soviet." *China Quarterly* 59 (July-Sept.): 477–490.
Hu Hanmin. 1920. "Cong jingji jichu guancha jiazu zhidu (An economic-based analysis of the family system)." *Jianshe* 2:4 (May 1).
Hu Hanmin. 1929. "The New Civil Code." *China Critic* 2:19–20 (May 9 and 16).
Hu Hanmin. 1930a. "Zenyang qu zuo da shiye (How to go about doing great things)." *Zhongyang ribao* (Apr. 25).
Hu Hanmin. 1930b. "Minfa qinshu jicheng liangbian zhong zhi jiazu zhidu (The family system in the civil code family and inheritance books)." *Zhongyang ribao* (Dec. 20–25).
Hu Hanmin. 1978. *Hu Hanmin xiansheng wenji* (Collected writings of Hu Hanmin). 4 vols. Taipei: Dangshi weiyuanhui.
Hu Hanmin, and Lin Sen. 1930. "Minfa qinshu jicheng bian ying zhuyi ge dian (Points to be attended to in the civil code family and inheritance books)." *Zhongyang ribao* (Apr. 16–17); also reprinted in *Dagongbao* (Apr. 24).
Hua Yougen. 1993. *Zhongguo jindai falü sixiang shi* (History of modern Chinese legal thought), vol. 2. Shanghai: Shanghai shehui kexueyuan.
Huang Jiping, ed. 1936. *Dangdai funü* (Contemporary women). Shanghai.
Huang, Philip C. C. 1996. *Civil Justice in China: Representation and Practice in the Qing.* Stanford, CA: Stanford University Press.

Huang, Philip C. C. 2001. *Code, Custom, and Legal Practice: The Qing and the Republic Compared*. Stanford, CA: Stanford University Press.

Huang, Philip C. C. 2008. "Introduction to 'The Nature of the Chinese State: Dialogues among Western and Chinese Scholars I." *Modern China* 34: 1(Jan.): 3–8.

Huang Shuxian. 1940. "Funü de zhengzhi diwei (The political status of women)." *Zhongguo nüqingnian* 1:2 (May 8): 3–5.

Huang, Yuansheng. 2009. *Yingyin Daliyuan minshi panli bai xuan* (Selected Daliyuan decisions). Taipei: Wu nan tu shu chuban.

Huang Yuansheng. 2011. *Minchu Daliyuan yu caipan* (Daliyuan judgments in the early republic). Taipei: Yuan zhao chuban youxian gongsi.

Huey, Herbert. 1984. "Law and Social Attitudes in 1920s Shanghai." *Hong Kong Law Journal* 14:3 (Sept.): 306–322.

Hunefeldt, Christine. 2000. *Liberalism in the Bedroom: Quarreling Spouses in Nineteenth-Century Lima*. University Park: Pennsylvania State University Press.

Hung, William S.H. (Shih-hao). 1934. *Outlines of Modern Chinese Law: Legal History, Contracts, Agency, Sales, Bailments and Carriers, Partnership, Property, Domestic Relations, Succession, Private Corporations, Negotiable Instruments, Criminal Law, Including List of Prevailing Laws and Table of Degrees of Punishment*. Shanghai: Kelly and Walsh.

International Journal of Asian Studies special issues on "Law, State and Society in China," 2004–2008.

Isaacs, Harold R. (1938) 1962. *The Tragedy of the Chinese Revolution.* Stanford, CA: Stanford University Press.

Isett, Christopher M. 2007. *State, Peasant, and Merchant in Qing Manchuria, 1644–1862.* Stanford, CA: Stanford University Press.

Jamieson, George. (1921) 1970. *Chinese Family and Commercial Law.* Hong Kong: Vetch and Lee.

Ji Qingyi. 1941. "Guanyu zinü xingshi wenti (On the issue of children's surnames)." *Funü gongming* 10:1 (Mar. 1): 14–15.

Jiang Liping and Lin Weiping. 2004. *Min jian de huisheng:* Xinminbao *chuangshiren Chen Mingde Deng Jixing zhuan* (The voice of the people: A biography of the founders of the New People's Daily Chen Mingde and Deng Jixing). Beijing: Xin shijie.

Jin Shiyin. 1931. "Du minfa qinshu bian hou zhi yiwen (Doubts on reading the Civil Code Family Book)." *Funü gongming* 39 (Jan. 1): 8–17.

Johnson, Kay Ann. 1983. *Women, the Family, and Peasant Revolution in China.* Chicago: University of Chicago Press.

Johnston, Reginald F. (1910) 1986. *Lion and Dragon in Northern China*. Hong Kong: Oxford University Press.

Jones, Peter. 1994. *Rights*. New York: St. Martin's Press.

Judd, Ellen R. 1989. "Niangjia: Chinese Women and Their Natal Families." *Journal of Asian Studies* 48:3 (Aug.): 525–544.

Judge, Joan. 2008. *The Precious Raft of History: The Past, the West, and the Woman Question in China.* Stanford, CA: Stanford University Press.

Karl, Rebecca E. 2000. "History and Gender in China." *Radical History Review* 77 (Spring): 142–156.

Key, Ellen. 1911. *Love and Marriage*. Translated by Arthur G. Chater. New York: G.P. Putnam's Sons.

Kiang Yung. 1924–1926. "The Development of Modern Legal Institutions and Judicial Reform in China." Translated by Yueng-li Liang. *China Law Review* 2: 19–31, 77–87, 117–134.

Ko, Dorothy. 2005. *Cinderella's Sisters: A Revisionist History of Footbinding.* Berkeley: University of California Press.

Ko, Dorothy. 1994. *Teachers of the Inner Chambers: Women and Culture in Seventeenth-Century China*. Stanford, CA: Stanford University Press.

Krebs, Edward S. 1998. *Shifu: Soul of Chinese Anarchism.* Lanham, MD: Rowman and Littlefield.

Kuhn, Philip A. 1990. *Soulstealers: The Chinese Sorcery Scare of 1768.* Cambridge, MA: Harvard University Press.

Kuryū Takeo. 1931. *Hunyin fa zhi jindaihua* (The modernization of marriage law). Translated by Hu Changqing. Nanjing: Falü pinglun she.

Lan, Hua R., and Vanessa L. Fong, eds. 1999. *Women in Republican China: A Sourcebook.* Armonk, NY: M.E. Sharpe.

Lary, Diana. 2007. *China's Republic.* Cambridge: Cambridge University Press.

Lean, Eugenia. 2007. *Public Passions: The Trial of Shi Jianqiao and the Rise of Public Sympathy.* Berkeley: University of California Press

Lee, Bernice J. 1975. "The Change in the Legal Status of Women in Civil Matters from Traditional Law to the Republican Civil Code." PhD diss., University of Sydney.

Leutner, Mechthild, and Nicola Spakowski, eds. 2005. *Women in China: The Republican Period in Historical Perspective.* New Brunswick: Transaction.

Levi, Werner. 1945. "The Family in Modern Chinese Law." *Far Eastern Quarterly* 4:3 (May): 263–273.

Levine, Marilyn A. 1993. *The Found Generation: Chinese Communists in Europe during the Twenties.* Seattle: University of Washington Press.

Li, Huaiyin. 2005. *Village Governance in North China, 1875–1936.* Stanford, CA: Stanford University Press.

Li Jingxi. 1948. "Lun xingming quan (On rights over names)." *Falü pinglun* 762 (Mar. 28): 1–5.

[Li] Yitao [Li Zhishan]. 1930. "Wo duiyu minfa zhong qinshu chengji liang bian de yijian (My views on the civil code family and inheritance books)." *Funü gongming* 28 (May 15): 6–9.

[Li] Zhishan. 1935. "Wo ye lai tantan yihun funü de xingshi (Let me also discuss married women's surnames)." *Funü gongming* 4:2 (Feb. 20): 30–31.

Li Zuyin. 1929. "Tongxing bu hun zhidu lun (On the system by which same-surnames do not marry)." *Falü pinglun* 284 (Mar. 21): 1–12.

Liang Huijin. 1997. "Minguo ershisan nian funü zhengqu nannü pingdeng kexing zhi jingguo: yi tongjian zui wei li (The women's struggle for gender equal sentencing: the example of adultery)." *Guoshiguan guankan* 23 (Feb.): 143–168.

Liang, Linxia. 2007. *Delivering Justice in Qing China: Civil Trials in the Magistrate's Court.* Oxford: British Academy, Oxford University Press.

Lifayuan gongbao.

Lin Zhenyong. 1930. "Zenyang jiejue Zhongguo de hunyin wenti (How to resolve China's marriage problem)." *Dadao* supplement to *Zhongyang ribao* (Dec. 23–24).

Lipkin, Zwia. 2006. *Useless to the State: "Social Problems" and Social Engineering in Nationalist Nanjing, 1927–1937.* Cambridge, MA: Harvard University Asia Center, distributed by Harvard University Press.

Liu fa quan shu (Complete text of the six codes). 1932. Shanghai: Shanghai faxue bianyishe.

Liu Fengfen. 1940. "Hunyin zhidu gailiang chuyi (My humble opinion on marriage reform)." *Zhongguo nü qingnian* 1:2 (May 8): 5–8.

Liu Hengjing. 1941. "Wo duiyu xingshi wenti de yijian (My opinion on the surname issue)." *Funü gongming* 10:1 (Mar. 1): 12–14.

Liu Hengjing. 1947. *Funü wenti wenji* (Collected writings on the women's question). Nanjing: Funü yuekan she.

Liu Lumin. 1930. "Duiyu qinshu jicheng bian xianjue wenti zhi yanjiu (Research on the preliminary issues to be resolved in the civil code family and inheritance books)." *Faxue congkan* 1:4:1–17.

Liu, Yu. 2010. "Maoist Discourse and the Mobilization of Emotions in Revolutionary China." *Modern China* 36: 3 (May): 329–62.

Lü Fangshang. 1994. "Kangzhan shiqi de nüquan lunbian (Arguments over women's rights during the war of resistance)." *Jindai Zhongguo funü shi yanjiu* 2 (June): 81–115.

Lü Fangshang. 1995. "Ling yi zhong 'wei zuzhi': kangzhan shiqi hunyin yu jiating wenti chutan (Another type of 'pseudo-institution': Preliminary investigation into questions of marriage and family during the war of resistance)." *Jindai Zhongguo funü shi yanjiu* 3 (Aug.): 97–121.

Lu, Hanchao. 1999. *Beyond the Neon Lights: Everyday Shanghai in the Early Twentieth Century.* Berkeley: University of California Press.

Lu, Hanchao. 2005. *Street Criers: A Cultural History of Chinese Beggars.* Stanford, CA: Stanford University Press.

Lubman, Stanley B. 2003. "The Study of Chinese Law in the United States: Reflections on the Past and Concerns About the Future." *Washington University Global Studies Law Review* 2 (Winter): 1- 36.

Luo Ding. 1946. *Qinshu fa gang yao* (Outline of family law). Shanghai: Dadong shuju.

Luo Suwen. 1996. *Nüxing yu jindai Zhongguo shehui* (Women and modern Chinese society). Shanghai: Shanghai renmin chubanshe.

Macauley, Melissa. 1998. *Social Power and Legal Culture: Litigation Masters in Late Imperial China.* Stanford, CA: Stanford University Press.

MacCormack, Geoffrey. 1996. *The Spirit of Traditional Chinese Law.* Athens, GA: University of Georgia Press.

Maine, Sir Henry S. (1864) 1986. *Ancient Law: Its Connection with the Early History of Society, and Its Relation to Modern Ideas.* Tucson: University of Arizona Press.

Mann, Susan. 1997. *Precious Records: Women in China's Long Eighteenth Century.* Stanford, CA: Stanford University Press.

McCann, Michael W. 1994. *Rights at Work: Pay Equity Reform and the Politics of Legal Mobilization.* Chicago: University of Chicago Press.

McKnight, Brian E. 1981. *The Quality of Mercy: Amnesties and Traditional Chinese Justice.* Honolulu: University of Hawaii Press.

McLaren, Angus. 2007. *Impotence: A Cultural History.* Chicago: University of Chicago Press.

Mei Shu. 1930. "Duiyu 'Hu Hanmin jiangyan' de ji ju hua (A few words on 'Hu Hanmin's speeches')." *Dagongbao* (May 10).

Meijer, Marinus J. (1950) 1976. *The Introduction of Modern Criminal Law in China.* Arlington, VA: University Publications of America.

Meijer, Marinus J. 1971. *Marriage Law and Policy in the Chinese People's Republic.* Hong Kong: Hong Kong University Press.

Merry, Sally Engle. 2006. *Human Rights and Gender Violence: Translating International Law into Local Practice.* Chicago: University of Chicago Press.

Michael, Franz. 1962. "The Role of Law in Traditional, Nationalist and Communist China." *China Quarterly* 9 (Jan.-Mar.): 124–148.

Million, Joelle. 2003. *Woman's Voice, Woman's Place: Lucy Stone and the Birth of the Woman's Rights Movement.* Westport, CT: Praeger.

Ming [pseudo.]. 1941. "Yonghu 'Wo duiyu xingshiwenti de yijian' he 'Guanyu zinü xingshi wenti' (In support of 'My opinion on the surname issue' and 'On the issue of children's surnames')." *Zhongguo nü qingnian* 1:5 (Apr. 30): 1–2.

Minguo renwu dacidian (Biographical dictionary of the Republic of China). (1991) 2007. Edited by Xu Youchun. Shijiazhuang: Hebei renmin chubanshe.

Minshi xiguan diaocha baogao lü. (1930) 2000. Compiled by the Sifa xingzheng bu. Beijing: Zhengfa daxue.

Mühlhahn, Klaus. 2009. *Criminal Justice in China: A History.* Cambridge, MA: Harvard University Press.

Nathan, Andrew J. 1976. *Peking Politics: Factionalism and the Failure of Constitutionalism.* Berkeley: University of California Press.

Nathan, Andrew J. 1986. "Sources of Chinese Rights Thinking." In *Human Rights in Contemporary China,* edited by R. Randle Edwards, Louis Henkin, and Andrew J. Nathan, 125–164. New York: Columbia University Press.

Nedostup, Rebecca. 2010. *Superstitious Regimes: Religion and the Politics of Chinese Modernity.* Cambridge, MA: Harvard University Asia Center, distributed by Harvard University Press.

Neighbors, Jennifer M. 2009. "The Long Arm of Qing Law? Qing Dynasty Homicide Rulings in Republican Courts." *Modern China* 35:1 (Jan.): 3–37.

O'Brien, Kevin J. and Lianjiang Li. 2006. *Rightful Resistance in Rural China.* New York: Cambridge University Press.

Ocko, Jonathan K. 1988. "I'll Take It All the Way to Beijing: Capital Appeals in the Qing." *Journal of Asian Studies* 47:2 (May): 291–315.

Ono, Kazuko. 1989. *Chinese Women in a Century of Revolution, 1850–1950*. Edited by Joshua A. Fogel. Stanford, CA: Stanford University Press.

Pan Yihong. 1997. "Feminism and Nationalism in China's War of Resistance against Japan." *International History Review* 19:1 (Feb.): 115–130.

Pateman, Carole. 1988. *The Sexual Contract*. Stanford, CA: Stanford University Press.

Peake, Cyrus H. 1937. "Recent Studies on Chinese Law." *Political Science Quarterly* 52:1 (Mar.): 117–138.

Peng Shi. 1935. "Ren'ge quan zhi yanjiu (Research on human personhood rights)." *Falü pinglun* 612 (Aug. 4).

Pepper, Suzanne. (1978) 1999. *Civil War in China: The Political Struggle, 1945–1949*. Lanham, MD: Rowman & Littlefield.

Perry, Elizabeth J. 2008a. "Chinese Conceptions of 'Rights': From Mencius to Mao—and Now." *Perspectives on Politics* 6:1 (Mar.): 37–50.

Perry, Elizabeth J. 2008b. "Reclaiming the Chinese Revolution." *Journal of Asian Studies* 67:4 (Nov.): 1147–1164.

Phillips, Roderick. 1988. *Putting Asunder: A History of Divorce in Western Society*. New York: Cambridge University Press.

Qian [pseud.]. 1934. "Tan yihun nüzi de xingming wenti (Discussing the question of married women's surnames)." *Nü sheng* 3:5 (Dec. 15): 3.

Qian Jianqiu. 1936. "Zhonghua minguo falü yu funü (Law and women in the Republic of China)." In *Dangdai funü*, edited by Huang Jiping, 39–45. Shanghai.

Reddy, William M. 1997. *The Invisible Code: Honor and Sentiment in Postrevolutionary France, 1815–1848*. Berkeley: University of California Press.

Reddy, William M. 2001. *The Navigation of Feeling: A Framework for the History of Emotions*. Cambridge: Cambridge University Press.

Reed, Bradly W. 2000. *Talons and Teeth: County Clerks and Runners in the Qing Dynasty*. Stanford, CA: Stanford University Press.

Riasanovsky, Valentin A. (1938) 1976. *Chinese Civil Law*. Arlington, VA: University Publications of America.

Ruskola, Teemu. 1994. "Law, Sexual Morality, and Gender Equality in Qing and Communist China." *Yale Law Journal* 103:8 (June): 2531–2565.

Scheingold, Stuart A. [1974] 2004. *The Politics of Rights: Lawyers, Public Policy, and Political Change*. Ann Arbor: University of Michigan Press.

Schneider, Helen M. 2011. *Keeping the Nation's House: Domestic Management and The Making of Modern China*. Vancouver: University of British Columbia Press.

Schwartz, Benjamin I. 1964. *In Search of Wealth and Power: Yen Fu and the West*. Cambridge, MA: Harvard University Press.

Scogin, Hugh T., Jr. 1994. "Civil 'Law' in Traditional China: History and Theory." In Bernhardt and Huang 1994, 13–41.

Scott, James C. 1998. *Seeing Like a State: How Certain Schemes to Improve the Human Condition Have Failed.* New Haven: Yale University Press.

Shapiro, Hugh. 1998. "The Puzzle of Spermatorrhea in Republican China." *positions* 6:3 (Winter): 551-595.

Shen Jiaben. 1982a. "Fan jin tonxing wei hun (Reverse the prohibition against same-surname marriage." In Wang 1982, 850.

Shen Jiaben. 1982b. "Biantong yixing wei si niyi (Proposal to allow different-surname succession)." In Wang 1982, 852.

Shenbao. 1930. "Zuo wu Lifayuan zhi shengyan: jiejue xing hunyin jiating wenti (Yesterday afternoon's grand banquet at the Legislative Yuan: solving the surname, marriage, and family problems)." (Apr. 19).

Sheng, R.C.W. 1930. "The Civil Code of China." *China Law Review* 4:4 (Apr.): 69–78.

Sheridan, James E. 1975. *China in Disintegration: The Republican Era in Chinese History, 1912–1949.* New York: Free Press.

Shi Shangkuan. (1964) 2000. *Qinshu fa lun* (Treatise on family law). Beijing: Zhengfa daxue chubanshe.

Shibao (The Truth Post). 1936. Beijing.

Shklar, Judith N. 1984. *Ordinary Vices*. Cambridge, MA: Harvard University Press.
Shue, Vivienne. 1988. *The Reach of the State: Sketches of the Chinese Body Politic*. Stanford, CA: Stanford University Press.
Sifa tongji: 1936. 1938. Chongqing: Sifa xinzhengbu.
Sifayuan jieshi huibian (Judicial Yuan digest of legal explanations). 1931–1935. 5 vols. Edited by Sifayuan canshichu. Nanjing: Sifayuan canshichu.
Sommer, Matthew H. 2000. *Sex, Law, and Society in Late Imperial China*. Stanford, CA: Stanford University Press.
Spence, Jonathan D. 1978. *The Death of Woman Wang*. New York: Viking Press.
Stacey, Judith. 1983. *Patriarchy and Socialist Revolution in China*. Berkeley: University of California Press.
Stannard, Una. 1977. *Mrs. Man*. San Francisco: Germainbooks.
Stapleton, Kristin. 2000. *Civilizing Chengdu: Chinese Urban Reform, 1895–1937*. Cambridge, MA: Harvard University Asia Center, distributed by Harvard University Press.
Stone, Lawrence. 1990. *Road to Divorce: England 1530–1987*. New York: Oxford University Press.
Stone, Lawrence. 1993. *Broken Lives: Separation and Divorce in England, 1660–1857*. New York: Oxford University Press.
Stranahan, Patricia. 1983. *Yan'an Women and the Communist Party*. Berkeley: Institute of East Asian Studies, University of California, Berkeley Center for Chinese Studies.
Strand, David. 1989. *Rickshaw Beijing: City People and Politics in the 1920s*. Berkeley: University of California Press.
Strand, David. 1997. "Community, Society, and History in Sun Yat-sen's *Sanmin zhuyi*." In *Culture and State in Chinese History: Conventions, Accommodations, and Critiques*, edited by Theodore Huters, R. Bin Wong, and Pauline Yu, 326–345. Stanford, CA: Stanford University Press.
Strand, David. 2011. *An Unfinished Republic: Leading by Word and Deed in Modern China*. Berkeley: University of California Press.
Strauss, Julia C. 1998. *Strong Institutions in Weak Polities: State Building in Republican China, 1927–1940*. New York: Oxford University Press.
Sun, Yat-Sen. 1927. *San min chu i: The Three Principles of the People*. Translated by Frank W. Price. Shanghai: China Committee.
Svensson, Marina. 2002. *Debating Human Rights in China: A Conceptual and Political History*. Lanham, MD: Rowman & Littlefield.
The Swiss Civil Code: English Version. 1925. Translated by Ivy Williams. Oxford: Oxford University Press, Humphrey Milford.
Tai Yen-hui. 1978. "Divorce in Traditional Chinese Law." In Buxbaum 1978, 75–106.
Tan Renjiu. 1932. *Zhongguo lihun de yanjiu* (Research on divorce in China). Shanghai: Zhonghua jidujiao nü qingnian hui quanguo xiehui.
Tan Sheying. 1930. "Nannü xingming pingdeng wenti (The issue of male-female surname equality)." *Funü gongming* 34 (Aug.15): 1–3.
Tan Sheying. 1936. *Zhongguo funü yundong tongshi* (General history of the Chinese women's movement). Nanjing: Funü gongming she.
Tao Huizeng [Tao Xisheng]. 1933. *Minfa qinshu lun* (On family law). Shanghai: Shanghai faxue bianyi she.
Tao Xisheng. (1934) 1992. *Hunyin yu jiazu* (Marriage and family). Shanghai: Shanghai shudian.
Telford, Ted A. 1992. "Covariates of Men's Ages at First Marriage: The Historical Demography of Chinese Lineages." *Population Studies* 46:1 (Mar.): 19–35.
Teng, S.Y. 1977. "The Role of the Family in the Chinese Legal System." *Journal of Asian History* 11:2: 121–155.
Theiss, Janet M. 2004. *Disgraceful Matters: The Politics of Chastity in Eighteenth-Century China*. Berkeley: University of California Press.
Theiss, Janet M. 2007. "Explaining the Shrew: Narratives of Spousal Violence and the Critique of Masculinity in Eighteenth-Century Criminal Cases." In *Writing and Law in Late Imperial*

China: Crime, Conflict, and Judgment, edited by Robert E. Hegel and Katherine Carlitz, 44-63. Seattle: University of Washington Press.

Three Five Law Society. 1930. "Minfa qinshubian xianjue gedian zhi yijian (Opinion on the preliminary issues in the civil code family book)." *Faxue jikan* (Law Review, Nanjing) 1:1 (Dec. 12): 241–245; also reprinted in *Faxue jikan* (Law Review, Shanghai) 4:5 (July): 428–432.

Thurston, Richard L. 1979. "China's Civil Law Reform Movement, 1912–1930." PhD diss., University of Virginia.

Tianjin Nü xing she: funü yundong shi ziliao xuanbian (The Tianjin Ladies' star society: selected material from the history of the women's movement). 1985. Edited by Zhonggong Tianjin shi wei. Beijing: Zhonggong dangshi ziliao chubanshe.

Tran, Lisa. 2009. "Sex and Equality in Republican China: The Debate over the Adultery Law." *Modern China* 35:2 (Mar.): 191–223.

Tseng, Yu-hao [Zeng Youhao]. 1930. *Modern Chinese Legal and Political Philosophy.* Shanghai: Commercial Press.

Tsin, Michael. 1999. *Nation, Governance, and Modernity in China: Canton 1900–1927.* Stanford, CA: Stanford University Press.

Turner, Karen G., James V. Feinerman, and R. Kent Guy, eds. 2000. *The Limits of the Rule of Law in China.* Seattle: University of Washington Press.

Tushnet, Mark. 1984. "An Essay on Rights." *Texas Law Review* 62:8 (May): 1363-1403.

van der Sprenkel, Sybille. 1962. *Legal Institutions in Manchu China*. London: Athlone.

van der Valk, Marc. 1938. "Freedom of Marriage in Modern Chinese Law." *Monumenta Serica* 3: 1–34.

van der Valk, Marc. 1939. *An Outline of Modern Chinese Family Law*. Beijing: Henry Vetch.

van der Valk, Marc. (1949) 1968. *Interpretations of the Supreme Court at Peking: Years 1915 and 1916*. Taipei: Chengwen.

Van Vorst, Bessie. 1926. *A Girl from China (Soumay Tcheng)*. New York: Frederick A. Stokes.

Wagner, William G. 1994. *Marriage, Property, and Law in Late Imperial Russia*. New York: Oxford University Press.

Wakefield, David. 1998. *Fenjia: Household Division and Inheritance in Qing and Republican China*. Honolulu: University of Hawaii Press.

Wakeman, Frederic, Jr., and Richard Louis Edmonds, eds. 2000. *Reappraising Republican China.* New York: Oxford University Press.

Wang Chonghui. 1917. "Law Reform in China." *Chinese Social and Political Science Review* 18: 13–21.

Wang Chonghui. 1957. *Kun xue zhai wen cun*. Taipei: Zhonghua congshu weiyuanhui.

Wang Chonghui. 1981. *Wang Chonghui xiansheng wenji* (Collected writings by Wang Chonghui). Taipei: Dangshi weiyuanhui.

Wang Jieqing, ed. 1982. *Zhongguo falü yu fazhi sixiang* (Chinese law and jurisprudence). Taipei: Sanmin shuju.

Wang Quangen. 2000. *Zhongguo xingshi de wenhua jiexi* (A cultural analysis of Chinese surnames). Beijing: Tuanjie chubanshe.

Wang Shijie. 1927. "Lihun wenti (The divorce problem)." *Falü pinglun* 190 (Feb. 20): 3–13.

Wang Yongbin. 1930. "Qi guan fuxing wenti (The issue of wives adding their husbands' surnames)." *Faxue jikan* 1:1 (Dec. 12): 27–48.

Wang Zecun. 1993. *Xingshi, minghao, biecheng—Zhongguo renwu mingming xisu* (Surnames, nicknames, alternative names—naming customs of Chinese personages). Chengdu: Sichuan renmin chubanshe.

Wang Zheng. 1999. *Women in the Chinese Enlightenment: Oral and Textual Histories*. Berkeley: University of California Press.

Watson, Rubie S. 1986. "The Named and the Nameless: Gender and Person in Chinese Society." *American Ethnologist* 13: 619–631.

Watson, Rubie S., and Patricia Buckley Ebrey, eds. 1991. *Marriage and Inequality in Chinese Society*. Berkeley: University of California Press.

Weatherley, Robert. 1999. *The Discourse of Human Rights in China: Historical and Ideological Perspectives*. New York: St. Martin's Press.

Wei, Madam Tao-Ming [Zheng Yuxiu]. 1943. *My Revolutionary Years: The Autobiography of Madame Wei Tao-Ming*. New York: Scribner's Sons.
West, Robin. 2001. "Introduction: Revitalizing Rights." In *Rights,* edited by Robin West, xi–xxxi. Burlington, VT: Ashgate.
Who's Who in China 1918–1950. 1982. Hong Kong: Chinese Materials Center.
Williams, Patricia J. 1991. *The Alchemy of Race and Rights*. Cambridge, MA: Harvard University Press.
Witke, Roxane H. 1970. "Transformation of Attitudes towards Women during the May Fourth Era of Modern China." PhD diss., University of California, Berkeley.
Wolf, Arthur P., and Chieh-shan Huang. 1980. *Marriage and Adoption in China, 1845–1945.* Stanford, CA: Stanford University Press.
Wolf, Margery. 1968. *The House of Lim: A Study of a Chinese Farm Family*. New York: Appleton-Century-Crofts.
Wolf, Margery. 1972. *Women and the Family in Rural Taiwan*. Stanford, CA: Stanford University Press.
Wolf, Margery. 1974. "Chinese Women: Old Skills in a New Context." In *Woman, Culture, and Society*, edited by Michelle Zimablist Rosaldo and Louise Lamphere, 157–172. Stanford, CA: Stanford University Press.
Wu, Chih-Fang Wu (T.F. Wu). 1934. *Chinese Government and Politics.* Shanghai: Commercial Press.
Wu, Ching-chao. 1927. "The Chinese Family: Organization, Names, and Kinship Terms." *American Anthropologist* 29: 316–325.
Wu, Jingxiong. 1930. "Guanyu bianding minfa zhi shangque (Discussion of the civil codification process)." *Faxue jikan* 4:1 (Jan.): 42–52.
Wu, Jingxiong. 1935. "Xianfa zhong renmin zhi quanli ji yiwu (People's rights and duties under constitutional law)." *Faling zhoukan* 235 (Jan. 2).
Wu, John C. H. [Wu Jingxiong]. 1928. *Juridical Essays and Studies*. Shanghai: Commercial Press.
Wu, John C. H. [Wu Jingxiong]. 1936. *The Art of Law and Other Essays Juridical and Literary*. Shanghai: Commercial Press.
Wu, John C. H. [Wu Jingxiong]. 1967a. "Chinese Legal and Political Philosophy." In *The Chinese Mind: Essentials of Chinese Philosophy and Culture,* edited by Charles A. Moore, 213–237. Honolulu: East-West Center Press.
Wu, John C. H. [Wu Jingxiong]. 1967b. "The Status of the Individual in the Political and Legal Traditions of Old and New China." In *The Chinese Mind: Essentials of Chinese Philosophy and Culture*, edited by Charles A. Moore, 340–364. Honolulu: East-West Center Press.
Wu, John C. H. [Wu Jingxiong]. 1971. *Sun Yat-Sen: The Man and His Ideas*. Taipei: Commercial Press.
Wu Jingxiong and Huang Gongjue. (1937) 1992. *Zhongguo zhi xian shi* (Chinese constitutional history). Shanghai: Shanghai shudian.
Wu Qi. 1947. *Zhongguo qinshu fa yuanli* (Principles of Chinese family law). Shanghai: Zhongguo wenhua fuwu she.
Xia Mei. (1922) 1973. "Ziyou lihun lun (On freedom of divorce)." *Funü zazhi.* Reprinted in *Lihun wenti lunping ji* (Collection of essays on the divorce problem). Hong Kong: Zhongshan tushu gongsi.
Xie Zhenmin. (1937) 1999. *Zhonghua minguo lifa shi* (The legislative history of the Republic of China). Beijing: Zhengfa daxue.
Xu Sida. 1932. *Lihun fa lun* (Treatise on divorce law). Tianjin: Yi shi bao guan.
Xu, Xiaoqun. 1998. "Between State and Society, between Professionalism and Politics: The Shanghai Bar Association in Republican China, 1912–1937." *Twentieth-Century China* 24:1 (Nov.): 1–29.
Xu, Xiaoqun. 2008. *Trial of Modernity: Judicial Reform in Early Twentieth-Century China.* Stanford, CA: Stanford University Press.
Xue Yunsheng. (1905) 1970. *Du li cun yi* (Doubts from studying the substatutes). 5 vols. Reprint. Edited by Huang Jingjia. Taipei: Chinese Materials and Research Aids Service Center.

Yang Youjiong. (1936) 1989. *Jindai Zhongguo lifa shi* (History of legislation in modern China). Shanghai: Shanghai shudian.

Ye, Weili. 1994. "'Nü Liuxuesheng': The Story of American-Educated Chinese Women, 1880s–1920s." *Modern China* 20:3 (July): 315–346.

Yeh, Wen-hsin. 2005. "The Paradox of Autonomy: Nation, Revolution, and Women through the Chinese Looking Glass." In *Women in China: The Republican Period in Historical Perspective,* edited by Mechthild Leutner and Nicola Spakowski, 40–56. New Brunswick: Transaction.

Yeh, Wen-hsin. 2007. *Shanghai Splendor: Economic Sentiments and the Making of Modern China, 1843–1949.* Berkeley: University of California Press.

Yick, Joseph K.S. 1995. *Making Urban Revolution in China: The CCP-GMD Struggle for Beiping-Tianjin, 1945–1949.* Armonk, NY: M.E. Sharpe.

Young, Mary Buck. 2004. "Law and Modern State-Building in Early Republican China: The Supreme Court of Peking (1911–1926)." PhD diss., Harvard University.

Yu Ni. 1927. "Zhong xi fazhi zhi chayi (Distinctions between Chinese and Western law)." *Falü pinglun* 210 (July 10): 1–8.

Yu Ni. 1932. *Qinshu fa yao lun* (Essentials of family law). Beijing: Chaoyang daxue chubanshe.

Yu Weixiong. 1987. *Wang Chonghui yu jindai Zhongguo* (Wang Chonghui and modern China). Taipei: Wenshizhe chubanshe.

Yu Zhengxie. 1982. "Nanü pingdeng (Gender equality)." In Wang 1982, 832.

Zanasi, Margherita. 2006. *Saving the Nation: Economic Modernity in Republican China.* Chicago: University of Chicago Press.

Zarrow, Peter. 1988. "He Zhen and Anarcho-Feminism in China." *Journal of Asian Studies* 47:4 (Nov.): 796-813.

Zarrow, Peter G. 1990. *Anarchism and Chinese Political Culture.* New York: Columbia University Press.

Zarrow, Peter. 2005. *China in War and Revolution, 1895–1949.* New York: Routledge.

Zarrow, Peter. 2008. "Anti-Despotism and 'Rights Talk': The Intellectual Origins of Modern Human Rights Thinking in the Late Qing." *Modern China* 34: 2 (Apr.): 179–209.

Zelin, Madeleine, Jonathan Ocko, and Robert Gardella, eds. 2004. *Contract and Property in Early Modern China.* Stanford, CA: Stanford University Press.

Zhang Huiquan. 1935. "Lun tong xing bu neng hun yu jiu lü ji minfa qinshu tong hun de xianzhi (On the restrictions against same-surname marriage under old law and the civil code family provisions)." *Fagui qikan* 2:1 (Jan.): 107–112.

Zhang Jixin. 1930. "Shiba nian lifa shiye zhi huigu (A look back at the 1929 legislative undertakings)." *Faxue jikan,* 4:3 (Jan./Feb.): 141–146.

Zhang Xipo. 2004. *Zhongguo hun yin li fa shi* (History of Chinese marriage legislation). Beijing: Renmin chubanshe.

Zhao Deren, and Xia Jingmin. 1929. "Funü jiehun hou de xingshi wenti (Women's problems with surnames after marriage)." *Falü pinglun* 290 (May 5): 14–19.

Zhao Fengjie. (1928) 1993. *Zhongguo funü zai falü shang zhi diwei* (The legal status of Chinese women). Banqiao: Daoxiang chubanshe.

Zhao Fengjie. (1937) 1993. "Zhongguo funü zai falü shang zhi diwei bupian (The legal status of Chinese women, revised edition)." *Qinghua daxue shehui kexue* 1:4: 153–204.

Zhao Fengjie. 1947. *Minfa qinshu lun* (On family law). Shanghai: Zheng zhong shuju faxing.

Zheng Baohua. 1931. "Falü shehuihua lun (On the socialization of law)." *Faxue jikan* 4:7 (Jan.): 637–677.

Zhongguo faxuejia cidian (Dictionary of Chinese legal scholars and lawyers). 1991. Beijing: Zhongguo laodong chubanshe.

Zhongguo funü yundong lishi ziliao 1921–1927 (Materials concerning the Chinese women's movement, 1921–1927). 1984. 2 vols. Edited by Zhonghua quanguo funü lianhehui funü yündong lishi yanjiu shi. Beijing: Renmin chubanshe.

Zhongguo Guomindang dangwu fazhan shiliao—funü gongzuo (GMD development of party work: women's department activities). 1996. Compiled by Chen Pengren and Lin Yangzhi. Taipei: Guomindang zhongyang weiyuanhui dangshi weiyuanhui.

Zhonghua minguo minfa zhiding shiliao huibian (Compilation of civil laws of the Republic of China). 1976. 2 vols. Taoyuan: Hongde.

Zhou Jianren. (1922) 1973. "Zhongguo lihun fa shang de san jue (Three questions about China's divorce law)." *Funü zazhi.* Reprinted in *Lihun wenti lunping ji* (Collection of essays on the divorce problem). Hong Kong: Zhongshan tushu gongsi.

Zuigao fayuan jieshi li quanwen (Complete texts of Supreme Court interpretations). 1946. Edited by Guo Wei. Shanghai: Shanghai faxue bianyishe.

Zuigao fayuan panli yaozhi (Excerpts from important Supreme Court decisions). 1954. Taipei: Zuigao fayuan panli yaozhi faxing weiyuanhui.

Glossary

aiqing de biaoxian 愛情的表現
an fei 案費
baiban nüedai 百般虐待
baishou xielao 白首偕老
beifu taohun 背夫逃婚
beifu zaitao 背夫哉逃
Beiping difang fayuan 北平地方法院
bianti chengshang 遍體成傷
bianti lingshang 遍體鱗傷
bieju 別居
bu dong chunse 不動春色
bufu jiaoxun 不服教訓
bu kan tongju zhi nüedai 不堪同居之虐待
buneng rendao 不能人道
caiding 裁定
caipan fei 裁判費
Cai Yuanpei 蔡元培
caolao guodu 操勞過度
chexiao hunyin 撤銷婚姻
Chen Bijun 陳碧君
Chen Changheng 陳長蘅
Chen Hengzhe 陳衡哲
Chen Yiyun 陳逸雲
chunü 處女
cong 從
congshuwu 從屬物
Dagongbao 大公報

Daliyuan 大理院
da ma 打罵
Danggang 黨綱
Deng Jixing 鄧季惺
dian 典
difang fayuan 地方法院
duda 毒打
enjue 恩绝
Fadian bianji hui 法典編輯會
Falü biancha hui 法律編查會
Falü guan 法律官
Falü pinglun 法律評論
falü zu 法律組
fanghai hunyin jiating zui 妨害婚姻家庭罪
Faxue jikan 法學季刊
Fayuan bianzhi fa 法院編制法
Fazhi ju 法治局
feida jima 非打即罵
feiren 非人
Fu Bingchang 傅秉常
fudao 婦道
Funü gongming 婦女共鳴
ganqing bu hemu 感情不和睦
ganqing huifu 感情恢復
ganqing polie 感情破裂
gaodeng fayuan 高等法院
gongwu 公務
gongye 工業
guanxing ouda 慣性毆打
guniang 姑娘
haohao guorizi 好好過日子
Hebei sheng gaodeng fayuan 河北省高等法院
he fang 和房
He Xiangning 何香凝
Hu Changqing 胡长清
Hu Hanmin 胡漢民
hui niangjia 回娘家
hunyin wuxiao 婚姻無效
huopo 活潑
jiadao pinhan 家道貧寒
jianchaguan 檢察官
jiandingshu 鑑定書
Jiang Menglin 蔣夢麟

Jiangsu sheng gaodeng fayuan 江蘇省高等法院
jiannu 兼怒
jiaotong yunshu 交通運輸
jicheng 繼承
jiechu hunyue 解除婚約
Jin Shiyin 金石音
kongyan 空言
Lifayuan 立法院
lihun 離婚
lijue 礼绝
Lin Sen 林森
Li Shizeng 李石曾
Li Zhishan 李峙山
Liang Zhao Maohua 梁趙茂華
lijiao zhi su 禮教之素
lingxin 另心
ling you qitu 另有企圖
Liu Wang Liming 劉王立明
liuzhiquan 留置權
longtong 籠統
lüeshi 略示
menhu budang 門互不當
mian'ao 棉襖
Minfa qicao weiyuanhui 民法起草委員會
minshi 民事
Minzheng bu 民政部
moumou furen 某某夫人
mu 畝
nage qingxing 那個情形
nanyi renshou 難以忍受
nanzi de nuli fuyong 男子的奴隸附庸
nanzunnübei de nanxizhidu de louxi 男尊女卑的男系制度的陋習
nianbao 年報
nianyou wu li dikang 年幼無力抵抗
ning 凝
nongye 農業
nüedai 虐待
nüquan 女權
Nü sheng 女聲
nüshi 女士
ouda 毆打
ouer ouda 偶爾毆打
panjue 判決

po fuyou 頗富有
qichi dawu 奇恥大辱
Qian 茜
qianque diaocha 欠缺調查
qi chu 七出
qingwei 輕微
qinshu 親屬
qipao 旗袍
qipian hunyin 欺騙婚姻
queren hunyin bu chengli 確認婚姻不成立
queren hunyin chengli 確認婚姻成立
renmin liyi 人民利益
renquan 人權
rensheng suowei shenger yangnü 人生所謂生兒養女
renshi fuwu 人事服務
ruming 乳名
ruo nű zi 弱女子
san buqu 三不去
sancong 三從
sancong side 三從四德
Sanmin zhuyi 三民主義
Sanwu faxueshe 三五法學社
shangdan 傷單
shangxin 傷心
shangye 商業
shangzi 上字
Shao Yuanchong 邵元沖
shehui liyi 社會利益
Shenbao 申報
shenghuofei 生活費
shenjing shuairuo 神經衰弱
shenpan feiyong 審判費用
shenpanguan 審判管
shi 氏
Shibao 實報
Shifu 師復
shin ű 石女
shiye 失業
shou qi 受氣
Sifa bu 司法部
Sifaxingzhengbu 司法行政部統計處
Song Meiling 宋美齡
Song Qingling 宋慶齡

susong feiyong 訴訟費用
taitai 太太
Tan Sheying 談社英
tianfu renquan 天賦人權
tianjingdiyi 天經地義
tianyan 天閹
tongfang zhi ye 同房之夜
tongju 同居
Tongmenghui 同盟會
tongyangxi 童養媳
tongzi hunyin 童子婚姻
tuishi 推事
Wang Yongbin 王用賓
Wu Jingxiong 吳經熊
wuquan 物權
wuquan xianfa 五權憲法
wuru 侮辱
wuye 無業
Wu Zhihui 吳稚暉
xian sifachu 縣司法處
xian zhengfu 縣政府
Xiangxia nü 鄉下女
xianpin aifu 嫌貧愛富
Xianxing minlü cao'an 現行民律草案
xiaobenying 小本營
xieyi liyi 協議離異
Xin funü zhoubao 新婦女週報
xingtong luren 形同路人
xinqing yiyuan 心情意願
xishi 細實
Xiuding falü guan 修訂法律官
xunwen 訊問
xushuo 敘說
yanci bianlun 言詞辯論
yanzhongding 眼中釘
yijue 义绝
ying ye 營業
yuan 元
zhaiwu 債務
Zhang Mojun 張默君
zaoda muma 早打暮罵
zhe zhong funü 這種婦女
zhengyi 正義

zhongshi 忠實
Zhongyang ribao 中央日報
Zhongyang zhengzhi huiyi 中央政治會議
zhuangyang yao 壯陽藥
zhuayao zhi shang 抓咬之傷
zixiu 自修
ziyou zhiye 自由職業
zongfa shehui 宗法社會
zongtiaozhuyi 宗祧主義
zongze 總則
Zuigao fayuan 最高法院

Index

About the Author

Margaret Kuo is an associate professor of history at California State University, Long Beach, and EDS-Stewart Fellow at the Center for the Pacific Rim, University of San Francisco.

www.ingramcontent.com/pod-product-compliance
Ingram Content Group UK Ltd.
Pitfield, Milton Keynes, MK11 3LW, UK
UKHW041631031026
15587UKWH00001B/217

9 781442 218406